CBT

VALUES AND ETHICS

Sara Miller McCune founded SAGE Publishing in 1965 to support the dissemination of usable knowledge and educate a global community. SAGE publishes more than 1000 journals and over 800 new books each year, spanning a wide range of subject areas. Our growing selection of library products includes archives, data, case studies and video. SAGE remains majority owned by our founder and after her lifetime will become owned by a charitable trust that secures the company's continued independence.

Los Angeles | London | New Delhi | Singapore | Washington DC | Melbourne

CBT

VALUES AND ETHICS

DAVID KINGDON | NICK MAGUIRE
DZINTRA STALMEISTERS | MICHAEL TOWNEND

Los Angeles | London | New Delhi
Singapore | Washington DC | Melbourne

Los Angeles | London | New Delhi
Singapore | Washington DC | Melbourne

SAGE Publications Ltd
1 Oliver's Yard
55 City Road
London EC1Y 1SP

SAGE Publications Inc.
2455 Teller Road
Thousand Oaks, California 91320

SAGE Publications India Pvt Ltd
B 1/I 1 Mohan Cooperative Industrial Area
Mathura Road
New Delhi 110 044

SAGE Publications Asia-Pacific Pte Ltd
3 Church Street
#10-04 Samsung Hub
Singapore 049483

Editor: Amy Jarrold
Editorial assistant: Edward Coats
Production editor: Rachel Burrows
Marketing manager: Camille Richmond
Cover design: Lisa Harper-Wells
Typeset by: C&M Digitals (P) Ltd, Chennai, India
Printed and bound by CPI Group (UK) Ltd,
Croydon, CR0 4YY

First published 2017

Library of Congress Control Number: 2016947439

British Library Cataloguing in Publication data

A catalogue record for this book is available from the British Library

ISBN 978-1-4462-7300-5
ISBN 978-1-4462-7301-2 (pbk)

CONTENTS

About the Authors vi
Acknowledgements viii
List of Abbreviations x

Introduction 1
1 General Principles of Values and Ethics 6
2 Concepts in Clinical Ethics 21
3 Implications for CBT Technique 41
4 Considering Therapist's Responsibilities and Boundaries 54
5 Confidentiality and Record Keeping 70
6 Professional and Therapeutic Competence in CBT 80
7 Research and Evidence 93
8 The Ethics of Using a CBT Approach 108
9 Specific Populations 120
Conclusion: Ethical Decision-Making 147

References 172
Index 180

ABOUT THE AUTHORS

David Kingdon is Professor of Mental Health Care Delivery at the University of Southampton, Clinical Services Director, Adult Mental Health, Southampton, and Honorary Consultant Adult Psychiatrist for Southern Health NHS Trust. He has previously worked as Senior Medical Officer (Severe Mental Illness) at the Department of Health and has participated in many policy initiatives over the past two decades. He chaired the Expert Working Group, leading to the Council of Europe's Recommendation 2004(10) on Psychiatry and Human Rights (1996–2003). His research interests are in cognitive therapy of severe mental health conditions and mental health service development, about which he has published over a hundred peer-reviewed papers and many articles, chapters and books. He received the Aaron T. Beck Award for Exceptional Cognitive Therapy in May 2015.

Nick Maguire is an Associate Professor in Clinical Psychology at the University of Southampton. He is currently the Deputy Head of Department responsible for Education, and has research and clinical interests in excluded populations. He teaches and researches psychological factors implicated in the causation and maintenance of social exclusion, and the implications for the adaptation of cognitive and behavioural therapies. He is a founder member of the Faculty for Homeless Healthcare and was on a support panel for the NHS Inclusion Health Board. He is passionate about enabling excluded populations with serious and enduring mental health problems to access health care, including much needed psychological provision.

Dzintra Stalmeisters is a Chartered Psychologist and Associate Fellow of the British Psychology Society (BPS). She is trained in Cognitive Behavioural Psychotherapy, Gestalt Psychotherapy and holds a BPS qualification in Counselling Psychology. Dzintra is an Independent Practitioner and is also a Senior Lecturer at the University of Derby. She works on the MSc Cognitive Behavioural Psychotherapy (CBP) course as the Module Leader for Ethics, Law and Research in CBP. Dzintra is also a Doctoral Supervisor and is currently active in research. She is keen to engage students and therapists in conversations and discussion about ethical practice, and quintessentially to make ethics more accessible.

Michael Townend is a Reader and Senior Lecturer in Cognitive Behavioural Psychotherapy at the University of Derby, where he teaches and researches cognitive behavioural psychotherapy. He also leads the Doctoral Programme in Health and Social Care Practice. He is a Consultant in Cognitive Behavioural Psychotherapy at the SPIRE Parkway Hospital Solihull. Michael was the Founding Editor of the BABCP journal, *The Cognitive Behaviour Therapist*. He is passionate about the development of values and ethical practice alongside evidence to underpin therapeutic work that has compassion, formulation and the therapeutic relationship at its heart.

ACKNOWLEDGEMENTS

There are a number of people who have contributed to the development of this book and whose interest, encouragement and support we wish to acknowledge.

We would first like to thank everyone at Sage who have worked with us to bring this project to completion. Particular thanks go to Amy Jarrold, Kate Wharton and Edward Coats – our editorial team – and all at SAGE who have been such a solid source of support throughout the process.

Beyond those directly connected with this project, we are deeply grateful to all those who, over the years, have shaped our understanding of our diverse professional fields and the values and ethics that we consider can underpin cognitive behaviour therapy alongside a research-based approach to practice. A particular mention goes to the many clients, teachers and supervisors, with whom we have had the good fortune to work and from whom we have learned so much. We also acknowledge our current and former students and colleagues, who continue to challenge us and who have in so many ways shaped this edition.

David Kingdon wishes to acknowledge the influence of many colleagues he has worked with over the years, especially Douglas Turkington, Shanaya Rathod, Lars Hansen and Farooq Naeem, and most of all, Marie, who appreciated how important it was for this book to be written.

Nick Maguire wishes to acknowledge Tess, Papa and Tanisha for their patience when dealing with a grumpy dad after a late night at the keyboard. He has learned an enormous amount from his Southampton Psychology Department colleagues about thinking ethically, and more from the homeless people who put up with him as their psychologist.

Dzintra Stalmeisters wishes to acknowledge her husband Michael and their children, Matthew, Sinead and Ruairi, for their continued support and encouragement. She is also grateful to the students who have taken part in the MSc Cognitive Behavioural and Psychotherapy, Ethics, Law and Research Module at the University of Derby: their engagement with the ethics part of the module has stimulated thought, contributing to the completion of this book.

Michael Townend wishes to acknowledge Jenny, his family and friends for their love, understanding and patience. His thanks also go to all his colleagues at the University of Derby, for their inspirational ideas and for helping to create the space to enable work on yet another book. Finally, he thanks his students and his clients, who, by their experiences and feedback, have contributed to this text. They also act as a continuous reminder that it is a privilege to be in a position to work with them all.

LIST OF ABBREVIATIONS

AACBT	Australian Association for Cognitive and Behaviour Therapy
AaCT	Acceptance and Commitment Therapy
ACT	Academy of Cognitive Therapy
APA	American Psychological Association
APS	Australian Psychology Society
BABCP	British Association for Behavioural and Cognitive Psychotherapies
BME	Black and Minority Ethnic
BPD	Borderline Personality Disorder
BPS	British Psychology Society
CBP	Cognitive Behavioural Psychotherapy
CBT	Cognitive Behavioural Therapy
CEBT	Cognitive Emotion and Behaviour Therapy
CICM	Chronic Illness Coping Model
COPD	Chronic Obstructive Pulmonary Disease
CPD	Continuing Professional Development
CT	Cognitive Therapy
DBT	Dialectical Behaviour Therapy
DH	Department of Health
DSM	Diagnostic and Statistical Manual
EABCT	European Association for Behavioural and Cognitive Therapies
EBMWG	Evidence-Based Medicine Working Group
EBT	Evidence-Based Therapy
EPR	Electronic Patient Records
HSCIC	Health and Social Care Information Centre
IAPT	Improving Access to Psychological Therapies
ICD	International Classification of Diseases
KSA	Knowledge, Skills and Attitudes
ME/CFS	Myalgic Encephalopathy/Chronic Fatigue Syndrome
MRC	Medical Research Council
NHRA	NHS Health Research Authority
NHSU	National Health Service University

NICE	National Institute for Health and Care Excellence
NIMHE	National Institute for Mental Health in England
NPSA	National Patient Safety Agency
OCD	Obsessive Compulsive Disorder
OT	Occupational Therapist
PORT	Schizophrenia Patient Outcomes Research Team
PTSD	Post-Traumatic Stress Disorder
RCT	Randomised Controlled Trial
RFT	Relational Frame Theory
ROMs	Routine Outcome Measures
SCIE	Social Care Institute for Excellence
SCMH	Sainsbury Centre for Mental Health
T-FCT	Trauma-Focused Cognitive Therapy
UNGA	United Nations General Assembly
WHO	World Health Organization
WMA	World Medical Association
WRAP	Wellness Recovery Action Plan

INTRODUCTION

When David was initially approached about the possibility of writing a book on cognitive behavioural therapy (CBT), ethics and values, his instant reaction was that there must be one already and why do you need more than one? He was also rather surprised at receiving the request to put such a book together – it arose, it seems, because he had coordinated work on CBT and diversity and had given an opening overview at a very successful and well-advertised conference on the subject. In fact, there wasn't one and it would clearly be a difficult and complex task for one individual, so, over time, it became an interdisciplinary collaboration.

This book has now been written and published because David's partner, a social worker, goaded him, saying: 'you CBT lot, you've got no ethics and values'. Her view was that CBT was frequently too individualistic, even mechanistic and lacking a social perspective and if this were ever to change, then such a book was needed. This was also the view of a national Mental Health Provider group, set up to consider issues about the perceived narrow focus of guidelines in the UK, in which he had been the 'token' CBT representative. Other members of the group had come from a range of psychotherapeutic backgrounds and there were clear differences between the views held. Yet, there was also a lot of commonality that emerged in considering the importance of the relationship in therapy and, more basically, our ethics and values.

On reflecting on the development of this book, it does seem remarkable that a text with this or a similar title has not apparently been written as such books exist in many areas of mental health work and relate to different modes of psychotherapy. Does it say anything about CBT that one doesn't currently exist? The need for such a book seems to us to be self-evident. The basis for any social or health care practice should be rooted in a set of ethics and values. Professional bodies proscribe these but they also deserve to be interpreted in different therapeutic contexts. This is important in enabling practitioners to reflect on their own approaches and is particularly important for new entrants to the field. The expansion in the numbers of cognitive therapists internationally is substantial, especially in the UK with the Improving Access to Psychological Therapies programme (IAPT; see fuller description later), which is training therapists in high- and low-intensity ways of working.

David's interest in the values and ethics of CB therapy flows from his recent work on considering cultural diversity and ethics and values. He also spent a period of time at the Council of Europe in Strasbourg, chairing a working group on a Recommendation on Human Rights and Psychiatry. This was a fascinating experience, involving immersing in philosophical and ethical discussion with the lawyers and other psychiatrists in the group and also the representations from a range of countries and organisations, including those led by service users.

David works primarily using CBT as part of his role as a psychiatrist rather than offering regular therapy sessions so, from the outset, he needed some help. Nick Maguire is a clinical psychologist, working in various settings in Southampton and London and with a range of projects, especially with marginalised people. This, as well as his professional background, his values and experience as a CBT trainer, seemed an excellent fit for this book and he agreed to co-author it.

However, David and Nick were struggling to complete the book until, coincidentally at a CBT conference in India, at a roof top restaurant, David and Michael discussed this project and its progress. Michael was originally a mental health nurse and has been involved in the training of CB therapists for over twenty years and was instantly hooked on the idea of the book. He was aware that there wasn't a similar text and that there needed to be one. The timing was perfect as Michael had just completed a book on assessment and formulation. Whilst he wasn't looking for a fresh challenge, he was rather excited about the book because, other than a brief period of contributing to the Ethics, Standards and Conduct some years previously with colleagues for the BABCP, he hadn't fully immersed himself in considerations of values and ethics since his student days. Thus, he felt it was time to think about some of these issues to inform his teaching and own practice and so to develop himself through engagement in this project. He was also keen to be involved because the book might influence others to do the same.

Michael also suggested the involvement of Dzintra from a psychology background, who is not only a CB therapist but is also influenced by gestalt philosophies. She also had the essential qualification of actually teaching a course on ethics and values at the University of Derby on the MSc in CB therapy. Dzintra noticed that many students initially approached ethics with a certain amount of trepidation, however, they soon engaged with the subject and were often surprised not only that they had developed a good grounding in ethics, and felt more confident, but also that they found the subject stimulating and enjoyable. Michael and Dzintra in particular have influenced and helped shape this book into what we hope is an easy-to-read text that is cohesive, challenging but practically focused.

If you have picked up this book and got this far, it is probable that you have little problem appreciating why ethics and values are so important to consider in clinical practice but it may still be worth just confirming those reasons. We expect CB therapists and trainees, other therapists, mental health workers using CB approaches, managers and some clients and carers to find this book of interest, as well as practitioners from a variety of disciplines: psychiatrists, clinical psychologists, nurses, occupational therapists (OTs), social workers, peer workers and case managers.

Ethics is a discursive discipline, where there are often no right answers. It operates best when there is an iterative dialogue which enables different perspectives to be articulated, aired and compared with each other, in order to, often identify a least worst solution. This operates by, at times proposing ethical issues with existing solutions, and at times providing a dialectic – an enquiry into apparent contradictions and their solutions – which may be addressed. Some solutions may be far from perfect, and the reader is invited to perhaps generate better ways of dealing with the issues.

In each chapter, we have included examples from our own experience from practice or supervision to try and bring what at times can be quite dry or difficult-to-grasp conceptual or philosophical issues to life with practical exercises and suggestions for further reading.

The chapters can stand alone but we have organised them into this Introduction, followed by a main section and then a Conclusion. More general issues come first, followed by specific applications. There is also a sequence through the book that lends itself to working from Chapter 1 onwards. We start by discussing what CBT is and then briefly and we hope, accessibly, relevant ethical principles and the relationship between ethics and values. In this chapter, we also consider which ethical ideas are most relevant to psychological therapy and to CB therapy, in particular. Chapter 2 deals with important issues that directly relate to CB practice such as autonomy, consent, capacity and safeguarding. Chapter 3 defines professional responsibilities, drawing on the codes of practice of national organisations. It also considers issues of consent to therapy and the management of professional boundaries. Whilst in Chapter 4 the focus is on considerations of confidentiality and record keeping in both handwritten and electronic forms, it also considers the use of recording of practice and how to manage the process effectively. Criticisms of the use of CBT techniques and considerations that need to be made are considered in depth in Chapter 5. Professional competence and maintenance of it forms the subject matter for the chapter, with particular reference to notions of fidelity. Chapter 6 considers ethical issues to do with competence in CBT, both professional and therapeutic. Chapter 7 considers ethical issues regarding research and evidence. Chapter 8 covers the ethics and values related to CB therapy and the general use of a CB approach in practice. Chapter 9 covers specific populations and situations. It commences with a discussion on how social and cultural issues influence, or should by adaptation influence, CBT. It describes ethical issues of working with people with learning disability and excluded populations and then those with chronic medical problems. Lastly, it is focused on how the safety of individuals is preserved where they may be suicidal. In the Conclusion, we have tried not only to bring the themes from the book together but have also included an ethical reasoning model with worked examples that we think will help people make consistent, well-thought-through ethical decisions. This can be used by professionals to make decisions when a rapid response is needed, moment by moment, with clients. It can also be used in supervision to help supervisors and supervisees arrive at a reasoned way to address ethical concerns. We have also found it a useful way to teach ethical reasoning with students and when working with more experienced therapists in continuous professional development contexts. In the Conclusion, we also included a reflective learning tool to help you to get the best of the material contained within this book.

We've tried to ensure that the values portrayed, the ethical principles and the legal procedural matters are sourced and accurate, but many areas exist where there are a number of perspectives and opinions and it is at times more an awareness of a prevailing opinion that dictates, so we are not expecting the reader to agree with everything that we have concluded. This reflects the subject matter of ethics and values when there is not always a single best way to conceptualise an issue or right way to address an issue. We have throughout the book attempted to cope with the differences in opinions and the changes that are occurring, by stressing either using broad principles or making explicit contrasting views which can be applied and be a guide in a changing global world. We are all working in the UK but have attempted to incorporate national guidelines from the USA and Australia in particular. International perspectives are very valuable as this is an area where assumptions about what is right and wrong may differ and dialogues around this are essential in moving the field forward as a whole ethically. *This is also a complex and rapidly changing area, e.g. in considerations of mental capacity and safeguarding, and practitioners should ensure that they are aware of and follow their professional and local organisations' processes and procedures, which will take precedence over statements made in this book.*

We would certainly appreciate comments and responses to the way in which we have handled issues in this book that are inevitably controversial and evolving. Finally, throughout the book, we have tried to create an integrated, consistent and practical approach. You can let us know if you think that we have got it right.

Confidentiality

The case studies and all additional case material included in this book have been inspired by dilemmas encountered in the context of training and the delivery of CBT in a variety of health care settings. However, steps have been taken to ensure anonymity in all cases. In order to preserve confidentiality, a number of potentially identifying features have been changed, with some issues representing a composite of several clients or dilemmas.

1

GENERAL PRINCIPLES OF VALUES AND ETHICS

Learning outcomes

After reading this chapter and completing the activities at the end of it, you should be able to:

1. Be aware of the range of cognitive behavioural therapies that have developed.
2. Understand why an appreciation of general principles of ethics matters.
3. Know what types of ethical theories are relevant.
4. Realise the importance of human rights, ethical and legal frameworks.
5. Know the sources of value statements for mental health care that can help.
6. Clarify the specific principles that relate to psychological treatment.
7. Use the sources for ethics particularly relevant to CBT.

We are going to begin by providing a broad description of cognitive behavioural therapy and then describe some broad ethical principles relevant to using it.

Cognitive behaviour therapy

Since Freud developed theories of the ways in which one's internal world may govern behaviours, a wide range of therapies have developed. Evidence to support the effectiveness of psychological therapies has followed – more for some than for others. This empirical approach formed part of the behavioural work of Thorndike (1905), Watson (1913) and later Skinner (1938, 1971), and was later operationalised as a formal psychological therapy by Wolpe (1968) and Marks (1987). Cognitive aspects of psychological therapies first appeared in Kelly's (1955) personal construct theories and then Ellis's rational emotive behaviour therapy (1962) and Beck's cognitive behaviour therapy (1963). Behavioural theories have proved robust over a century of experimental investigation, with cognitive processing research being comparatively younger with 30 to 40 years of work.

There are, very broadly, three schools of psychological therapy based on distinct theories of pathology and change. Psychoanalytic and psychodynamic therapies were until perhaps the mid-1980s dominant in the field of talking therapies. However, a lack of empirical validation of theory and effectiveness, with a growing evidence base for both cognitive and behavioural therapies, led to a significant shift, culminating in the government-sponsored Improving Access to Psychological Therapies programme (IAPT) making CBT the main model. More recently, evidence has developed for related therapies, including brief interpersonal therapy (Klerman and Weissman, 1994) and mentalisation-based therapy (Bateman and Fonagy, 2012).

There are now around fifty or more interventions based on the expression of the relationship between thoughts, feelings and behaviours. The interventions make use of techniques which enable a number of change processes, particularly important among them is 'metacognition' (the ability to reflect on one's own thoughts and internal world) and cognitive/behavioural habituation. Most of these therapies are based on theories that have received empirical attention to demonstrate their validity. These therapies fall into two basic groups, sometimes referred to as 'second' and 'third wave' cognitive therapies, the first wave being therapies based on behavioural principles. The different forms of CBT often have different theoretical foci, but overlap in significant ways. Below is a brief consideration of the main families of cognitive and behavioural therapies, which arguably have coherent theories and effectiveness evidence bases.

Families of cognitive and behavioural therapies

The most widely used approaches were developed by the 'father' of CBT, Aaron Beck, who first published a fully formulated treatment approach for anxiety and depression in 1979 (Beck et al., 1979). The theory proposes that the negative content of thoughts is important, originally expressed as thinking errors. It is these that lead to and maintain distress and maladaptive safety behaviours, which in turn maintain the thought system. Cognitive processing is acknowledged in terms of distortions, and it is theorised that problematic ways of thinking due to fundamental (core) beliefs and 'rules for living' formed in interaction with childhood experience then lead to 'safety behaviours' that enable the avoidance of distress. Therapeutic interventions involve identifying problematic ways of thinking in terms of content, and testing them and emotion intensity using behavioural experiments. It may be delivered in individual and group formats.

Schema-focused cognitive therapy (Young et al., 2003) was developed to treat the complex interpersonal issues inherent within personality disorder. Young et al. identified 18 fundamental 'schema' from patient records, i.e. clusters of beliefs about the self and others that drive perceptions and maladaptive behaviours. The theory posits different 'modes' of operating (behavioural repertoire subsets), to which people move, depending on contextual factors, and that there are three broad ways of attempting to cope with distress: schema avoidance, overcompensation and surrender.

Dialectical Behaviour Therapy (DBT; see Linehan, 1993) focuses on reducing maladaptive behaviours (particularly self-harming behaviours) and increasing functioning for people with complex trauma issues. The premise is that clients have not yet acquired certain skills, e.g. managing emotions, establishing and maintaining relationships (perhaps due to attachment disruption and/or inconsistent, punishing or neglectful parenting). Emotion dysregulation is a key issue and interventions develop skills to manage anger and anxiety. The biosocial model theorises that the set of symptoms termed 'personality disorder' stem from a combination of an early invalidating environment, together with a biological predisposition to high arousal. The therapeutic relationship is an intrinsic aspect of DBT treatment as a model of a healthy relationship and also to reinforce behaviours that are less harmful to the individual. 'Mindfulness' techniques are used to enable clients to notice the negative judgements that they make about themselves and others.

Acceptance and Commitment Therapy (AaCT; see Hayes et al., 1999) is based on an empirical theory, Relational Frame Theory (RFT), which associates language (internal dialogue) with distressing experience. The useful concept of 'cognitive fusion' is described, i.e. that our emotional experience becomes 'fused' with the words we use to describe it. Treatment makes use of techniques to enable the individual to accept difficult life events and defuse from troubling experience. This may be enabled by experiential 'defusion' from meaning of words and concepts. Articulation of an individual's values is important, which may enable the individual to be clear about behaviours in which they engage that are in the service of those values.

Mindfulness-Based Cognitive Therapy (e.g. Segal et al., 2012) has an evidence base in treating recurrent and severe depression. The practice of mindfulness (purposefully paying attention to experience, including thoughts) has been found to be particularly useful in reducing the intensity of depression experienced, and the lengths and frequency of depressive episodes. The therapy makes use of theoretical findings, indicating that negative moods can increase the likelihood of negative images and thoughts, thereby exacerbating the depressed mood.

Values and ethics

So, that describes CBT. Now we will move on to discuss values and ethics. You may ask why you need to know about general principles of values and ethics? It is quite likely that in your day-to-day practice, these can all seem to be a bit distant and irrelevant. But, you may meet a problem that we have not covered or a combination of issues that seem to need apparently conflicting approaches. You may need to explain the reasons behind your chosen approach to a client or trainee. In these circumstances, you can sometimes find it very helpful to be able to speak from first principles – if you can remember them. We will keep it simple for that reason and, by the end of the chapter, we hope that you might even find it interesting – we have, and have learnt a lot in the process.

Two distinct types of rights are defined by philosophers: natural and legal rights. Natural rights are viewed as more basic 'elemental' and therefore not related to laws, culture or beliefs but fundamental and universal. Legal rights are those which come from specific legal systems derived from individual cultural norms and expectations and so can vary between countries. However, there are also legal rights which transcend national systems: the Universal Declaration of Human Rights is the most prominent of these. In Europe, the Council of Europe also has considerable influence. Each has enshrined natural rights into international law, with the highest priority being given to the right to life and to liberty. There are also specific provisions for people with mental health problems, e.g. in the Council of Europe Committee of Ministers Recommendation on Human Rights and Psychiatry (2004: 11; Kingdon, Jones and Lönnqvist, 2004).

There is a history to this: John Locke (1841) held life, liberty and property to be primary considerations in describing rights:

- Life: Everyone is entitled to live once they have been created.
- Liberty: Everyone is entitled to do anything they want to as long as it does not conflict with the first right. (You might also think that there is a trade-off with other people's rights, and not just of their right to live, but we'll come to that later.)
- Property (or 'Estate'): Everyone is entitled to own all they create or gain through gift or trade, so long as it does not conflict with the first two rights.

However, property has been deemed in some frameworks to be subordinate to 'pursuit of happiness'. In the 1776 United States Declaration of Independence, these rights were famously condensed to:

> We hold these truths to be self-evident, that all men are created equal, that they are endowed by their Creator with certain unalienable Rights ...

The signers of the Declaration of Independence deemed it a 'self-evident truth' that all men are 'endowed by their Creator with certain unalienable rights'. 'Unalienable' means 'incontrovertible' – or, if that doesn't help explain it, 'absolute rights'. However, it may not matter because Rousseau (1920) believed that the existence of unalienable rights, whatever they are, is unnecessary for the existence of a constitution or a set of laws and rights. His idea was of a 'social contract', which is the most widely recognised alternative to unalienable rights. The social contract describes the agreement between members of a country to live within a shared system of laws and that rights and responsibilities are derived from a consensual, agreed, contract between the government and the people. Specific actions of government are the result of the decisions made by members acting in their joint collective capacity. Government is instituted to make laws that protect the three natural rights mentioned previously, i.e. to life, liberty and property. However, if a government does not properly protect these rights, the populous, the people, has the right to overthrow it.

Hutcheson, on this theme, also placed clear limits on the notion of unalienable rights, declaring that: 'there can be no Right, or Limitation of Right, inconsistent with, or opposite to the greatest public Good'. He elaborated on this idea of unalienable rights in *A System of Moral Philosophy* (Hutcheson, 1755), based on the principle of the liberty of conscience. This had come about because of the Reformation of the Church which had bought to prominence the idea that there were further rights that were important and acting according to your conscience was one of these rights.

This is getting nearer to, but does complicate, the discussion about rights as it relates to professional practice. This idea meant that you could not give up the capacity for private judgement, e.g. about religious questions, regardless of any external contracts or oaths to religious or secular authorities, so that right is also, here we go again, 'unalienable' according to Hutcheson (1755):

> Thus no man can really change his sentiments, judgments, and inward affections, at the pleasure of another; nor can it tend to any good to make him profess what is contrary to his heart. The right of private judgment is therefore unalienable. (Hutcheson, 1755: 261–2)

In contrast, a thing, say, a piece of property, can, in fact, be transferred from one person to another. According to Hegel, the same would not apply to those aspects that make one a person:

> The right to what is in essence inalienable is imprescriptible, since the act whereby I take possession of my personality, of my substantive essence, and make myself a responsible being, capable of possessing rights and with a moral and religious life, takes away from these characteristics of mine just that externality which alone made them capable of passing into the possession of someone else. When I have thus annulled their externality, I cannot lose them through lapse of time or from any other reason drawn from my prior consent or willingness to alienate them. (Hegel, 1967: 66)

In discussion of social contract theory, 'inalienable rights' were said to be those rights that could not be surrendered by citizens to the sovereign. Such rights were thought to be *natural rights*, independent of positive law. Some social contract theorists reasoned, however, that in the natural state, only the strongest could benefit from their rights. Thus, people form an implicit social contract, giving up their natural rights to the governing authority to protect the people from abuse, and living under the legal rights of that authority.

As no people can lawfully surrender their religious liberty by giving up their right of judging for themselves in religion, or by allowing any human beings to prescribe to them what faith they shall embrace, or what mode of worship they shall practise, then neither can any civil societies lawfully surrender their civil liberty by giving up to any external body their power of legislating for themselves and disposing of their property. In other words, no group of people can give up their right to choose a religion – or not to choose one – or set laws for them or dispose of their own property.

The 1948 Universal Declaration of Human Rights asserts that rights are inalienable:

> recognition of the inherent dignity and of the equal and inalienable rights of all members of the human family is the foundation of freedom, justice and peace in the world.

The Council of Europe was established in 1949 after the Second World War to promote human rights, democracy and the rule of law in its member states and essentially be a barrier against further devastating conflicts. It includes the European Convention on Human Rights 1950, which has been incorporated into UK law by way of the Human Rights Act 1998. The European Court on Human Rights has jurisdiction over UK law and appeal to it is possible, especially for human rights issues.

The Committee against Torture is a monitoring body which includes oversight of mental hospitals and regularly visits countries to inspect them. It does not have the resources to inspect all hospitals but does have the right to do so. The Council of Ministers of the Council of Europe issued a recommendation on psychiatry and human rights in 2004 and this has implications for mental health services. It includes reference to the importance of professional standards and regulatory bodies (referred to later) and also an oversight commission in each country. This was the Mental Health Act Commission in the UK but this function now forms part of the remit of the Care Quality Commission.

International documents establishing legal rights

The Magna Carta (1215, England) required the King of England to renounce certain rights and respect certain legal procedures, and to accept that the will of the King could be bound by law.

The Declaration of Arbroath (1320, Scotland) established the right of the people to choose a head of state (see Popular Sovereignty).

The Bill of Rights (1689, England) declared that Englishmen, as embodied by Parliament, possess certain civil and political rights.

The Claim of Right (1689, Scotland) was one of the key documents of Scottish constitutional law.

Virginia Declaration of Rights (1776) by George Mason declared the inherent natural rights and separation of powers.

United States Declaration of Independence (1776) succinctly defined the rights of man as including, but not limited to, 'Life, liberty, and the pursuit of happiness', which later influenced 'liberté, égalité, fraternité' (liberty, equality, fraternity) in France.

The phrase can also be found in Chapter III, Article 13 of the 1947 Constitution of Japan.

Also, Article 3 of the Universal Declaration of Human Rights reads: 'Everyone has the right to life, liberty and security of person'.

The Declaration of the Rights of Man and of the Citizen (1789, France) was one of the fundamental documents of the French Revolution, defining a set of individual rights and collective rights of the people.

The Universal Declaration of Human Rights (1948) is a comprehensive set of standards by which governments, organisations and individuals would measure their behaviour towards each other. It declares that the 'recognition of the inherent dignity and of the equal and inalienable rights of all members of the human family is the foundation of freedom, justice and peace in the world ...'.

The European Convention on Human Rights (1950, Europe) was adopted under the auspices of the Council of Europe to protect human rights and fundamental freedoms.

The International Covenant on Civil and Political Rights (1966) is a follow-up to the Universal Declaration of Human Rights, concerning civil and political rights.

The International Covenant on Economic, Social and Cultural Rights (1966) is another follow-up to the Universal Declaration of Human Rights, concerning economic, social and cultural rights.

The Charter of Fundamental Rights of the European Union (2000) is one of the most recent legal instruments concerning human rights.

Rights in relation to acts on the person are important in mental health settings as these affect consideration of what level of intrusion and the circumstances involved and sanctioned is appropriate in physical but also psychological terms. This protects therapists in circumstances where they are asking about personal issues and provides the protections and rights that the client has.

At an extreme level, the libertarian non-aggression principle is relevant as it holds that only the initiation of force is prohibited; defensive, restitutive or even retaliatory force is not. Clearly, physical coercion will not be appropriate in therapeutic encounters. However, as effective interventions are developed in circumstances where patients are severely unwell, psychiatrists, nurses and psychologists can be acting, at least partially, as 'therapists' with people who lack insight into a need for treatment, and will be involved in situations where force is used, e.g. to administer medication and detain people in hospital. It is therefore important to be aware of the principles involved where this is occurring. Even if physical coercion is not likely to feature in their practice circumstances, all therapists need to be aware of the potential for psychological coercion and similar principles apply.

The provisions of the Helsinki Agreement, again established after the Second World War, govern specific issues regarding research. The World Medical Association (WMA) developed the Declaration of Helsinki (1913) as a statement of ethical principles for medical research involving human subjects, including research on identifiable human material and data. It forms the foundation for the ethical conduct of research and, so, is relevant to any research activity involving human beings and hence underpins Research Ethics Committees.

Safeguarding of clients is now receiving much greater attention than previously due to, sadly, numerous occasions where rights of vulnerable people have been seriously infringed by people caring for them, including therapists, and others who have been in a position of power over them. Social and health care helps people with care and support needs to live full lives, free from abuse and neglect. This includes preventing abuse, minimising risk without taking control away from individuals, and responding proportionately if abuse or neglect has occurred. Health services, including therapists and mental health practitioners, local authorities, other care providers, housing providers and criminal justice agencies, are all important safeguarding partners who collaborate to protect clients whilst also empowering them (see Chapter 2).

The Care Act 2014 in England introduced new safeguarding duties for local authorities, including leading a multi-agency local adult safeguarding system, making or causing enquiries to be made where there is a safeguarding concern, hosting safeguarding adults boards, carrying out safeguarding adults reviews and arranging for the provision of independent advocates. Within health organisations, safeguarding processes are, or have been, developed to make sure that where there are concerns about vulnerability, neglect or abuse, there is a robust route to see that action is taken to remedy or protect the individual.

Empowerment and safeguarding are amongst the key sources of values described for mental health practitioners. Ten Essential Shared Capabilities (Hope, 2004) have been described, defining service user rights and responsibilities, values-based practice and recovery principles.

Ten Essential Shared Capabilities

1. Working in Partnership
2. Respecting Diversity
3. Practising Ethically
4. Challenging Inequality
5. Promoting Recovery
6. Identifying People's Needs and Strengths
7. Providing Service User Centred Care
8. Making a Difference
9. Promoting Safety and Positive Risk Management
10. Personal Development and Learning

(Hope, 2004)

Cognitive behaviour therapy: collective values and personal values

The values that are embedded in psychotherapy, such as anti-discriminatory practice, empowerment of clients, respect of diversity, have consistency with these legal rights as expressed by the Universal Declaration of Human Rights (1948). However, it is worth considering to what extent the CBT theoretical model fits with the Human Rights Act's notion of justice and anti-oppressive values, and also with the values depicted in the Ten Essential Shared Capabilities (Hope, 2004), chiefly challenging inequality. There is no argument that, as therapists, we endeavour to act in accordance with such worthy values, however, it can be beneficial for all to sometimes question the theoretical model that is employed. Within CBT, whilst importance is placed on the client and therapist working together to develop more helpful thinking styles and behaviour, the 'problem' is predominantly located at the level of the client. The CBT theoretical model emphasises the interaction of cognitions, physiology, emotions and behaviours within a context. However, given that structural oppression and inequality exist in society (Lago, 2006), is the role of the environment sufficiently developed in the model? Is structural oppression that may be relevant to the client adequately taken into account? Does it need to be? These are perhaps the sorts of questions that CB therapists need to reflect on to ensure that they are not unwittingly perpetuating values or standards of behaviour that they have little regard for, in this case, inequality and oppression.

This said, therapists' values are influenced by the professional code of practice and ethics that the therapist adheres to. The British Association for Behavioural and Cognitive Psychotherapies (BABCP) code of Standards of Conduct, Performance and Ethics, like other codes of practice, not only communicates the collective values of the profession it represents (Francis and Dugger, 2014), but also shapes values. Although, the BABCP's code does not make a clear statement about the values that underpin it, like, for instance, the Australian Code of Ethics (APS, 2007), which names the underpinning values as:

- Respect for the rights and dignity of people and peoples
- Propriety
- Integrity

The BABCP's values are, nevertheless, evident. It is apparent from reading the document that the values that are significant within the BABCP code relate to:

- Honesty and integrity
- Respect for the dignity of others
- Co-operation
- Responsibility and accountability
- Protection of service users
- Effectiveness

The values held within the BABCP code of Standards of Conduct, Performance and Ethics are unsurprisingly consistent with the inherent values of the CBT theoretical model that accentuates working collaboratively, with respect for the client's subjective meaning and safety, while employing empirically informed techniques. Whilst these values inform our practice, we have to remember also that, in the socialisation process, values from our personal history, private life and culture may also influence our practice. It is not improbable, therefore, that the values that the therapist holds might at times be challenged within the therapeutic context. Tension could be experienced in relation to the differing values held by the client, or even with those endorsed by the employing agency, particularly if the employer's values are firmly linked to commercial priorities (Shillito-Clarke, 2003). Although therapists recognise the importance of not dismissing the client's values (Barnes and Murdin, 2001), it remains possible that the therapist's personal values may unintentionally enter the therapy room, particularly when working with vulnerable clients. The therapist's response to the client's disclosures, either verbally or via non-verbal communication, may reveal their conflicting personal values, and hence disempower or confuse the client.

Just as it is important to question the values underpinning the CBT model, so is it of course beneficial for therapists to reflect on their own value system. For instance, they may question what their current values are and how they have changed. Upon reflection, it becomes possible to prioritise which values hold greater personal significance and how they are congruent with those of the profession. What is more, is that it is suggested that reflecting on values can facilitate deeper self-knowledge and develop ethical thinking (Ellis, 2015).

Ethical theories

Ethics is concerned with conduct. It questions the rights and wrongs of behaviour, and therefore pervades every aspect of our life. Within the health care profession, the ethical theories of Deontology, Utilitarianism and Virtue Ethics are evident. Although they can be somewhat aspirational in nature, these theories help in the decision-making process of which action to follow. While the theories may lead to the same action, the reasoning behind them will differ. There are a range of perspectives within each theory, however having an understanding of the basic theories will enable the therapist to reflect upon the values that underpin them, and identify which are congruent with their own values. We will briefly look at these theories now as an overview, but in-depth reading is recommended.

Deontology

Deontology, derived from the work of Immanuel Kant (1724–1804), is concern with 'duty': a duty to certain principles or rules. It utilises reasoning to create rules and gives prominence to the agent's intention behind an act (Playford et al., 2015). It does not, however, focus on consequences. Kant's Categorical Imperative states: 'Act only according to the maxim by which you can at the same time follow will that it should become a universal law' (cited in Van Staveren, 2007: 23). This fundamental rule is associated with a number of underlying principles, which include the Principle of Universalisability and the Principle of Humanity.

The Principle of Universalisability suggests that a moral rule for living is one that can be applied to anyone, all of the time. This, arguably, could be problematic, given the diversity of society and the range of value systems that are evident. Nevertheless, from this perspective, it is deemed that some actions are intrinsically good and others intrinsically bad. It suggests that we have a duty to do what is intrinsically good, such as telling the truth, and avoid what is intrinsically bad, such as telling lies. It is not too difficult, though, to imagine that following such a rule could lead to harm. It might be difficult to follow this rule if, for instance, someone was at risk of harm from a perpetrator, and to tell the truth might endanger them. Even though it may be less challenging to understand how some action or inactions, for example refraining from killing someone may be sensible and perceived as intrinsically good, do such rules translate to all situations? Consider life-threatening situations.

Act Deontology, a branch of Deontology, in some ways moderates traditional Rule Deontology by formulating rules that take into consideration the situation. If we look at the Principle of Universalisability and the action of keeping confidentiality within the therapeutic context, a maxim or principle from an Act Deontologist perspective might be: 'Keep confidentiality unless someone will suffer serious harm'. The intention behind keeping confidentiality within the therapeutic situation is based on the need for trust. If therapists were to breach confidentiality with no regard for their clients, then trust or fidelity would have no meaning in therapy.

Deontological principles can be observed in ethical codes. A list of obligations for therapists to adhere to, for instance, appear in the BABCP's code under the heading: 'Your Duties as a Member of the BABCP' (p. 3). The duty, for example, 'You must act in the best interest of your client', is a universal principle for all therapists to follow. Moreover, duties that are consistent with the Principle of Humanity which communicates the value of equality and justice, are also communicated in ethical codes. By example, the APS Code of Ethics (2007) states under the principle of Justice, 'Psychologists assist their clients to address unfair discrimination or prejudice that is directed against their client' (A.1.3). The obligation to treat others with respect principally draws attention to the need to treat people as an end in themselves, and not as a means to an end. In other words, not to use or manipulate people to fulfil our needs. So, again, if we look at this principle in relation to CBT, it could be argued that its emphasis on collaboration helps to negate treating people as a means. However, when we look at the same principle in relation to certain procedures, treating clients as an end in themselves might be less discernible. From a Deontological perspective, collecting measures each week without fail from clients in order to demonstrate the effectiveness of a service could be construed as treating people as a means to an end.

Although Deontology employs reason and reflection to discover which principle or rule should be followed, determining the appropriate rule or the weightier duty can be problematic. This can be particularly challenging in the therapeutic situation where there can be a number of competing duties.

Utilitarianism

In contrast to Deontology, Utilitarianism, also known as Consequentialism, relates moral actions with outcomes. Carefully assessing the consequence of actions are fundamental to this theory. Utilitarianism was derived from the work of Jeremy Bentham (1748–1832) and of John Stuart Mill (1806–73). It proposes that an action is right if it produces the best outcome for the greatest number, or, as Mill advocated, 'the greatest happiness for the greatest number' (cited in Playford et al., 2015). So, if we consider the therapeutic setting again, and the example above of collecting data from each client after every session to demonstrate the effectiveness of a service, it could be argued from this perspective to be a good thing. If the data demonstrates that the service is effective, then, as a consequence, the service remains available to benefit many people.

Even if the data reveals that the service is not effective, then funding could be redirected to a more useful service, again to the greater good of many people. (Assuming, of course, that the tools employed measure what they are supposed to measure.) It would seem that collecting the data potentially benefits many, and outweighs the inconvenience that the client and therapist may experience.

Similar to Deontology, Utilitarianism can be separated into Rule and Act. Briefly, the former, Rule Utilitarianism, advocates that rules for moral actions can be derived at by calculating outcomes, the rules can then be generalised to other situations to produce good outcomes. Although Act Utilitarianism also recognises the need to calculate the best outcomes, it proposes that to derive the best outcome necessitates a calculation of consequences in each situation. Although it might appear to be a straightforward approach simply calculating the best outcome for the greatest number, it can be problematical in assessing or predicting outcomes. Short-term consequences may be very different to long-term ones. Moreover, maximising benefits for the greatest number could result in the minority being overlooked, thus undermining the values of justice and equality.

Virtue Ethics

The ethical theories discussed so far have been concerned with formulating and following rules. However, Virtue Ethics, originating from the work of Aristotle (384–322 BC), rather than being guided by principles and rules, focuses its attention on the qualities or traits of the moral agent. The moral agent currently under discussion is the therapist. Characteristics or virtues, such as kindness, patience, honesty, having integrity, are valued. Consideration of how someone with such virtuous characteristics may behave in a given situation, guides action. A virtuous agent is naturally inclined to do good (Dalal, 2014), and, according to Meara et al. (1996), they possess vision and discernment and will therefore behave morally. Although it is 'person-centred' in nature as the focus is on the virtuous agent (Begley, 2005), it also recognises the meaning of significant relationships, social relations and context as affecting decisions and actions (Shillito-Clarke, 2003).

Cultivating good habits, such as integrity and respect for others, and hence developing the self, is consistent with many ethical codes of practice, and are observed within the BABCP's ethical code and the APS Code of Ethics. However, it is not clear how being a virtuous agent enables objective decision-making. Indeed, it is questionable if a good person with good motives always produces the best or right outcome.

Moreover, it is necessary to be able to justify actions, particular when faced with an ethical dilemma. Virtue Ethics does not provide a guide to decision-making. Nonetheless, the virtuous qualities advocated by Virtue Ethics are valued within the therapeutic context, and are certainly sought when recruiting CB therapists (BABCP, Knowledge, Skills and Attitudes (KSA)).

Activities

- Consider what values you hold as important. How do they fit with being a CB therapist?
- How are measures and targets used in your organisation? Does this fit with a Deontological or an Utilitarianism approach?
- Reflect on the values that are predominant in your current employment. How congruent are they with your values?
- What would you do if you felt that working in your client's best interest conflicted with your agency's policies? How would you resolve this dilemma? Do the ethical principles compete? What are your responsibilities in this situation?

2

CONCEPTS IN CLINICAL ETHICS

Learning outcomes

After reading this chapter and completing the activities at the end of it, you should be able to:

1. Understand some of the basic ethical concepts governing practice.
2. Be better equipped to balance autonomy and 'best interests'.
3. Be aware of the importance that clients' rights are safeguarded.
4. Understand the concept of clinical negligence in relation to CBT practice.

This chapter will cover a number of concepts that need definition and understanding in relation to a broad understanding of ethics and values. They will be dealt with separately but will be drawn together near the end of the chapter.

Autonomy

Autonomy comes from the words for 'self' and 'law', so it literally means: 'one who gives oneself their own law'. Autonomy is therefore the ability of the person to make his or her own decisions. This is a very important principle in any therapeutic work and especially in cognitive behavioural approaches, which stress collaboration and self-individuation.

It is a concept found in moral, political and bioethical philosophy, describing the capacity of a rational individual to make an informed decision without coercion – i.e. pressure – from others. In moral and political philosophy, autonomy is often used as the basis for determining moral responsibility for one's actions.

In medicine, respect for the autonomy of patients is an important goal of deontology (duty-based ethics). Duty-based ethics are concerned with what people do, not with the consequences of their actions. Simply:

- Do the right thing.
- Do it because it's the right thing to do.
- Don't do wrong things.
- Avoid wrong things because they are wrong.

Under this form of ethics, you can't justify an action by showing that it produced good consequences, which is why it is sometimes called 'non-Consequentialist'. In other words, the 'ends do not justify the means'. This may seem to conflict with a competing ethical principle, namely beneficence – 'best interests' – which involves seeing that actions taken result in the most positive outcome for an individual. The latter can therefore be seen as being in contrast to autonomy or perhaps it might be better appreciated as providing a balance to it. Because you or others think that something is right for someone and make a strong case for it, it does not mean that they should be compelled to comply.

Many definitions of autonomy place the individual in a social context, e.g. relational autonomy: a person is defined through their relationships with others; supported autonomy differs in that, in certain specific circumstances, it may be necessary to temporarily compromise the autonomy of the person in the short term in order to preserve their autonomy in the long term, e.g. when ill, dependence on others for assistance can allow healing and recovery to take place so that a return to independence or autonomy is possible. Other definitions of autonomy see the person as a contained and self-sufficient being whose rights should not be compromised under any circumstance. The Convention on the Rights of Persons with Disabilities (United Nations, 2007) also defines autonomy as principles of rights of person with disability, including: 'the freedom to make one's own choices, and independence of persons'. In social psychology, autonomy is a personality trait, focusing on a personal achievement of independence, and a preference for solitude, often associated with sociotropy (social avoidance).

In health care, this was initially framed in a medical context – respect for a patient's personal autonomy is considered one of many fundamental ethical principles. This faith in autonomy is the central premise in the concepts of informed consent and shared decision-making. This idea has emerged and been refined in the last 50 to 100 years to the extent where it is considered essential to today's practice of medicine and broader health and social care. Highly influential here were the Nuremberg trials that detailed accounts of horrifyingly exploitative medical 'experiments' that violated the subjects' physical integrity and personal autonomy. These incidences prompted calls for safeguards in medical research and clinical practice and have led to current legislation and codes of conduct (see Helsinki Principles in Chapter 1).

Users of the health care system have the right to be treated with respect for their autonomy: concern about abuses and also more subtle domination and coercion by the power and authority of the physician has driven this process. But, it also applies to all those in positions of power, including as exerted by therapists, over others specifically in a health care context where individuals are vulnerable due to health and social reasons. This is amplified for specific populations, e.g. children, old people and those with learning disabilities (known in many countries as mental handicap or retardation) or mental health problems.

Through the therapeutic relationship, a collaborative dialogue between the client and the practitioner can lead to better outcomes for the client as he or she is more of a participant in decision-making. The concept of expert-by-experience signifies the relationship that seems most likely to be effective.

Informed consent

Informed consent is a protection against coercion and infringements of autonomy.

The seven elements of informed consent include:

- Threshold elements: Competence and Voluntariness
- Information elements: Disclosure, Recommendation and Understanding
- Consent elements: Decision and Authorisation

In certain unique circumstances, the government may have defined the right in law to temporarily override the right to bodily integrity, autonomy, in order to preserve the life and well-being of the person. Such action can be described using the principle of supported autonomy, a concept that was developed to describe unique situations in mental health (examples include the forced feeding of a person dying from the eating disorder anorexia nervosa, or the temporary treatment of a person living with a psychotic disorder with anti-psychotic medication). While controversial, the principle of supported autonomy is consistent with the role of government to protect the life and liberty of its citizens. Forced psychological therapy is, of course, much more difficult to envisage, let alone implement, but coercion to participate can occur in many forms and equally affect autonomy. For example, commitment by the courts to attend therapy as an alternative to custody, 'therapy for benefits' (see Chapter 9), or intensive family or mental health team pressure, involve influence that can amount to coercion. Persuasion is acceptable, coercion into therapy is not - but when does one become the other? This can be judged by the amount of repetition, threatened consequences and persistence of encouragement to participate, the robustness of the response not to do so - but this can be influenced by personal unassertiveness, ambivalence or actions consistent or inconsistent with participating. Arguments given by families can merge into 'emotional blackmail' - 'I'll leave you if you don't go to therapy,' although the comment that 'unless you seek help, it will inevitably endanger our relationship' could be considered simply a factual one. Sometimes, someone may clearly say that they do not want to participate in therapy but then turn up and start to become involved. It is important to understand why and allow the possibility of change but not assist in coercion.

Pressure from family - 'do it for us' - can be reasonable but also contribute to a coercive approach. Financial and other incentives complicate matters still further - 'I'll let you have your welfare benefits if you go' - whether from family or government is very suspect in terms of interfering with autonomy. There is a contrary argument that those receiving such assistance have a duty to do all they can to improve their mental state and capabilities and, if not, it is reasonable not to provide them with as much, if any, support (see Chapter 9).

Best interests

'Best interests' is the doctrine used by courts to determine a wide range of issues relating to the well-being of children and vulnerable people. Important amongst these include questions that arise on the divorce or separation of the children's parents or death of a carer. But there are similarities in the considerations of children with vulnerable people, including those with mental health problems, and also differences to highlight.

In English law, the Children Act 1989 makes the interests of any child the paramount concern of the court in all proceedings and, having indicated that delay is likely to prejudice the interests of any child, it requires the court to consider the 'welfare checklist', i.e. the court (and therefore others involved with a child's care) must consider:

- The needs, wishes and the ascertainable wishes and feelings of each child concerned (considered in light of their age and understanding).
- Physical, emotional and/or educational needs now and in the future.
- The likely effect on any change in the circumstances now and in the future.
- Age, sex, background and any other characteristics that the court considers relevant.
- Any harm suffered or at risk of suffering now and in the future.
- How capable each parent, and other person in relation to whom the court considers the question to be relevant, is of meeting the child's needs.
- The range of powers available to the court under the Children Act 1989 in the proceedings in question.

The rights of vulnerable people are not framed in the same way, i.e. that they are paramount, but similar considerations to those above apply.

Feelings of the child or vulnerable person should be elicited and the analysis of these is vital to ensure that their human rights are always in the forefront of all considerations. The welfare checklist provides a comprehensive list of issues that need to be considered in order to ensure that those who come into court proceedings are fully safeguarded and that their rights as citizens are promoted.

The Best Interests standard has received considerable criticism by certain groups within the privacy rights and family law reform movement, particularly with regard to how it unlawfully marginalises children from one of their parents and often cultivates protracted litigation. Critics argue that a higher evidentiary standard should be applied to fit parents, and that the Best Interests standard should only be applied in cases where a termination of parental rights has already occurred (Social Care Institute for Excellence (SCIE), undated).

In therapy with children and vulnerable people, the above considerations need to apply and therapists may become involved in decision-making in relation to providing advice on what is in the best interests of individuals.

Mental capacity

If a person has a mental disorder, this may affect their capacity to make decisions, and an assessment of their capacity to do so will be necessary.

However, this is relatively unusual and can be assumed wrongly - just because someone has a mental disorder does not mean that they cannot make decisions for themselves. The presumption must always be that someone has the capacity to decide on any specific decision, exert autonomy, unless the contrary can be demonstrated. Assessment of such capacity requires establishing that the person can understand relevant information on which the decision is based and that they can retain the information for long enough to come to a decision, reason about it and communicate their decision to others.

Assessment of such capacity requires:

1. Consideration of whether a person has a mental disorder.
2. Establishing that the person can understand relevant information on which the decision is based.
3. That they can retain the information for long enough to come to a decision.
4. That they can weigh up the evidence and so reason about it.
5. That they can communicate their decision to others.

The Mental Capacity Act 2005 in England and 'best interests' meeting was established to plan actions to ensure that people are fully involved, protected and supported in the decisions that affect them. Specific decisions are considered: in some circumstances, it can be the situation that the person has difficulty making any decisions but, more frequently, some decision-making is possible but specific individual decisions are either too complex or emotionally laden to be taken in a capacitous manner, i.e. the person does not have the capacity to decide on specific matters such as the use of finances or where to live.

Safeguarding involves protection from abuse and, in this safeguarding context, mental capacity is the ability of a person to understand the implications of their situation and the risks to themselves, take action themselves to prevent abuse and anticipate to the fullest extent what is possible in decision-making about interventions involving them, be they life-changing events or everyday matters.

The Mental Capacity Act 2005 in England is an example of developed legislation in this area. It is based on several key principles:

1. Assumption of capacity: All adults, even those felt to be lacking in mental capacity, have the right to make their own decisions and must be assumed to have capacity to make decisions about their own safety unless it is proved (on a balance of probabilities) otherwise.
2. Support to make decisions: Adults at risk must receive all appropriate help and support to make decisions before anyone concludes that they cannot make their own decisions.

3. Right to make unwise decisions: Adults at risk have the right to make decisions that others might regard as being unwise or eccentric and a person cannot be treated as lacking capacity for these reasons.
4. Best interests: Decisions made on behalf of a person who lacks mental capacity must be done in their best interests and should be the least restrictive of their basic rights and freedoms.
5. Least restrictive option: Someone making a decision or acting on behalf of a person who lacks capacity must consider whether it is possible to act in a way that would interfere less with the person's rights and freedoms of action.

Communicating the decision could be done by talking, using sign language or even simple muscle movements such as blinking an eye or squeezing a hand. Every effort should be made to find ways of communicating with someone before deciding that they lack capacity to make a decision based solely on their inability to communicate. Also, you will need to involve family, friends, carers or other professionals, according to the individual's consent.

The assessment must be made on the balance of probabilities - is it more likely than not that the person lacks capacity? You should be able to show in your records why you have come to your conclusion that capacity is lacking for the particular decision.

The person who assesses an individual's capacity to make a decision will usually be the person who is directly concerned with dealing with the outcome of the decision that is made. This means that different people will be involved in assessing someone's capacity to make different decisions at different times. For the majority of day-to-day decisions, this is most likely to be the person caring for them at the time when a decision must be made.

A care worker might need to assess whether the person can agree to being bathed, whereas a district nurse might assess whether the person can consent to having a pressure sore cleaned. When assessing a person's capacity to consent to care or treatment, the assessor must have a 'reasonable belief' that the person lacks capacity to agree to the action or decision to be taken. While it is generally one person making the assessment, complex decisions may involve the multidisciplinary team (the team of people from different professional backgrounds who provide support to a person). In many settings, it is best practice to devise a written care plan setting out in advance with the individual and their family members what their preferred decisions are so that these are clear to all staff.

Similarly, solicitors and legal staff must assess the client's capacity to instruct them on legal transactions (for example, making a will).

More complex decisions are likely to need more formal assessments. This means that any assessor should have the skills and ability to communicate effectively with the person. If necessary, they should get professional help to communicate with the person.

The Mental Capacity Act 2005 provides the following guidance when assessing a person's ability to make their own decisions:

1. Does the person have all the relevant information they need to make the decision?
2. If they are making a decision that involves choosing between alternatives, do they have information on all the different options?
3. Would the person have a better understanding if information was explained or presented in another way?
4. Are there times of day when the person's understanding is better?
5. Are there locations where they may feel more at ease?
6. Can the decision be put off until the circumstances are different and the person concerned may be able to make the decision?
7. Can anyone else help the person to make choices or express a view (for example, a family member or carer, an advocate or someone to help with communication)?

We all have the right to make unwise choices. Choosing something out of the ordinary is not an indication of a lack of capacity, nor necessarily is choosing something that involves risk. However, if someone consistently makes unwise decisions that place them at significant risk, this might be sufficient grounds to question their capacity. It is important to remember that everyone has their own values, beliefs and preferences, which may not be the same as yours. You cannot treat people as lacking capacity because they hold different values, beliefs or preferences from your own.

We need to do our best to understand the beliefs and values of the person whose capacity to make decisions is under question. We do this by seeking evidence of a person's beliefs and values, which can be found in things like their cultural background, religious beliefs, political convictions and past behaviour or habits.

Best interests considerations do not discriminate: do not make assumptions about someone's best interests merely on the basis of the person's age or appearance, condition or any aspect of their behaviour – take into account all relevant circumstances. It involves determining, as far as possible, what an adult would do if they had capacity. So, you decide not on what is best for them in your judgement (as you would with children) but by asking those who know them and consulting any advanced directive or other relevant communication what their decisions would be. An example might be when one of our partners loses capacity, she has expressed that it is in her best interests to eat cake when she gets stressed, even if it may not be to the benefit of her physical health, because that is what she does now.

If faced with a particularly difficult or contentious decision, it is recommended that practitioners adopt a 'balance sheet' approach (weighing up the advantages and disadvantages of each option, in turn). Will the person regain capacity? If so, can the decision wait? Involve the individual as fully as possible and take into account the individual's past and present wishes and feelings, and any beliefs and values likely to have a bearing on the decision. It is advisable to consult as far and as widely as possible.

The principle of taking the least restrictive option is a central one. If you make a best interests decision on behalf of someone judged to lack capacity, it is important that you make the choice that least restricts the person's liberty. This means that, before you make a decision or act on behalf of a person who lacks capacity to make that decision or consent to the act, you must always question whether you can do something else that would interfere less with the person's basic rights and freedoms (and would not close down or reduce the future choices available to them). This includes considering whether there is a need to act or make a decision at all.

The Deprivation of Liberty Safeguards are an amendment to the Mental Capacity Act 2005. They apply in England and Wales only. The Mental Capacity Act allows restraint and restrictions to be used – but only if they are in a person's best interests. Extra safeguards are needed if the restraint and restrictions used will deprive a person of their liberty and they do not have the capacity to consent; these are called the Deprivation of Liberty Safeguards. The Deprivation of Liberty Safeguards can only be used if the person will be deprived of their liberty in a care home or hospital. In other settings, the Court of Protection can be asked if a person can be deprived of their liberty.

The ways in which people's freedoms are curtailed include: using locks or key pads, which stop a person going out or into different areas of a building; the use of some medication, for example to calm a person; close supervision in the home or requiring a person to be supervised when out; restricting contact with family, friends and acquaintances, including if they could cause the person harm; physically stopping a person from doing something that could cause them harm; removing items from a person that could cause them harm; holding a person so that they can be given care or treatment; use of bedrails, wheelchair straps and splints; the person having to stay somewhere against their wishes or against the wishes of a family member.

Abuse

Abuse is about the misuse of the power and control that one person has over another and intent is not the central issue. Abuse can occur through lack of consideration of consequences of actions, even if there is no intent to misuse power or control.

Types of abuse include: physical abuse, emotional abuse: threats, deprivation of contact, shouting, ignoring, cruelty, bullying, humiliation, coercion, negating the right of the adult at risk to make choices and undermining self-esteem; sexual abuse.

Sexual abuse is the direct or indirect involvement of the adult at risk in sexual activity or relationships, which they do not want or have not consented to or cannot understand and lack the mental capacity to be able to give consent to or have been coerced into because the other person is in a position of trust, power or authority (for example, a care worker or therapist). It can lead directly to mental health problems (e.g. Larkin and Morrison, 2007), although this is certainly not inevitable.

Abuse includes: neglect and acts of omission - things that should have been done and are not; and financial exploitation - the use of a person's property, assets, income, funds or any resources without their informed consent or authorisation.

Discriminatory abuse occurs when someone's cultural beliefs or rituals result in a misuse of power that denies opportunity to some groups or individuals. It can be a feature of any form of abuse of an adult at risk, but can also be motivated because of age, gender, sexuality, disability, religion, class, culture, language and race or ethnic origin. It can result from situations that exploit a person's vulnerability by treating the person in a way that excludes them from opportunities which they should have as equal citizens, for example education, health, justice and access to services and protection. Institutional abuse occurs when the routines, systems and regimes of an institution result in poor or inadequate standards of care and poor practice.

Abuse may be a single act or repeated acts. Abuse may take the form of a single act that has abusive consequences for the vulnerable adult or may comprise a series of acts, large or small, whose cumulative impact adversely affects the individual. It can be unintentional: sometimes, the abusive act was wilful on the part of the perpetrator but, sometimes, it may be unintentional. Causing harm may be unintentional but, nevertheless, harm was caused and therefore abuse has taken place, requiring a response under the safeguarding adults procedures. The nature of the response is likely to depend on whether the act was intentional or not.

An act of neglect or a failure to act includes abuse caused as a result of a person with caring responsibilities acting in a way that is harmful to a dependent person. Failure to act so as to provide the level of care that a reasonable person would be expected to provide, which results in harm to an adult at risk, is also abuse and requires a response under the safeguarding procedures.

Multiple acts can occur – an individual may experience several types of abuse simultaneously. Although the different forms of abuse are presented below as though they are discreet categories, there is often a lot of overlap between them.

In considering abuse, it is necessary to think about whether the adult at risk gave their consent to the abusive act and, if they did, was it informed consent? You might reach the conclusion that the person concerned either did or did not have the mental capacity to make that choice. You need to consider whether consent was given under duress, for example as a result of exploitation, pressure, fear or intimidation. If this is apparent, consent to the abuse is likely to be disregarded. Consent issues need to be addressed with the vulnerable adult at each stage of any investigation – disclosure, interview, referral, investigation, medical examination and the taking of protective action, including the involvement of the police.

The degree of harm is relevant. The seriousness of harm or the extent of the abuse is not always clear at the point when suspicions are raised or concerns come to light. All reports of suspicions or concerns should be approached with an open mind and could give rise to action under the safeguarding adults policies and procedures.

While it is the responsibility of the safeguarding professionals to determine whether or not abuse has taken place, it can be helpful to understand the concept of 'significant harm' on which their decision will be based. 'Significant harm' is a legal concept but is not defined. Rather, practitioners are encouraged to consider: the degree of the vulnerability of the person, the nature and extent of the abuse or neglect; the length of time that the abuse or neglect has been occurring; the impact of the alleged abuse on the adult at risk; the risk of repeated or increasingly serious acts of abuse or neglect; the risk that serious harm could result if no action was taken; the illegality of the act or acts; and the involvement of the police – some abusive acts are clearly criminal and require the involvement of the police. Others may be less easy to categorise. All situations of abuse by a professional are likely to result in police involvement. Where there are allegations against carers who are relatives or friends, a distinction will be made between unintentional harm caused inadvertently by a carer and a deliberate act.

In cases where unintentional harm has occurred, this may be due to lack of knowledge or due to the fact that the carer's own physical or emotional frailties make them unable to care adequately for the adult at risk. The carer may also be an adult at risk.

In this situation, the aim will be to support the carer and to help make changes in their behaviour in order to decrease the risk of further harm to the person they are caring for.

Safeguarding

In safeguarding the individual, services provided should be appropriate to the adult and not discriminate because of disability, age, gender, sexual orientation, race, religion, culture or lifestyle. Individuals must be allowed to make their own decisions as far as possible – and supported to make choices. They should be offered advocacy services as appropriate to their needs.

Ethical scenario

Julie, aged 25, was referred as having emotional problems – distressed, angry and anxious – which had been going on for a number of years but seemed to be getting worse. Her partner was very concerned about her and having difficulties continuing to support her and their 3-year-old daughter.

She had missed her first assessment appointment but turned up a bit late for the second one, saying that she wasn't sure that therapy was going to help. However, she eventually started to talk about how she was feeling, how fed up she was, how nobody cared and how she couldn't see the point in going on. As the assessment developed, she began to talk about her childhood and 'bad things' that had happened to her. She then left the room.

However, she returned for the next appointment and began to talk in more detail about her experiences and disclosed that her uncle had sexually abused her between the ages of 10 and 13. She said that her uncle lives nearby.

Ethical questions

1. What safeguarding responsibilities do you have?
2. How are you going to proceed?

An 'adult at risk' is defined in the UK as a person aged 18 years or older, who is or may be in need of community care services by reason of mental or other disability, age or illness; and who is or may be unable to take care of him or herself, or unable to protect him or herself against significant harm or exploitation. The term 'vulnerable adult' may wrongly imply that some of the fault for the abuse lies with the abused adult. The term 'adult at risk' is used as an exact replacement for 'vulnerable adult', i.e. someone not having the mental capacity to make decisions about their own safety – including having fluctuating mental capacity associated with mental illness, or with communication difficulties, physical dependency – being dependent on others for personal care and activities of daily life, low self-esteem or experience of abuse, including in childhood.

Safeguarding adults at risk applies, even when the person has the capacity to give informed consent to abusive situations. The issue of a person having a lack of assertiveness may also be relevant and thus has to be considered. Some people may also need help in order to express their wishes fully. Assertiveness training can be of help here. The issue of capacity is, of course, crucial in determining action taken but it needs to be clear that action has to be considered even when adults make a capacitous decision, for example not to inform the police. Professionals can then help with a risk reduction plan instead. This is philosophically interesting in relation to autonomy and 'welfarist' considerations, but it is how professionals are expected to operate (at least in the UK) as an adult at risk is one who qualifies for secondary services, not necessarily lacking capacity but entitled to support and treatment.

Factors about a situation that might make someone more at risk of harm include: being cared for in a care setting where they are more or less dependent on others; not getting the right amount or the right kind of care that they need; living in a family with multiple problems, isolation and social exclusion, subject to stigma and discrimination; lack of access to information and support; and being the focus of anti-social behaviour.

Key principles of safeguarding adults include: empowerment; presumption of individual-led decision-making and informed consent; protection – support and representation for those in greatest need; prevention – better to take action before harm occurs; proportionality – least intrusive response appropriate to the risk presented; partnership – working with communities; accountability and transparency in providing protections.

As this can frequently happen in therapy, managing disclosure will be part of the basic skills developed during training. Simply, in responding to someone who is making a disclosure of abuse, it can be helpful to explicitly let them know that they are being taken seriously, being listened to carefully, and being enabled to tell their story with minimal interruption.

Adults at risk should be given information, advice and support in a form that they can understand. Their views and desired outcomes remain central to safeguarding decisions about their lives. All decisions taken by professionals about a person's life should be timely, reasonable, justified, proportionate and ethical.

In mental health practice, it is most commonly the issues of retention of information and reasoning that most often interfere. Retention can be affected by organic disorders, for example dementia and brain damage, but there are potential issues where depression or psychosis are so severe that memory is affected or concentration can be so poor that information is not retained. Reasoning can also be affected by mental health problems and, whilst there are clear-cut examples where decision-making is affected by depression or psychosis, this can sometimes be quite complex, especially where emotional difficulties ('personality disorder') are involved.

For psychosis, the decision under consideration might be affected by voices telling the person to act in a way that is against their best interests and they may feel compelled to comply, or by a delusional belief, e.g. that they are stupendously wealthy, may lead to them spending money they don't have. With depression, they may feel so negative about life and the future, that decisions which affect their well-being and interests are either neglected, made without reasoning on the basis that they are pointless, or acting in a way which affects them, and sometimes others, negatively.

People with persistent emotional difficulties or who are affected by childhood trauma histories ('personality disordered') can present with difficulties in decision-making through indecisiveness, undue concern about the effects on others or need for support from others (which may not be conveyed directly through, for example, fear of disparagement or rejection). Their needs can be great and requests for assistance in decision-making can be a way of seeking validation and support from others that may not have been previously available to them through parental and other relationships. The person themselves may be seeking reassurance or wanting the decision to be made for them. This may be because their decision-making has been taken from them or never given to them in the past and they have become dependent on others as a result. Alternatively, it may be that the decisions that they have made have been ignored, derided or discounted, such that they have come to the conclusion that whatever they say does not influence their situation. A key component of managing capacity to decision-make is that of assisting, encouraging, even training the individual to make those decisions that they are capable of making themselves, and this applies here. It is fully consistent with therapeutic approaches used in these situations (e.g. DBT and CBT).

Decisions about self-harm can be especially complex in this situation. When is it appropriate not to intervene? The automatic response to someone attempting to harm themselves is to try to prevent them from doing so, and where someone is seriously depressed and suicidal or psychotic and acting according to delusional beliefs or voices, this is wholly appropriate. Where the nature of the decision is such that serious harm can ensue, it is perfectly reasonable, ethically and legally (under common law, if not already subject to Mental Health Act provisions), to prevent such harm. It becomes much more complex when a full assessment has been made and the conclusion reached that, at that moment, the individual has the capacity to make the decision about harming themselves and is doing so (see Chapter 9 Suicide and Suicide Prevention Section).

The key message is that safeguarding is everyone's business, especially of those involved in therapeutic interactions. Key things to ensure are that ownership of the safeguarding agenda is acknowledged - being explicit about responsibilities as an individual and as an organisation and disseminating it. Maintaining accurate records is vital - ensuring that clear and up-to-date details are kept on adults being supported, including age, date of birth, address, contact details and emergency contacts. It is also important to list the next of kin (and ask the person for the name of the individual whom they would like to be listed). Maintain and review a record of concerns: all concerns that arise need to be documented with the action taken in response. These need to be reviewed regularly as it may be possible to see patterns of behaviour emerging, which can suggest episodic or accumulating abuse.

Organisations need to follow safe recruitment procedures, including Criminal Records checks or equivalent and so therapists can expect to need to cooperate with these and routinely expect take-up and checking of references.

When a safeguarding issue arises, i.e. when there is concern that somebody is being exploited or abused, this needs to be acted upon. In emergencies, in order to prevent immediate serious harm, the police may be the most appropriate agency to contact. Usually, however, discussion with supervisors, managers or colleagues to clarify the situation and actions to take would be the first step. Agency procedures can be consulted and followed. Where a child or vulnerable person is involved, this may mean contacting an agency with specific responsibilities, e.g. social services or welfare departments. A meeting of all those concerned will often be the way to determine appropriate action. The individual's autonomy and capacity to make the specific decisions involved needs to be fully considered, and often help and guidance are effective in alerting the individual to the potential, and concerning, consequences and they may then adjust accordingly. Where they do not do so, their capacity to make such decisions needs to be assessed and action taken - or not - in response.

Circumstances can arise where clients disclose information but do not want it acted upon, e.g. in relation to abuse. The perpetrator may remain in a position to continue to abuse children or vulnerable adults.

Where identifiable information has been given, this has to be discussed with responsible agencies, e.g. social services, who can then judge what action needs to be taken. Where information provided is more general, it may be appropriate to discuss with the client whether they have access to more specific information and should provide it to protect others. They may be concerned about consequences for themselves and need support for this.

Sometimes, clients will say that they want to discuss something that they want kept totally confidential between them and the therapist. Although it can seem that providing such an assurance can allow communication of material which will not otherwise be disclosed, doing so can lead to major difficulties, if not dangers, and there are certainly no circumstances in which a trainee should agree to this - and probably none for experienced therapists. An ability to discuss with a supervisor or colleague is an essential safeguard and it will always be necessary to explain that certain disclosures would have to be reported onwards. Promises of complete confidentiality, therefore, need to be responded to by explaining the duty to tell others, e.g. managers or other designated people, and possibly social services and the police if concerns are such that this is necessary in protecting them and others. But they will be involved in decisions about what will happen and steps will be taken and support offered to protect them or others from further abuse or neglect. Confidentiality concerns need to be dealt with through discussion and cannot be used simply to withdraw support (see Chapter 5 on Confidentiality).

The safeguarding lead and/or manager in an organisation should be clearly identified, visible and accessible, ensuring that those with concerns can go straight to the person who can do something about them and involve straightforward reporting procedures. A protection plan may be put in place as part of a process to ensure that abuse does not occur and all agencies providing services to the individual, including therapists, can expect to be bound to cooperate with the plan by agreements made by their organisation.

If there is concern that a member of staff has abused an adult at risk, there is a duty to report these concerns and inform a senior manager in your organisation, or another designated manager for safeguarding adults, without delay.

So, in the scenario provided, we need to make explicit that the childhood abuse by the uncle puts the client's child, and potentially others, at risk and would need reporting to the relevant safeguarding authorities to ensure safety due to the risk to the child. It is essential, although too often does not happen, that therapists think about other potential victims, just because the client may be safe now, you cannot assume that all is okay. Risk to other children will also override confidentiality requests, although there will need to be support offered to the client if this leads to, for example, family conflict.

Reporting concerns about colleagues and organisations

'Whistle-blowing' has been highly controversial but is very important: whoever provides care, their first priority is to the person they support and not to their colleagues or their organisation. Organisations and managers need to demonstrate their commitment to a policy where reporting on poor performance of staff or organisations is supported. Processes should be in place and staff should have confidence in them but reporting to external organisations such as the Care Quality Commission and Medical or Nursing Councils is available. Advice from professional bodies, defence organisations, as well as unions, can also be sought on ways to proceed. Reporting to media, e.g. press, radio or TV, has led to the uncovering of serious deficiencies in care in the past but it has to be better for those with management and professional responsibilities to try to resolve issues before escalation to the media.

Organisations potentially affected will include private ones providing psychological services or public ones, e.g. hospitals, community services, NHS Trusts or Improving Access to Psychological Therapies (IAPT) services.

Safety assessment and management

Risk or more positively, safety management involves consideration of factors involving clients: assessment of risk to self or towards others will be a component of management of any client offered CBT and will be a continuing process, although with some, risks will be assessed as very low. Where these are higher, good practice needs to be followed (see Chapter 9). Compliance with statutory regulations can help to improve patient safety. In addition, client risks can be minimised by making sure that systems are regularly reviewed and issues arising dealt with. For example, systems of critical incident review and audit of outcomes and actions from such reviews can improve practice and also development of effective procedures and learning from complaints. Adherence to health care professionals' and therapists' ethical standards are also a key factor in maintaining client and public safety and well-being.

Ensuring safety of practitioners requires quality assurance considerations such that clinicians do not develop physical or mental health problems themselves from the often intense contact with clients, e.g. leading to secondary post-traumatic stress disorder (PTSD) and stress. Mental health management needs to be considered along with ensuring that work occurs in a safe environment, e.g. effective lone-working policies when required, and physical precautions, e.g. whether immunisation against infectious diseases are relevant to their job, and the practitioners are helped to keep up to date with continuing professional development (CPD).

Safety of the organisation is threatened by poor quality of service – leading to poor client outcomes or experiences – and inadequate safeguarding processes. In addition to reducing risks to patients and practitioners, organisations need to: reduce their own risks by ensuring high-quality employment practice, including locum procedures and reviews of individual and team workloads and performance; a safe environment, including effective health and safety policies and training and safe estates; and attention to privacy and well-designed policies on public involvement.

Negligence

Negligence is a failure to exercise the care that a reasonably careful person would exercise in similar circumstances. Medical negligence is professional negligence by act or omission by a health care provider, in which the treatment provided falls below the accepted standard of practice in the medical community and causes injury or death to the patient, with most cases involving medical error. Standards and regulations for medical malpractice vary by country and jurisdiction within countries. Professionals may obtain professional liability insurances to offset the risk and costs of lawsuits based on medical malpractice. The public sector may provide coverage for individuals whilst working for them – but not at other times. However, such insurance will be mandatory in private practice.

A successful medical malpractice claim requires that a duty was owed to the individual claiming. This may be the legal duty that exists whenever a hospital, therapist or health care provider undertakes care or treatment of a patient. If that duty was breached, it means that: the provider failed to conform to the relevant standard care. The breach that occurred caused an injury. Without damage – financial, physical or emotional – there is no basis for a claim, regardless of whether the medical provider was negligent. Damage can occur and does so frequently without negligence, for example when someone dies from a fatal disease.

Circumstances where someone dies from suicide are especially relevant to practice in mental health settings. Coroners are becoming more questioning of whether safety assessments and delivery of care has been adequate by services and, whilst negligence claims in the court are rare, criticisms of organisations and individuals is becoming common. The recognition that people with mental health problems die an estimated 10–20 years earlier than others is also focusing attention on whether the monitoring of their physical health, lifestyle interventions offered and health care provided has been sufficient when they do die prematurely. The ethical concept of 'parity of esteem' for mental and physical health has been accepted by the UK (Health and Social Care Act 2012) and US governments and the consequences are that this is a goal to achieve.

The 'relevant standard care' that should be met is judged in courts by expert opinions based on four questions (Daubert *v.* Merrell Dow Pharmaceuticals, Inc., 1993): whether a 'theory or technique ... can be (and has been) tested'; 'has been subjected to peer review and publication'; in respect to a particular technique, is there a high 'known or potential rate of error'; and are there 'standards controlling the technique's operation'? Such standards would include National Institute for Health ad Care Excellence (NICE) guidelines in the UK or similar ones in the USA, Australia and New Zealand, as well as those from other national and international professional organisations.

Activities

- Balancing autonomy and acting in someone's best interests is often quite complex. Reflect on an instance where you have acted in someone's best interest affecting their autonomy. List the considerations that you took into account and why you decided to act.
- Recall an instance where someone disclosed to you a situation where advantage has been taken of them. Detail how you elicited information and reflect on the actions you took.
- Acting in an optimal fashion at all times is impossible but there is a boundary between adequate and negligent practice. Consider how that boundary is defined in your own clinical practice.

Further reading

Allen, N. (1998) *Making Sense of the Children Act: A Guide for Social and Welfare Services*, 3rd edn. Chichester: Wiley.

Brindle, N., Branton, T., Stansfield, A. and Zigmond, T. (eds) (2013) *A Clinician's Brief Guide to the Mental Capacity Act*. London: RCPsych Publications.

(Continued)

(Continued)

Department of Health (2009) *Reference Guide to Consent for Examination or Treatment: Second Edition*. London: COI for the Department of Health. Available at: www.gov.uk/government/uploads/system/uploads/attachment_data/file/138296/dh_103653__1_.pdf (accessed 18 June 2016.)

Department of Health and Home Office (2000) *No Secrets: Guidance on Developing and Implementing Multi-agency Policies and Procedures to Protect Vulnerable Adults from Abuse*. London: Department of Health.

Kingdon, D.G. and Finn, M. (2006) *Tackling Mental Health Crises*. Abingdon: Routledge.

Social Care Institute for Excellence (undated) *Adult Safeguarding Resource*. Available at: www.scie.org.uk/publications/elearning/adultsafeguarding/resource/2_study_area.html (accessed 15 May 2016).

3

IMPLICATIONS FOR CBT TECHNIQUE

Learning outcomes

After reading this chapter and completing the activities at the end of it, you should be able to:

1. Understand the common ethical criticisms of CBT in regards to therapeutic strategy and techniques.
2. Critically analyse the validity of the criticisms of CBT using the Professional Standards of Conduct, Performance and Ethics frameworks.
3. Consider the strategies for the enhancement of appropriate ethical clinical practice from a CB perspective.

The terms 'cognitive behaviour therapy' and 'cognitive therapy' have tended to be used interchangeably in the literature with the latter, perhaps, emphasising a centrality to cognition whilst the former reflecting that behaviour change is also a key component in the objective of reducing distress and disability. In this book, we have used CBT throughout for consistency, although the issues we will be discussing are equally applicable to all the approaches used within the behavioural and cognitive fields.

As described in the Chapter 1, cognitive behaviour therapy developed from work particularly by Aaron Beck and Albert Ellis in the 1960s that linked thoughts, feelings and behaviours. It was initially introduced for anxiety and depression but is now used across the range of psychiatric conditions. So, not only has CBT been established as an effective therapy for anxiety and depression, but it has also established itself as an evidence-based approach for other conditions. Randomised Controlled Trials (RCTs) and subsequent meta-analyses have demonstrated its effectiveness for the treatment of eating disorders, psychosis and borderline personality disorder (BPD; Corrie et al., 2016). Thus, it can be argued that it would be unethical for mental health services not to provide or to withhold such provision to those with mental health problems – who are some of the most disadvantaged in society (Pilgrim, 1997).

However, CBT, despite its evidence base, or perhaps because of its adherence to a scientific approach, has been criticised for a number of reasons. In this chapter, we will explore and discuss these criticisms in depth. This will include consideration of why these criticisms have arisen and how valid we think they are, and we will offer some suggestions as to why their use might be considered an ethical approach to practice. Where relevant, we will also refer to the well-developed BABCP (2010) code of Standards of Conduct, including its Performance and Ethics framework, and other similar codes of practice.

Diagnosis and language

There are some ethical considerations around the use of diagnostic terms. Diagnosis itself has been extensively criticised by non-medical practitioners and therapists both within and outside of CBT for being reductionist and at times for being unreliable and lacking validity. The purpose of diagnosis is to try and categorise problems into discreet groupings that have common features and processes associated with them. Arguments against this are that this categorisation process can depersonalise people through a dismissal of their complex unique individual histories and stories (Corrie et al., 2016). We agree that, if used unquestioningly and in a rigid form, diagnosis can depersonalise and dehumanise individual experience, but we would equally argue that this is actually poor practice and misuse of the diagnostic process. Thus formulation is essential to meet broad therapeutic needs but diagnosis is necessary for descriptive, legal and communication purposes.

To be ethical and meet BABCP standards, practice needs to be personalised to the individual with diagnosis helping the therapist and the client make a start on this process. Thus, it can help with communication in situations where clients do ask for a label for their problem and where it is necessary for administrative purposes, such as claiming welfare or sickness benefits. It is very difficult to get away from the inevitable tendency to group and name phenomena, experiences and material things – e.g. flowers, animals and football teams – our clients are no exception to this. They inevitably want answers to the question of 'what is wrong with me' and, thus, it would in our view be wrong to sidestep such questions. It can allow them to seek appropriate self-help material, books and Internet-based publications, and/or communicate with friends, relatives and employers, although issues of stigma and misunderstanding need to be addressed.

Yet, equally, acceptance is needed of the limitations of such processes. In our view, it is far better to consider diagnosis as being the start of a process, although following a full assessment, which will often take more than one session, that begins with a diagnosis for initial tentative guidance and then moves to the core underpinning practices within CBT which is the utilisation of the individualised formulation. Formulation can be argued as the bedrock of individualised practice and has been highlighted as an alternative, but essential, way of understanding a client's problems at the idiosyncratic level. Formulation alongside diagnosis can also be seen as an effective way of communicating in both a meaningful and acceptable manner.

What is more of an issue is whether mental disorders are appropriately classified, and the continued controversies over the *Diagnostic and Statistical Manual* (*DSM*) and *International Classification of Diseases* (*ICD*) classifications suggests that there remain doubts about this. This is perhaps inevitable as our understanding of human problems develops and can be seen to be systematically evolving through the various iterations of these classification systems. It will be many years before these systems reach their final state of maturity and something, even if limited, does need to be used in the interim for the purpose of research and teaching and to underpin broad categories such as those used in treatment guidelines, e.g. from the UK NICE and US Schizophrenia Patient Outcomes Research Team (PORT), that have been widely accepted and appear to do much good through the description and dissemination of quality practice and services.

It is our position that the onus is on the individual CB therapist to be aware of both the strengths and limitations of the diagnosis systems and equally not to shy away from using them. They are not the preserve of psychiatrists or psychologists but are there to be used by all health care professions to achieve what might be considered the 'greater good' in ethical terms. Some of the other concerns can be addressed by careful and thoughtful practice such as the remaining concerns about the terminology that is used at times within the various classifications such as 'schizophrenia' (Kingdon et al., 2013) or 'personality disorder' (Kingdon, 2007) that have been particularly criticised in this context as stigmatising or even, for the latter, rather insulting. This is not the fault of the systems of classification per se, but of how society has come to misunderstand those terms. Thus, for the moment, alternative terms seem more acceptable to clients and include 'psychosis', 'learning disability, 'emotional dysregulation' or trauma-related difficulties, although a consensus has yet to be reached in this area.

A further ethical concern related to diagnosis is that they do reflect a specific Westernised view of mental disorder. Awareness of this is again important in communication with clients or colleagues from non-Western societies. Finally, language is also important in relation to terms that abound in CB therapy such as 'dysfunctional', 'pathological' or even 'clinical', which might all best be avoided as potentially having pejorative connotations. Some language such as 'dichotomous reasoning', 'selective abstraction' and 'arbitrary inference' might also be better understood by terms in more common use such as 'black-and-white thinking', 'getting things out of proportion' and 'taking things out of context'.

The therapeutic relationship

CBT builds on the foundation of a therapeutic relationship providing specific techniques for developing and maintaining well-being. In this respect, it is no different from other approaches to counselling and psychotherapy, although Beck has stated that the therapy relationship is 'necessary but not sufficient to produce an optimum therapeutic effect' (Beck et al., 1979: 45). It has subsequently been argued that the concept of the 'therapeutic relationship' ought to be considered a philosophical, rather than a theoretical, issue given the problems of specificity and defining what is actually meant by it (Alford and Beck, 1997). Nevertheless, it is a term that seems well understood by therapists of all modalities.

CB therapists are often characterised or even caricatured as aloof and distant from their clients and as being more interested in the latest techniques or research evidence than in developing a therapeutic relationship. This is a stereotype, and a style of working that is certainly not what is communicated through contemporary training courses or texts (Dryden and Branch, 2012; Corrie et al., 2016). There is also no empirical data that suggests that CB therapists are mechanical in their approach or lacking in empathy (Holtforth and Castonguay, 2005).

These sources suggest an equal importance for relationship-building with individual formulation as the vehicle for the delivery of evidence-based strategies within a professional and ethical framework (Alford and Beck, 1997; Gilbert and Leahy, 2007; Dryden and Branch, 2012; Corrie et al., 2016). This can be seen in attention to such areas as collaborating 'shoulder to shoulder' with clients as a way of promoting and developing autonomy. Other areas where CB therapists are taking a leading role is in the therapeutic use in practice and the teaching of empathy. This is through a four-element approach in order to address a variety of functions that empathy serves in a therapeutic process. These four elements are: empathic attunement, empathic attitude, empathic communication and empathy knowledge (Thwaites and Bennett-Levy, 2007).

Likewise, self-disclosure is probably more acceptable in CBT than in some other therapies because it is seen as an appropriate way of developing the relationship with people with who it may be very difficult to engage or who are socially unskilled or excluded. The use of 'befriending' as a component of therapy has been included in the engagement processes for people with psychosis (Kingdon and Turkington, 2005) who may find sustaining up to an hour of therapy difficult and who are suspicious by the nature of their problems. Self-disclosure can humanise and allow conversation to flow whilst limited to appropriate areas. The major practical and ethical issue is about the degree of disclosure that is appropriate which will vary with the situation, patient and therapist. Broadly speaking, it should not involve intimate details or identifiable information, e.g. where the therapist lived or family details, but might include discussion of interests and leisure activities. Certainly, the therapist and client should be comfortable with the level of disclosure provided and with the effect on the personal boundaries that have been set (see Chapter 5).

Ethical scenario

Paul had sought out some CBT through his family doctor for feeling low and not liking himself very much. He had read about CBT on a website and thought that a practical therapy might be just what he needed. He attended the initial appointment that was an assessment and the therapist explained that it was a screening appointment to see if the approach would be suitable for him. He was pleased when he was told that he would be able to have up to six sessions of CBT through the local service. He found the therapist professional and personable and was looking forward to starting therapy.

When he started therapy four weeks later, it was with a different therapist, whom he found more detached and less empathic. He did find her to be professional but was happy to continue the therapy. At the end of the first therapy session, he was told that he had 'moderate depression and low self-esteem' and that he might need more sessions than he might be able to have from the service. This did not help Paul's mood; he did not really

(Continued)

(Continued)

understand what being depressed was or what was meant by low self-esteem. At subsequent sessions, these questions were answered and the therapist was able to help him understand what was keeping his mood so low. He was, however, very anxious about the limit on the number of sessions. His evidence-based therapy (EBT) was behavioural activation. He found this very difficult but worked as hard as he could to cope with his low mood and do what he was instructed to do by his therapist. At the end of the six sessions he was offered another two sessions, on the grounds of seeing if he could make further progress. At each session, he completed some questionnaires that were called 'Routine Outcome Measures' (ROMs), but he did not know what this meant or what their purpose was. After eight sessions, he was told that he was going to be discharged at the next session as he had not made much progress. He was also told that the problem seemed to be his dysfunctional schema and that he might need to see a therapist who 'worked in a different way'.

Paul left the session feeling helpless and confused. He felt that he now had even more problems than when he started. He decided not to attend his final appointment as he did not think that he would get anything out of it. He contacted the clinic to say that he would not be attending. A few weeks later, he received a letter to let him know that he had been discharged from the service. There was no further contact from the service.

Ethical questions

1. Is it ethical for one therapist to do the initial assessment and then, without the client being made aware, to have the client seen by another therapist for therapy?
2. What ethical issues are raised by the therapeutic relationship and diagnostic processes?
3. What are the ethical issues of being offered a limited number of sessions when most studies of depression are in clinical trials of 12–15 sessions?
4. What ethical concerns does the choice of language of the therapist raise, for example 'low self-esteem', 'dysfunctional' and 'schema'?
5. What needs to be considered in regards to the timing of giving information to the client and being able to allay any fears or misconceptions?
6. What ethical issues are raised in respect to the use of outcome measures?
7. What are the ethical concerns about the ending of the therapy process?

Technique

There are potential criticisms that can be made of CBT which relate directly to the techniques used and these particularly relate to concerns that CBT does not take an individual focus, does not adapt to the needs of the person and is too rigid in its application. The implication is that CBT is a 'cookbook' therapy that uses the same ingredients for presenting conditions, e.g. depression, anxiety or PTSD, whatever the individual says or does. These are all-important considerations and, as we have argued, far from accurate where therapy is being offered in a skilled and effective way. Cookbook therapy is 'bad therapy' and is not intrinsic to the method used.

This view can, however, be reinforced in the eyes of some critics by the pre-specification of the number of sessions being offered and the style of therapy, along with assessment and outcome measures which focus on symptoms without assessing individual needs. In thinking about these issues from an ethical perspective, our argument is that specifying the number of sessions initially helps with focusing expectations, and taking into account progress from ROMs in IAPT services, for example, prevents overzealous or open-ended therapy approaches that might create a dependency or simply use precious therapy time ineffectively. It ensures that the maximum number of people can access therapy in a situation of scarce therapeutic resource that accords with the evidence base. We also argue that the use of assessment and outcome measures and instruments are important supplements to the necessary dialogue concerning the client's problems and needs and, if used sensitively and appropriately, are a crucial system of feedback on progress and collaborative decision-making.

The emphasis in CBT on establishing an agenda can seem to be more about 'doing the business' than attempting to build the relationship. However, structuring the session can clarify the process for the client, provide much needed support, guidance and boundaries for the client, and give confidence that specific issues will be dealt with. It must, however, be collaborative and address their issues, rather than just those proposed by the therapist.

The focus on 'here and now' can seem to be ignoring the richness and importance of prior experience, the 'then and there'. However, the purpose of the initial assessment is to establish a full picture of the problems presenting in order to develop a formulation – including considerations of past experiences. The point of focusing on the 'here and now' is to ensure that the impact on the current situation is the focus, although there may still be connections made between past and current thoughts and feelings.

Homework suggests a teacher–pupil relationship, rather than that of equals striving to find a way through the complexities of human experience and interaction. The principle of focusing on specific targets and activities to work on outside of the therapy sessions maximises effectiveness by ensuring that 'real-life' circumstances improve. However, it can be argued that the term may not be the best to use for 'tasks' occurring between sessions.

If the client does not agree with the model proposed or is unable to collaborate on tasks, there is a danger that they can be deemed non-responsive. Collaboration can, paradoxically, be used wrongly to make the client responsible if therapy does not work. It can shift towards leading the client in a way that becomes overly persuasive. The recognition that, if it is done, completing tasks correlates with good outcome but this can become coercive and may be in part a reflection of levels of motivation. The expert may correct client's misunderstandings – that is, educate the patient or persuade them – and if they don't respond, there is a danger that they can come close to 'blaming' them. Nevertheless, an important counter to this is a quote attributed to Padesky (2015): 'If a client doesn't do the homework, 90 per cent of the time it is due to the therapist, not the client.' When asked if she could clarify this powerful statement, Dr Padesky made the the following point:

> Therapists make many errors in assigning homework that account for most of the variance in whether clients do homework or not. If homework is routinely collaboratively devised, started in session, explicitly linked to client goals, written down and begun in session, devised to be interesting, developed to be within the client's skill level and time available, the client agrees to do it, and it is debriefed with great interest by the therapist in the following session ... then clients almost always do homework. (Personal communication, 2016)

In a sense, this goes beyond collaboration, relocating responsibility in the therapist to ensure that tasks are fully understood, that they think and work creatively and that all homework is agreed and not simply accepted due to acquiescence by, or worse, subtle coercion of the client.

Another common ethical dilemma for therapists who use exposure therapy is what is both acceptable and tolerable. For example, in Obsessive Compulsive Disorder (OCD), the client may over many years have lost sight of what would be considered a normal washing or checking behaviour. This can usually be addressed through discussion and perhaps a survey technique of the behaviour of others in similar situations. A problem can arise if the client is not improving or might be at risk of relapse and requires some overlearning. Overlearning is a strategy that would require the client to do something that would not be classed as normal in day-to-day behaviour (Rachman and Lopatka, 1988). The classic example is of people touching the toilet bowl or, for a client with a fear of contamination, carrying a specimen of something they fear. This difficult situation can usually be resolved by a discussion of the pros and cons of undertaking the exposure practice, alongside it being something that the therapist themselves would be willing to model. Further issues can also arise if the exposure or behavioural experiments might place the patient in a situation of real or potential danger. This might arise if the task involved challenging a potentially violent partner or perhaps venturing out at night in an area that may not be safe. Here, the ethical issue would be about balancing out the risks posed and the potential benefit that might be accrued.

As well as the above issues with exposure-based approaches, another area of contention is with the use of imaginal exposure in PTSD. Some therapists, despite evidence to the contrary, avoid the use of this approach, fearing re-traumatising the client or considering it an unsuitable approach in the context of comorbid problems (van Minnen et al., 2012). Hence, the ethical issue is concerned with not using an evidence-based strategy, when the evidence suggests that one ought to do so. This is a matter that can be addressed through supervision and by considering what is in the client's best interest. Also, in PTSD, there can be other complications if there is an outstanding compensation claim or, in the case of historical events, the use of some reliving techniques might have to be delayed due to the possibility of recovered memory syndrome (see Hall and Hall, 2012; and Brewin, 2003, which is a specialist text that considers these debates and potential complications).

The utilisation of aversive techniques can also court controversy. The field has shifted considerably over the last fifty or so years for ethical, moral and evidence reasons. There is very limited evidence that aversive techniques produce robust long-term positive outcomes. The exception to this is the utilisation of grounding techniques in the context of 'personality disorder' or PTSD. A grounding technique seeks to aid a client to stay in the 'here and now', rather than to dissociate, in order to enable them to learn to tolerate strong affect. It is used as a harm reduction strategy in the case of someone who self-harms or engages in imaginal exposure in the context of PTSD. These are very mild self-applied strategies such as the use of smelling salts, holding melting ice or even the mild pain from pinging an elastic band. Ethically, it is again a case of balancing the risks and the benefits, with the client making the final decision (Davidson and Townend, 2016).

Behavioural activation sounds like something that might be a process for bringing a robot to life – again, mechanistic and lacking subtlety. Any process involving re-motivating and developing activities to improve mood or test cognitions needs to be fully collaborative. General criticisms about diagnostic language have been made earlier in this chapter. Similar criticisms could be made about some behavioural approaches or practices over the years and can certainly be applied to the B in CBT if not understood in context or with full reference to the literature or codes of practice. The BABCP Standards of Conduct, Performance and Ethics specifically state that the practitioner must act in the best interests of service users, communicate properly and get informed consent for any therapy or treatment. So, approaches such as exposure have to be carefully explained to clients and the responsibility is on the therapist to ensure that the client fully understands the rationale for the why a particular approach is being advocated.

Techniques such as the use of the 'Downward Arrow' involve exploring the implications of beliefs and working down to core and often quite disturbing and distressing underlying assumptions or schema. How humane is this and is it necessarily warranted in achieving the individual's goals? Schema work that explores and, indeed, tries to modify assumptions, has lacked empirical evidence of effectiveness, although some has emerged recently in relation to personality disorder, but it is at least looking more deeply and potentially at meaningful personal material. Is this psychodynamic therapy based on analytical principles by another name? This specific ethical issue has been discussed in a critique of schema work (James, 2001). His arguments were threefold. The first argument was that the unquestioned utilisation of schema work in CBT is unwarranted unless there is clear empirical evidence or traditional CBT has been ineffective. He also argues that schema work can increase a client's distress if used indiscriminately or the therapist is not prepared to deal with the schemas that they have sought to elicit. This work would not therefore be appropriate to use, for example in a time-limited service, and certainly not if the therapist does not have the skill to do so. Whether or not it should be offered in a more extended service with trained therapists is a debate that needs to be considered if the evidence justifies it.

Inclusion criteria for CBT may be narrow and symptomatically or diagnostically defined which can seem contrary to holistic principles, but, equally, applying an approach that is not indicated would be an ethical violation. The use of diagnosis in setting criteria can be criticised as being too narrow on its own (see above) with formulation being proposed as a more appropriate approach although it may be more difficult to relate to the evidence base. Both are used in CBT but it is argued that they have different functions. Criteria for inclusion may be derived from their use for research purposes but can be more difficult to use in 'real life', e.g. with BPD, the requirement not to be self-harming or the individual may be ejected from the programme can seem harsh and impractical, although it may be based on the evidence that a therapy is effective only where such restrictions have been imposed. However, it can then mean that therapy is limited to a group who already have good prognosis. 'Absence of evidence is not evidence for absence' of effect. Gaps between criteria for different CBT approaches may lead to absence of services for those who do not fit into the 'pigeonholes' provided. This is a legitimate concern and one that needs to be addressed in research and by service planners in the commissioning of joined-up services in conjunction with clinicians and people who use such services.

CBT can be criticised for a lack of focus on emotions – as demonstrated by its name. The focus seemingly is on behaviour and cognition with emotions is, at best, an afterthought. In fact, consideration of emotions is key to CBT but identifying dysfunctional thoughts and behaviours is a method to manage them. This is certainly not a new idea and was extensively discussed by Alford and Beck (1997) in their seminal text concerning the integrative power of cognitive therapy. The argument presented was that CBT was essentially based around learning how to regulate and adjust the automatic survival systems such as emotions or physiological responses (in anxiety fight–flight) through the more conscious control and meta-cognitive systems. Thus, the term 'CBT' ought in reality to be renamed 'cognitive emotion and behaviour therapy' (CEBT). This argument has recently been strengthened with the development of third wave therapists such as in compassion-focused therapy, acceptance and commitment therapy, mindfulness-based cognitive therapy and behavioural dialectic therapy.

Developing and maintaining competency and fidelity standards are of importance as ethical issues. The ethics of offering brief training, e.g. in workshops, needs consideration as there is a danger of people attending and then using therapy and claiming competence (see Chapter 3). Acceptance of supervision is a professional requirement whether individual or peer on a regular and consistent basis and is expected to take place to retain accreditation with CBT bodies. This is probably not much different from other modalities but, whilst reflection on practice is expected, personal therapy as such is not a requirement.

Studies of brief interventions and the use of manualised approaches have been developed in anxiety, depression and psychosis. They are useful in that they can be evaluated and shown to have benefit but are potentially non-individualised. They describe very specific ways of working within limited timescales and these may not accord with the views of the individual therapist. Is it ethical to follow the manual or to act independently? And how does this fit with the BABCP code of Standards of Conduct, Performance and Ethics for acting in the best interests of service users. Thus, a balance needs to be struck between following manuals that have an evidence base and the apparent needs of the individual. Each of these considerations has a degree of subjectivity – the individual may differ from those involved in the original trials and so some variation may be reasonable. However, acting in a way that is therapist-determined and lacks any support from evaluation is even more problematic and has been a major problem over many years, with hopes lifted and then dashed and resources wasted on ineffective interventions.

How long should therapy be? Trials are constrained by funding and the practicalities, so that they will tend to be shorter than their architects would have ideally liked them to be. For example, we have constructed studies which provide up to a year of therapy for people with psychosis, but we are well aware that in our clinical practice, we usually offer, albeit infrequent, support and booster sessions for as long as the individual continues to want them and seem to benefit from them. Clinical trials cannot be constructed in this way because of the cost of follow-up of clients and, also, the lack of a defined end point means that results never accrue. Therapist involvement will discontinue as it is more economic to concentrate highly skilled resources on providing a restricted number of sessions, however this does not stop us from offering such longer-term support through mental health services.

One area of reasonable criticism of CBT is that therapy does tend to be individually based, rather than having a family or even group focus. It is reasonable to criticise practitioners as tending to neglect interpersonal issues and carer aspects/support, although both approaches are described. It is pragmatic as well as considerate to families to provide some contact as agreed with the client. Duties of confidentiality clearly exist (see Chapter 6) but can be used as an excuse not to involve them and consider their needs. Here, the ethical issue concerns, not just confidentiality, but the wider question also of 'whose problem is it' and to whom does the therapist owe their duty of care and responsibility. The BABCP Standards of Conduct, Performance and Ethics refer to respecting the confidentiality of the service user and make no mention of family members. Yet, family members might be affected by the therapy. If the client has reservations or does not want contact with family members, a negotiated approach can often be acceptable to them, with agreement over specific issues that can be discussed and messages that can be given about the therapy approach. It is certainly important not to coerce or bypass client wishes but discussion usually allows acceptable ways forward, although, ultimately, the duty is to the presenting client.

Scapegoating of individuals by families has been described in the literature, especially in relation to psychosis but in practice seems to be extremely rare and any decision that this is happening warrants very careful consideration through supervisory and multidisciplinary processes. Clear abuse, where disclosed, will necessitate consideration of safeguarding procedures for the individual and also others who might be at risk.

Contact with others, such as employers, can also make a major difference to the individual's situation and well-being and therapists' tendency not wanting to be involved in such contacts can be more to do with the time this takes than any ethical reasons not to do so.

Conclusion

There are some specific aspects of CBT theory and practice that raise ethical issues over and above those which are relevant to all mental health practitioners and therapists. These relate to the interpretation of distress in a social and cultural context and the use of techniques that have the potential to cause unnecessary distress. This chapter has provided the opportunity to review this area, about which relatively little has been written. CBT has taken a very pragmatic approach to therapy and focused strongly on research and evaluation of practice – a focus on ethics and values is probably overdue.

Activities

- Taking on board what you have read, reflect on whether you think that the therapeutic relationship is essential but not sufficient for effective therapy.
- Consider any therapeutic technique that might have a negative effect, e.g. differences of opinion, on the relationship with the patient, e.g. exposure work, downward arrow, behavioural activation. How do you judge the use of the technique? How do you introduce it? How long do you use it for and any other alternative choices?

Further reading

House, R. and Loewenthal, D. (eds) (2008) *Against and for Cognitive Therapy: Towards a Constructive Dialogue?* Ross-on-Wye: PCCS Books.

4

CONSIDERING THERAPIST'S RESPONSIBILITIES AND BOUNDARIES

Learning outcomes

After reading this chapter and completing the activities at the end of it, you should be able to:

1. Develop an understanding of what is meant by 'therapist's responsibility' in terms of accountability, collaboration, power and the BABCP Standards of Conduct, Performance and Ethics.
2. Explain the therapist's responsibilities in terms of informed consent.
3. Recognise how therapists might cross or violate boundaries and therefore not meet their responsibilities.
4. Appreciate how therapists might respect and manage these responsibilities.

Being a responsible professional begins from the moment that training as a cognitive behavioural therapist begins, if it has not already done so in another capacity. Many students enter cognitive behavioural therapy (CBT) training from another profession and so already adhere to a code of ethics. However, it is not always apparent what is meant by 'professional responsibilities' and how these relate to the cognitive behaviour therapists' practice. This chapter will explore some of the issues around professional responsibility, notably in relation to accountability, collaboration, power, the BABCP code of Standards of Conduct, Performance and Ethics, and potential violation of responsibilities. It will make comparisons with an international code of ethics, that of the APS (Australian Psychological Society, 2007): many CB therapists in Australia are psychologists and adhere to this code of ethics. The chapter endeavours to encourage good practice in terms of responsibility.

Responsibility and accountability

Responsibility involves: 'having an obligation to do something or having control over or care for someone' (*Oxford English Dictionary*, 2016); it is said to be more than 'mere accountability' (Solbrekke and Englund, 2011: 859). Importantly, being responsible involves adopting a proactive stance, whilst accountability involves taking ownership of action taken, and is the place of justification: giving an explanation of an action taken, or to be taken, or, indeed, of an action not taken. Within CBT, the responsible professional adopts a mindset where he/she employs his/her capacity to behave morally and legally towards others. This responsibility extends beyond the client, as depicted in Figure 4.1. However, the interpretation of responsibility emphasises 'to' others, rather than 'for' others. Whilst it is the responsibility of the therapist to create a safe non-exploitive environment for their *clients*, where the client can share and explore their vulnerabilities and work towards his/her

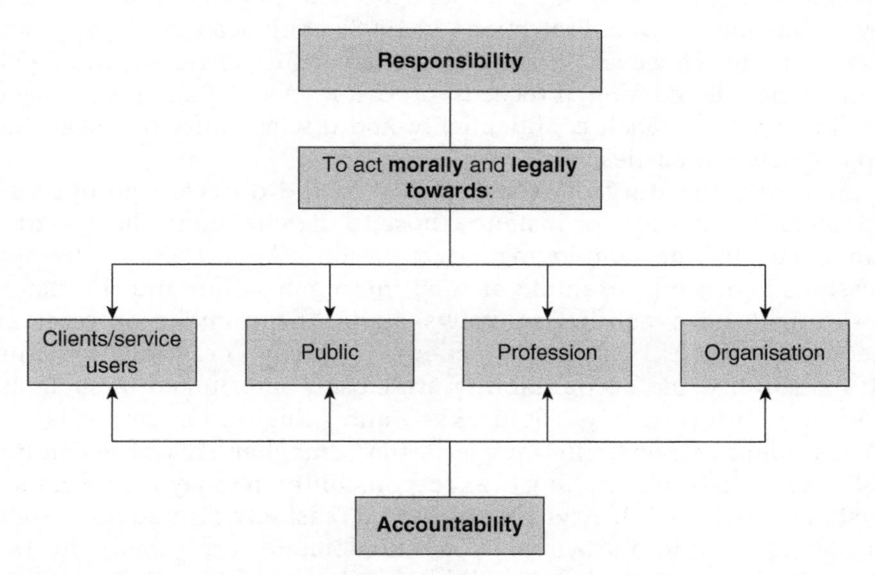

Figure 4.1 A diagrammatic representation of a CB therapist's framework of responsibility

goals, the therapists cannot be responsible 'for' their client. The latter position potentially competes with the ethical principle of respecting the autonomy of others (Beauchamp and Childress, 2013). Within the therapeutic encounter, this means valuing the client's right to make their own choices.

Professional responsibility extends to the therapist's employing organisation, to the profession and to the public. By the terms of his/her employment contract, the CB therapist will have responsibilities to the *employing organisation*. This involves an obligation to comply with the organisation's policies, for instance those related to confidentiality. Moreover, responsibility in terms of the *profession* requires that the therapist: 'acts in such a way that does not corrode the public confidence in the profession' (BABCP, Standards of Conduct, 4.1). Although, the therapist's primary responsibility is to the client, a duty of care broadly extends to the public, in working within the scope of the public interest. However, determining what is meant by 'public interest' is not always clear (ESRC, 2015). Whilst the BABCP Standards of Conduct explicitly relates the therapist's responsibility to others in the UK, in the context of protection and safety (BABCP, Standards of Conduct, 1.3–1.5), Jenkins et al. point out that: 'there is always a degree of uncertainty as to how the courts will actually apply the concept of public interest' (2004: 66). This said, the therapist needs to be aware that failing to uphold their duty of care, being negligent, being discriminative (i.e. breaching the Race Relation Act 2000), not protecting confidentiality (breaching the Data Protection Act 1998), could lead to a legal action against them. However, in the case of terrorism (Terrorism Act 2000) and money laundering (Proceeds of Crime Act 2002), it is a legal requirement to breach confidentiality and disclose information to the appropriate authorities.

At times, the duty of responsibility to the different groups can compete for priority, for instance those to the client and those simultaneously to the employing organisation. Apportioning therapy sessions is a useful example of this: the organisation and the therapist might have conflicting views about the number of sessions necessary for a particular client, thereby creating tension. Responsibility and accountability are closely interlinked in such situations. Interestingly, Solbrekke and Englund's analysis of professional responsibility suggests that: 'mechanisms of accountability seem to be triumphing over responsibility in today's governance systems' (2011: 847). Arguably, in an increasingly risk adverse society, in addition to one where economic demands are prominent, the therapist's professional responsibility in the decision-making process may seem somewhat diluted.

Responsibility and collaboration

A key element of CB therapy is collaboration. Values of collaboration include amongst others: 'equity, inclusion and transparency' (Jones, 2012: 17). Such values, particularly equity, can sit uncomfortably when considering the following definition of responsibility: 'having control and authority over something or someone and the duty of taking care of it, or him or her' (*Cambridge Dictionary*, 2015). Control and authority are linked to power. Indeed, it is argued that: 'responsibility is the partner of power' (Proctor, 2014: 77). Whilst the intent of adopting a collaborative approach may be to share responsibility with the client for the treatment plan and activities, including homework, as soon as is feasible, the imbalance of power may influence the nature of the collaboration. In keeping with this, it has been suggested that collaboration can be used to obscure the power differentials in CBT (Proctor, 2008). There is a possibility that collaboration can be employed as a way of obtaining the client's compliance with the therapist's wishes, rather than of developing an actual partnership. Indeed, although Gilbert and Leahy articulate the importance of putting the client 'at the centre of the recovery process, with the therapist as a guide' (2007: 10). It would seem that they, too, acknowledge that power can subtly influence collaboration because they also state that: 'The concept of collaboration becomes hazy in the shadow of the power dynamics' (ibid.: 11).

Even though some clients perceive themselves as consumers who are neither dependent, meek nor powerless (Zur, 2008), in order to prevent power from being unwittingly used, and to thoroughly engage in the collaborative approach, it is necessary for CB therapists to reflect upon the power differentials that inherently exist in the therapeutic encounter. This reflection on power enables the therapist to subtly adjust their practice to the needs of the client. Although the client is the expert of their experience, and may pay for therapy, the distribution of power favours the therapist, as illustrated in Figure 4.2. The therapist is viewed as the expert in the therapeutic context. Indeed, it is suggested that the client may attribute greater positive qualities, such as competence and well-being and the 'power to cure', to the therapist (Bond, 2015). In addition, therapy usually takes place in the therapist's environment, the therapist has more knowledge about the development of therapy and the process and, what is more, the therapist can often dictate the extent of therapy. Essentially, it should be recognised that the therapist has authority bestowed on them by the organisation for which they work, and by society due to their professional status. Accumulatively, these aspects of power sit like an elephant in the room.

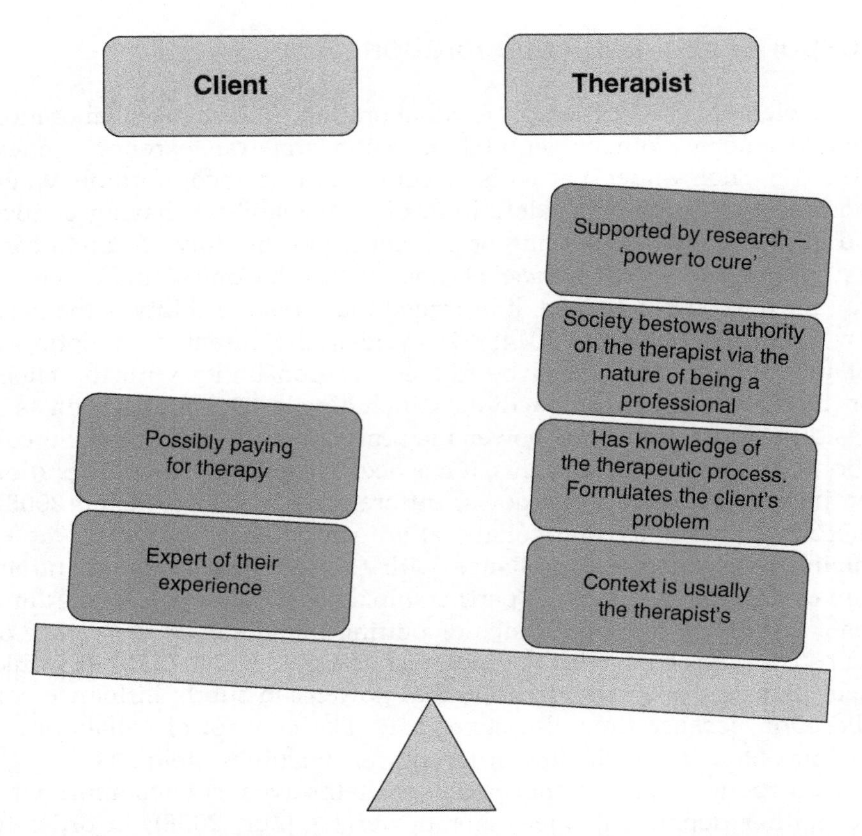

Figure 4.2 Elements of the power imbalance in the CBT therapeutic encounter

Although it has been purported that within CBT, the therapist's control and authority is usually greater at the start of therapy, this is progressively transferred to the client as the client takes more responsibility for the therapeutic treatment (Marshall, 1996). It would be appropriate that a discussion with the client takes place about the nature of power and collaboration, whilst emphasising how valued the client's views and participation in the process is. The latter point is important. A recent systematic review identified that knowledge on its own was not sufficient to facilitate shared decision-making in doctor–patient dyads (Joseph-Williams et al., 2014). It was also necessary for the patient to have power to participate in the shared decision-making process. Transparency and openness will help ensure that the therapist does not assume responsibility 'for' the client and/or directing the client's life (Corey, 2009), whilst, correspondingly, respecting and facilitating the client's autonomy and enhancing collaboration.

Responsibility in relation to the BABCP Standards of Conduct, Performance and Ethics

Professionals are guided by their ethical codes of practice, which provides both the public and its members with a statement of which behaviours are considered correct and which behaviours should be avoided. Although the guidelines can be prescriptive, offering guidance on what actions to take in certain situations, it would be impossible for them to cover every situation and provide absolute answers (Moleski and Kiselica, 2005). Moreover, they often do not consider any client responsibility (Gabriel, 2005). The BABCP Standards of Conduct, Performance and Ethics that UK CB therapists adhere to is no different in this respect. While it endeavours not to dictate how its standards should be met (ibid.: 4), it is prescriptive, in that it adopts an authoritarian voice, describing behaviours that 'must' be avoided or engaged with, yet at the same time it is vague because guidance for resolving ethical dilemmas is limited. In comparison, the Australian Psychological Society (APS) Code of Ethics (2007) is a comprehensive document, covering many areas. The language employed throughout subtly guides its members to what is considered ethical professional conduct. This said, the authoritarian voice is clearly heard in relation to non-exploitation of the client, for instance it states that: 'Psychologists: *do not* engage in sexual activity with a client or anybody who is closely related to one of their clients' (Standard C.4.3.a, emphasis added), and '*do not* accept as a client a person with whom they have engaged in sexual activity' (Standard C.4.3.d, emphasis added).

Whilst the notion of responsibility is implicit within both the BABCP's code and the APS's Code of Ethics, it is only explicitly referred to in the former six instances (1.1; 1.4 twice; 5.1; 9; 15.3). In contrast, the APS provide a useful section, making direct reference to professional responsibility (Standard B.3). Importantly, though, both the APS Code of Ethics and the BABCP's draw attention to the personal responsibility of the therapist. The APS states that: 'Psychologists: are *personally responsible* for the professional decisions they make' (Standard B.3.e); and, similarly, the BABCP asserts that: 'You are *personally responsible* for making sure that you promote and protect the best interest of your service user' (BABCP 1.1). Also, 'You are *responsible* for your professional conduct, any care or advice you provide, and failure to act' (BABCP 1.4) (emphasis added). Clearly, the boundaries between the personal and professional become merged here, personal responsibility is emphasised whilst in a professional capacity and context. Moreover, the interpretation of 'responsibility' in these clauses appears closely linked to accountability, that ultimately the therapist will be held accountable for their actions or inaction, to the client and to others. It is not impossible to envisage that the therapist's notion of being personally responsible could shape the therapist's decision-making process to a position of self-protection.

Moreover, it is possible to conceive that a conflict of responsibility could occur within an employing agency. As the therapist strives to promote and protect the best interest of their client, they can be brought into conflict with the employing agency. For example, a client who has issues related to trust discloses information concerning self-harming behaviours and is adamant that he does not want this information shared. In order to maintain a fragile but significant therapeutic alliance, the therapist may consider it beneficial to keep client confidentiality in accordance with the ethical principle of fidelity. However, such action could conflict with the agency policies. Appropriately, the APS Code of Ethics acknowledge that a tension can arise between an organisation and the therapist's values and principles as articulated in the Code of Ethics, and address this by providing some direction in order to achieve a resolution (Standard B.12).

The BABCP code connects, in the example above, the therapist's personal responsibility in relation to the 'best interest' of the service user (1.1). This commitment to best interest is also evident within the APS's Code under the principle of integrity (Standards, C.3.2 and C.6.2). Yet, how is 'best interest' defined and determined and from whose perspective? What happens when/if the client holds a conflicting opinion to that of the therapist, or to the organisation providing the therapy? How is the client's autonomy respected, if the therapist considers that the client's chosen action is not in their best interest? These are the sorts of questions that the responsible therapist needs to consider.

Whilst the codes provide a useful framework for ethical decision-making, and both the BABCP's and the APS Code of Ethics appear to define the boundaries of the therapist's responsibilities, it becomes apparent that the therapist's responsibilities can compete, potentially creating a dilemma.

Ethical scenario

Jenny, a 35-year-old woman, was receiving therapy from a CB therapist to help her manage the social anxiety she experienced. In the fifth session, Jenny disclosed that she had been sexually violated by her grandfather when she was a child. The abuse happened on a number of occasions. Her grandfather said that bad things would happen if she told anyone, it was to be their secret. Although Jenny was extremely upset when she shared this information, she was very clear that she did not want to tell anyone else about it. She said that she had given this a lot of thought, particularly in the light of the number of celebrities who were emerging in the media as paedophiles. Importantly, though, she could not tolerate the unhappiness that such a revelation would cause her family. Her grandfather was still alive, and lived with her grandmother in a town 50 miles away.

Ethical questions

1. What are the therapist's legal responsibilities in this situation?
2. Do the responsibilities differ if the therapist is employed by an organisation or works as a private practitioner?
3. What is the function of 'informed consent' in this scenario?
4. What does your ethical code of practice advise in such a situation?
5. How would you decide what action to take if you where the therapist?
6. How would you justify your action?

Informed consent

It is the therapist's responsibility to communicate to the client sufficient details about the therapeutic process, so that the client can make an informed decision about whether or not to take part in therapy (see the broad discussion of this in Chapter 2). Obtaining informed consent from the client is fundamental to the therapeutic encounter, particularly to the development of trust and, hence, the principle of fidelity. However, it is not appropriate for the therapist to make the assumption that, because a client has agreed to enter therapy, for instance at the assessment, and turns up for therapy, that this is a 'green light' for the therapist to do whatever they think is therapeutically appropriate (Jenkins et al., 2004). 'Informed consent' needs to be obtained, not only before the commencement of therapy, but also when any changes to the treatment plan are anticipated. In keeping with this, Barnett et al. (2007) point out that informed consent should not be considered as a one-off event that takes place prior to treatment, but should be perceived as 'a process' (ibid.: 180). This is echoed in the BABCP code of practice (Section 10.3). Not only is the client's autonomy then respected, but also adherence is made to the principles of beneficence and non-maleficence.

Both the BABCP code of practice (Section 10) and the APS Code of Ethics (Section A.3) make clear that the therapist must articulate to the client the aims of the proposed treatment and the rationale for it and any risks involved. Additionally, the BABCP include information about alternative treatment. The code's employment of informed consent is consistent with Beauchamp and Childress's (2013) conceptualisation of informed consent. Beauchamp and Childress separated informed consent into five areas:

- Competence
- Disclosure
- Understanding
- Voluntariness
- Consent

These areas involve the therapist reflecting on such questions as:

- Is the client competent to give consent?
- Does he/she understand what has been discussed?
- Can the information be made any clearer?
- Has sufficient information about CBT treatment, plus its techniques and the boundaries of confidentiality been given?
- Has consent been given freely without pressure or coercion?
- Has the client consented to CBT based on these elements?

Including research information concerning the effectiveness of CBT in the informed consent procedure can help the client to weigh up the potential benefits of whether or not to take part in therapy. Again, this is in keeping with the ethical principles of respect of autonomy and beneficence. However, it is stressed that this should include research that acknowledges the success of treatment to common factors found in talking therapies. These elements include a commitment to the aims and goals of treatment and the strength of the therapeutic relationship (Blease, 2015: 753). To do this may at first seem unhelpful, especially if the therapist is trying to increase the client's motivation to participate in CBT, but it is coherent with developing fidelity and beneficence. It is also consistent with the BABCP requirement to provide information about alternative treatments. Importantly, the therapist is demonstrating their ability to be open and their endeavour to work in the client's best interest. As a result, trust and confidence in the CBT approach might actually be enhanced.

It has to be remembered, though, that at the initial consenting stage, the client may be distressed with a reduced capacity to concentrate, arguably less able to establish their rights or to negotiate. Moreover, the power imbalance between the therapist and the client can be more acute at this stage, potentially affecting the client's decision-making process (Younggren et al., 2011: 166). Given this, what is shared and how it is discussed is significant. It is important to be sensitive to the role language plays, ensuring that the language used is at a level that the client can understand and is culturally appropriate. Although a verbal contract is deemed adequate (Jenkins et al., 2004), it is sensible to record the shared information in a written document. Written information enables the client to consider the information in their own time and may prevent the client from feeling potentially overwhelmed, and is consistent then with the ethical principles of beneficence and non-maleficence.

Certainly, the informed consent process can be seen as more than just clarifying a contract, but as a way of sharing responsibility. Moreover, not only is the client's autonomy respected, but the potential for harm and exploitation is reduced. Importantly, a foundation for collaboration is constructed and further strengthened as the ongoing consent process is adhered to.

Boundary crossing

It is widely agreed that, in order to create a safe therapeutic environment for the client, it is the therapist's responsibility to establish and maintain the 'metaphoric boundaries' of therapy and of the therapeutic relationship (Williams, 1997: 238). Although the BABCP code does not include the term 'boundaries' in its document, unlike the APS Code of Ethics, it identifies limits of acceptable and unacceptable behaviour throughout the code. Moreover, Section 5.4 highlights behaviours that can lead to dismissal from the association, such as offences including dishonesty.

It would seem that there are a number of actions that have been identified as the therapist stepping over the therapeutic boundary. These include the therapist accepting a gift, any kind of touch, self-disclosure and engaging in non-sexual socialising, even 'making a cup of tea for the client' has been viewed as boundary crossing (Feltham, 2007). However, in some models of therapy, such behaviours would not be considered as boundary crossing, for instance giving a client a comforting hug is not unusual practice within gestalt psychotherapy. Similarly, some of these behaviours are a normal practice within CBT treatment. Exposure work with a client who experienced social anxiety disorder, for instance, might involve visiting a social setting with the client. Additionally, self-disclosure can be helpful with some CBT techniques (Gibson, 2012). Given this, it is sensible to ensure, whenever possible, what might be anticipated as boundary crossing and that this is discussed and, if feasible, supported with theory and/or research, and then included in the therapeutic contract. However, Proctor (2014) points out that boundary crossing is unavoidable at times, for instance when inadvertently meeting a client outside of therapy. Additionally, boundary crossing by therapists who are members of some communities such as rural or religious communities or some minority groups, can be difficult to prevent (Syme, 2006). Furthermore, it has to be remembered that the giving of gifts in a number of cultures is associated with polite manners and a demonstration of gratitude (Zur, 2008). The therapist refusing to accept a gift from the client could be deemed impolite, and potentially lead to a rupture in the therapeutic relationship (Syme, 2006). Anticipating and managing such situations then requires sensitivity on the part of the therapist and a consideration of what is a proportional response.

Without question, it is the therapist's responsibility to ensure that the client's space is respected. Even though physical touch can bring comfort (Panksepp, 1998), the use of touch should only be employed when the therapist has a strong sense of holding and understanding boundaries. The therapist needs to be mindful that the use of touch might be misinterpreted by the client, and that clients from some cultural backgrounds may find the use of touch inappropriate. It is crucial that the therapist ensures that the use of touch is seen as acceptable by the client (Jenkins et al., 2004). At all times, it is the therapist's responsibility to justify their use of touch and to ensure that the client consents, without being coerced. A general principle is to avoid touch, especially where this involves male–female or female–male contact, unless you are sure that it will be acceptable and this often means that the client, rather than you yourself, takes the initiative.

Ethical scenario

Jane is a CB therapist and lives and works in a small market town. She has been working with a 30-year-old man, David, concerning anxiety issues related to his employment. However, he revealed in therapy that he has been diagnosed with Chlamydia.

On a night out with a group of girlfriends, one of Jane's friends excitedly showed her a picture of her latest boyfriend. Jane recognised that it was David, her client. Jane's friend is hoping that this relationship will develop into something really special, and she is thinking about suggesting to David that they have a weekend away in London. It seemed clear to Jane that her friend had no idea that David had a sexually transmitted disease.

Ethical questions

1. What is Jane's professional responsibility in this scenario?
2. Who is she accountable to?
3. Does Jane have the right to breach her client's confidentiality?
4. What does your ethical code advice in such a situation?
5. What is your organisation's protocol in the event that such a scenario occurred in your organisation?
6. What would you do and how would you justify your action?

Dual relationships

Dual relationships have been known to cause therapists anxiety (Gabriel, 2005). They occur when a therapist has more than one role in their relationship with the client, either concurrently or sequentially (Syme, 2006). On a professional level, it is not uncommon for trainee CB therapists to be engaged in a dual relationship with a client within their place of work. It is evident that some trainee CB therapists are, for instance, contracted to work as a mental health nurse on certain days, whilst being employed as a trainee CB therapist on other days with the same client/service user. Although, such roles might be viewed to be compatible, it is likely that some blurring of boundaries occur, causing a degree of role confusion for both the client and the therapist. The therapist's ability to be objective can be compromised, as information taken from the non-therapeutic role influences the therapeutic work, wittingly or non-wittingly. It could, of course, be argued that some information or the dual relationship might enhance the therapeutic work. Essentially, whilst not all dual relationships are harmful, all dual relations must be consensual (Proctor, 2002). Clinical supervision is imperative in such circumstances, and it is the therapist's responsibility to ensure that the opportunity to explore the dual relationship within supervision is utilised.

The necessity for the therapists to take responsibility to set clear boundaries at the beginning of therapy so that the client is able to recognise the therapeutic relationship is fundamentally a professional relationship and not one based on friendship is highlighted by Jenkins et al. (2004). However, it is quite possible to imagine that a client might extend an invitation to the therapist to attend a celebratory social event with them, or a former client might invite the therapist to develop a friendship. Indeed, the prevalence of social media increases the possibility of the latter. Although, it is not uncommon in some professions for a professional to socialise with their client/patient, entering such dual relationships needs careful consideration. Even though professional guidelines cannot account for the nuances of each individual situation (Gabriel, 2005), they should be consulted together with the employing organisations policies. The recommendation made in the BABCP code is: 'to make a clear distinction between personal and professional relationships' (Section 1.1). This may be viewed as an ideal position to take by some CB therapists, rather than a realistic position, because it does not fit with the complexities of the context in which they work. Nonetheless, dual relationships do obscure boundaries. Therefore, anticipating such situations and working through their consequences, with peers and in supervision, in advance of them occurring, can develop the therapist's confidence in establishing and justifying a dual relationship.

Boundary violation

Whilst it is argued that boundary crossing is a natural part of therapy that should not be avoided, and is not inevitably bad (Zur, 2008), it is also reasoned that a series of minor boundary crossing can be perceived as a pattern of negligence (Williams, 1997: 238). Importantly, distress leading to complaints and litigation can occur when the client believes that their boundaries have not been respected (Jenkins et al., 2004).

Within therapy, a boundary violation occurs when a therapist exploits their client (Gutheil and Brodsky, 2008). The BABCP's code makes clear that the therapist: 'must not abuse the relationship ... sexually, emotionally, financially or in other ways' (Section 1.1). Correspondingly, the APS Code of Ethics provides details of non-exploitation of clients and others under 'General Principle C: Integrity'. Such behaviour causes harm to the client, and subsequently to trust in the profession. All the ethical principles are disregarded. Fidelity, the client's trust in the relationship, will ultimately be destroyed as the principle of non-maleficence (do no harm) is ignored. Moreover, the client's autonomy in the decision-making process is challenged. Beneficence (working for the therapeutic benefit of the client) is no longer the main concern because the therapist's needs take priority. A sexual relationship with a client is a clear example of a boundary violation, and is unacceptable. The therapist takes advantage of the imbalance of power in the therapeutic relationship, the client's trust and vulnerability, for their own gratification.

Moreover, starting a sexual relationship with a *former client* is not advisable. Although the BABCP do not give guidance about this, the APS Code of Ethics give a guideline of at least two years before commencing a sexual relationship with a former client. Standard C.4.3 stipulates that:

> Psychologists: who wish to engage in sexual activity with former clients after a period of two years from the termination of the service, first explore with a senior psychologist the possibility that the former client may be vulnerable and at risk of exploitation, and encourage the former client to seek independent counselling on the matter.

However, the legal case between Pates *v.* Dungey (2007) draws attention to the risk involved in entering a relationship with a former client, even after a substantial period of time. According to newspaper reports, Pates, a psychologist, had a sexual relationship with Dungey, a former client, three years and eight months after the end of their therapeutic relationship. Dungey claimed that the therapist: 'took advantage of her mental and emotional fragility', 'breaching his professional obligations'. Although Dungey was found to have initiated the sexual relationship and the case was dismissed by the Appeals Court, Pates is reported to have said that, as a consequence, he lost his career and reputation (Savill, 2009). With this in mind, very careful consideration needs to be given to how best to maintain boundaries once therapy has ended, particularly in small communities. Discussing such issues with a senior colleague, and encouraging the former client to engage in independent therapy, as recommended by the APS Code of Ethics, offers some protection to all parties.

Respecting and managing responsibilities

It is necessary to acknowledge that all therapists, trainee and experienced, are vulnerable to making an inappropriate decision at times. But, it is important for the therapist to take responsibility for their decisions and subsequent actions in relation to their clients, the profession, their employing organisation and to society. At each stage of therapy, the CB therapist needs to ensure that they take responsibility to develop a shared understanding with their client about the therapeutic process and treatment. Documenting this protects all those involved (see Chapter 6 on Confidentiality). Supervision should provide an opportunity to explore, not just treatment, but also the therapeutic relationship, enabling the therapist to deepen their awareness of their feelings and thoughts that motivate their actions with therapy. CB therapists, in particular, need to be vigilant about boundary crossing when they step outside of the therapy room to conduct behaviour experiments or exposure work with the client, adhering wherever possible to the BABCP's recommendation to separate the professional from the personal (Section 1.1). Although a degree of boundary crossing might be inevitable at such times, the therapist should be mindful of the purpose of the boundary crossing and how this might be interpreted by the client. Feltham advises: 'Do no deliberate harm' (Feltham, 2007: 6). By being proactive and considering their responsibilities, particularly connecting them to the ethical principles, the therapist will be less susceptible to boundary violation.

'The special patient'

Most therapists at some stage in their career will be asked to see a professional, colleague, former or current trainee, relative of a colleague, celebrity or other 'special patient' and this raises a number of complex issues. Initially, it can be seen as simply 'helping the person out' or their colleague who has made the request. It can be flattering that you have been chosen to assist. It may be that your previous relationship with the person is seen as meaning that they can feel that they can trust you when they are going through a crisis in their lives.

However, there are a number of considerations that need to be taken into account. It may not be unethical to provide therapy in these circumstances but a previous relationship or relationship with their family may complicate or bias it, e.g. the family may expect a level of disclosure which breaches the client's autonomy – and when they don't receive it, can become aggrieved. Previous acquaintanceship may prejudice the assessment and affect treatment. The individual therapist may not involve the local mental health team or use supervision in the way that they might have done otherwise – sometimes, because of the requests of the client and family. It is most important that the therapist in such circumstances receives supervision and is able to access an independent view of therapy progress to enable them to reflect accurately on the interactions occurring with client and family. Most, if not all, professional organisations do now prohibit therapists or similar practitioners from working with members of their own families because perspective is much too affected in these circumstances.

Conclusion

The concept of therapist responsibility within CB therapy is complex, and can sit uncomfortably with the notion of collaboration and equalisation of power. However, considering what the therapist's responsibilities are, and how they relate to the ethical principles and the BABCP code of practice or other relevant code of ethics, can help ensure that the therapist does not violate their responsibilities. Supportive supervision that enables and allows time for the supervisee to explore these issues, including crossing boundaries and dual relationships, will develop the therapist's, the client's and the public's confidence in CBT. Importantly, therapists need to be aware that their responsibilities extend beyond the CB therapy room, and being able to justify and account for the decisions that they make and the actions taken is necessary.

Activities

- Consider how power is expressed in your work environment. Reflect upon its influence in the therapeutic encounter, supervision and at management level. Question whether power sits like an elephant in the room.
- How are the requirements of informed consent adhered to in your work context? How do you ensure that the client understands the therapeutic process and treatment? What is the set protocol in your agency?
- What does your employment contract say about professional and personal responsibilities?
- What would you do if you felt that working in your client's best interest conflicted with your agency's policies? How would you resolve this dilemma? Do the ethical principles compete? What are your responsibilities in this situation?
- What do you need to consider if a 'special patient', i.e. a fellow professional or relative of a friend, is referred to you?

Further reading

Bond, T. (2015) *Standards and Ethics for Counselling in Action* (4th edn). London: Sage.

Gabriel, L. (2005) *Speaking the Unspeakable: The Ethics of Dual Relationship in Counselling and Psychotherapy*. London: Routledge.

Grunberger, B. and Main, T. (1989) *The Ailment and Other Psychoanalytic Essays*. London: Free Association Books.

Gutheil, T. and Brodsky, A. (2008) *Preventing Boundary Violations in Clinical Practice*. New York: Guilford Press.

Jenkins, P., Keter, V. and Stone, J. (2004) *Psychotherapy and the Law: Questions & Answers for Counsellors & Therapists*. London: Whurr.

Younggren, J., Fisher, M., Foote, W. and Hjelt, S. (2011) 'A legal and ethical review patient responsibilities and psychotherapist duties', *Professional Psychology: Research and Practice*, 42(2): 160–8.

5

CONFIDENTIALITY AND RECORD KEEPING

Learning outcomes

After reading this chapter and completing the activities at the end of it, you should be able to understand:

1. Responsibilities to preserve confidentiality and circumstances where disclosure is appropriate.
2. The potential, but also limitations, imposed in relation to contact with the media.
3. Limitations in publishing case studies and in the use of training materials, e.g. video and audiotapes.
4. Issues around separate therapy record keeping and disclosure of records to clients and/or carers.
5. Confidentiality and the use of electronic patient records (EPR).

Confidentiality is a complex and often confusing area. What you need for dealing with therapeutic situations is much the same as is required in health care practice generally, that is, a sound working knowledge of the principles involved and how they affect the process of assessment, intervention and communication with others. Also needed is knowledge of the legal issues around capacity and, rarely but occasionally relevant with severe mental illness, mental health legislation because it affects decisions about the sharing of information in some circumstances.

When therapists hold in their minds the 'why' of confidentiality, they are bound to be closer to acting ethically. A therapist is likely to hear information about a client that is intensely personal, about their present situation and also about past experiences, including traumatic events. Information given by the client belongs to the client and should therefore be treated with utmost respect. How far it is shared should be the client's choice, with the caveat that there are rare exceptions to do with the welfare of the client and other people and also with certain legal obligations to share.

Rules around confidentiality differ for crises where the assessment takes place under mental health legislation. This is because there are certain obligations placed on therapists acting under various legislations to consult with and/or inform certain relatives, and we will examine these situations later. For all other crises where the client has capacity, the rules of thumb are relatively straightforward. Every client is assumed to have capacity unless otherwise demonstrated. (See later for a discussion on capacity issues, including what happens if there is evidence that a client lacks capacity.)

Under data protection guidelines, it is the client's right to have information about them kept within the health care team. Permission to share within the team needs to be explicitly sought as it cannot be assumed that the client will realise that this is the way in which services operate. Sharing is necessary for the allocation of appropriate services and staff members to provide cover out-of-hours for emergencies and when the main staff member is on leave. It is also necessary for supervision and training purposes. Information is used in data gathering, although this will be anonymised as far as appropriate to the circumstances. Research usage is evolving but, unless ruled otherwise, specific consent is needed for use of individual data. This is considered in the chapter on evidence (Chapter 7), where the role of Research Ethics Committees is discussed.

Where routinely referred to services or to an individual practitioner, information about confidentiality should be made available to them and they should know what this actually entails. It can in reality mean a number of people having access to it - doctors, nurses, social workers, administration staff and managers. The client is asked to take on trust that all of these people will treat this information professionally and with sensitivity and not disclose it beyond those covered by confidentiality provisions. In crisis situations, detailed explanations about confidentiality may not be possible or appropriate, but simple statements and responses to inquiries about confidentiality need to be made. In general, clients expect what is said to a social or health care worker to be kept confidentially within the social or health care system, but if the client seems to be unaware of this or there is doubt for any other reason, then it may be worth reiterating it. This is especially where someone seems reluctant to disclose information as confidentiality concerns may be contributing factors.

Clients should also know what the exclusions are. If a client may suffer or cause those around them to suffer significant harm, then there is no option for professionals but to work out who needs to know what information for safety purposes, e.g. children's services will need to be told if there is concern for children's welfare. They need to inform the client of this, except in those rare cases when to tell the client would immediately increase the risk, in this example to the children. Clients should ordinarily be told this and be involved in the process, but if the client is saying, for example, that they would hide the children away somewhere, then there may be consideration given to not telling the client before childcare colleagues are alerted. Similarly, informing the client may not occur immediately if they have made serious threats against others that need to be acted upon.

It is also the client's right to agree to information being shared with others. A confidentiality policy is not a secrecy policy. A client may want certain information about their situation to be shared with others, for example with their care coordinator/case manager, housing support worker, a friend or some family members. A common misunderstanding about confidentiality is that it is a blanket provision, meaning that information should not be given out. The point is that it is the client's choice what is given out and to whom it is given. This can be an essential part of mobilising a client's social support system. The key people in this system can be instrumental in supporting the client while they move through to crisis resolution. Sometimes, the presence of mental health workers can alert family to the gravity of a situation that the client had felt unable to communicate previously. In practical terms, in order to avoid disagreement at a later date, and to keep with the client as far as possible, it is often better to:

- Support the client to tell the relevant people themselves.
- Document what is agreed to prevent doubt later: many organisational procedures will obtain a client's signature to confirm that they wish information to be shared.

Many mental health teams and social services departments have standard 'Permission to Share' information and consent forms that are useful for such circumstances. These need revisiting and updating, though, as people's lives change and their views about whom they want to help them can alter radically over time.

For those clients who do not wish to have any information shared outside of their professional care team, there can be stresses when carers, family or friends wish to be involved. Many carers can feel excluded when professionals use confidentiality to avoid speaking with them at all. However, confidentiality means not sharing information without permission, it does not mean neglecting to listen to the information and concerns expressed by others. It is quite all right to tell a client that you are going to listen to their carer's views but that you will not be disclosing information, so they can be reassured. It is also acceptable to tell carers that you are unable to share information of what the client says but that you are happy to hear their views and worries. In fact, what carers overwhelmingly want is to make sure that their views are heard and to receive advice on the best ways to handle their situation and care for the client – 'What can I do to help?' is a frequently asked question, as are questions about what to do in response to certain changes in the client's behaviour, e.g. withdrawing, not eating, getting upset or responding to voices. Therapists can agree on a line to take with the client beforehand or, often better, bring client and carer together so that a plan of support is openly discussed. General advice can be given and can be found in any carer guide, or on relevant websites, to helping someone with a mental health problem (see Further reading).

There are times when a client may be assessed as lacking capacity to make his or her own decision about whether information should be shared (see later). Where a person is assessed as lacking sufficient capacity to make a reasoned decision about who is told about their crisis, the first question to ask is about whether the client has an advance directive in place. Alternatively, the person may have written and signed up to something less formal, such as a crisis plan or an advance directive as part of the multidisciplinary review process or a Wellness Recovery Action Plan (WRAP). If a person loses capacity, then it is consistent with the principle of respecting information – discussed earlier – to go along with their recorded wishes, in so far as this is ethically and legally possible, and to act in their best interests.

If someone has no such plan or it is a first presentation of a client formerly unknown to services, a decision has to be made about who needs to know what. There are probably good grounds for giving the carers general information about responding to the symptoms that the client has disclosed to them, particularly if they are helping in any treatment plan. Professional carers, e.g. hostel workers, will also usually be bound by confidentiality, family are not, but, of necessity, need to know about what to do and why. For example, if a client is so depressed that they are barely communicating and are not taking fluid and food, his or her family will need to be told of the need for the client to have fluids to prevent the life-threatening risks of dehydration and will be given advice on the administration of medication. A discussion will need to take place with the family about whether this can be achieved in the family home and, if so, what professional input they will need. They may also need to be told at what stage a hospital admission may become necessary. Key people need to know certain information to protect the client's welfare and this needs to be taken into account in relation to confidentiality constraints. Understanding the effects of these constraints on the support that can be offered will often lead to an acceptance by the client of the need to provide relevant information.

When assessments take place under mental health legislation in many countries, and specifically in the UK at present, the practitioner coordinating the assessment has certain obligations. Legislation usually obliges them to take into account the views of relevant relatives. While this implies listening to the views of those relatives, the very fact that you have contacted them as a nearest relative is giving away the fact that assessment under mental health legislation is taking place, whether or not the client has consented to them knowing this.

Where clients specifically do not want relatives to be contacted, there have been difficulties in the past if this clashes with the requirements of legislation. Clients may have relatives who have abused them previously and the need for background information for an assessment could be immensely traumatising if it involves discussing the situation with such a relative. The ratification of the European Convention on Human Rights in many European countries has been helpful in obliging countries with conflicting legislation to develop processes that respect a client's choice about who should be contacted in their family when compulsory admission is being considered. Particularly relevant here is Article 8, about the right to privacy and family life. Mental health legislation needs to encapsulate the need for carers and family to be consulted about compulsory admissions but to give as much control as possible back to the client as to whom the relevant people to consult may be.

Ethical scenario

John, aged 35, has been seeing you for therapy over the past six weeks. Progress has been very slow and you feel that he is holding something back. At this session, he seems more focused and eventually says, 'If I were to tell you something, would you promise me that you would never, ever, tell anyone else?'

Ethical questions

1. How do you proceed?
2. How do you preserve and continue to develop the therapeutic relationship?

Contact with the media

Newspapers, radio, TV and the Internet are an important part of most people's lives and can inform, and misinform, and connect people and entertain. They are very important in shaping views about subjects and people. They can do harm by misinforming, reinforcing prejudice and intruding into private matters.

Their role in reinforcing stigma and discrimination has led to concerted attempts to replace negative images with more positive balanced views. In the UK, Time for Change (www.TimeforChange.org) has been producing Internet and TV material for a number of years in conjunction with local campaigns to try to correct these images. Many mental health practitioners get involved in local work or are approached by TV or radio to assist in programmes. Positive examples where people have successfully managed mental health issues are very helpful in combatting stigma but care does need to be taken in ensuring that there is no breach of a client's confidentiality without their explicit consent, nor that they feel coerced into participating or are unaware of potential negative consequences. For example, there may be a risk that their disclosures may lead to individual stigmatisation by friends, employer, neighbours, even family, or that when fully recovered, they might regret being involved. Balancing that, individuals have the right to express their views. Broadcasters have codes of conduct to follow. Employing organisations have communications departments or access to such advice, and practitioners should always consult and use their guidance about media contacts relating to clients.

The Internet, and especially social media sites, need to be considered as public forums and confidentiality considerations need to be followed in exactly the same way as is the case in any communication with others. Secure servers have been developed for the purpose of emailing confidential information in health services, e.g. for the NHS (nhs.net).

Published case studies

Psychotherapy has a long tradition, from Freud onwards, of publishing detailed case histories of individual clients (e.g. Judge Shreber). This has been an invaluable way of researching, training and evaluating practice. Concrete examples can demonstrate techniques more effectively than theoretical descriptions. It has become less common, and some journals no longer publish such cases, but some continue to do so. Books, especially training manuals, use them as examples to guide practice.

However, once committed to print, there is no turning back, so provisions to protect confidentiality are essential. Clients may give full permission to publish and there are some circumstances where this is appropriate, e.g. where celebrities have specifically wished to be associated with anti-stigma campaigns. Stephen Fry, the actor and TV host, has notably changed the public perception of bipolar disorder through his writings and programmes about it.

Nevertheless, unless there is such a specific reason for disclosure, anonymising material can achieve the same aims whilst protecting identity. Identifiable characteristics, e.g. name, town, occupation, even gender, can often be altered without changing the messages which the case study is trying to convey. Clients themselves may still be able to identify themselves and, in these circumstances, their permission to publish and perhaps their suggestions on further anonymisation should be sought.

In practice, most authors use examples for which specific permission is not sought - this can be because anonymisation is deemed in these circumstances to provide sufficient protection. Cases may have been modified or combined so that they do not relate to any individual. It is clearly important that confidentiality is fully protected and if there is any doubt, then advice from data protection sources must be sought or permission obtained from the client.

Training materials, e.g. video and audiotapes

Very similar provisions hold with video and audiotapes used in workshops and other training venues. These are inevitably more difficult to anonymise, although ensuring that workshop/training attendees are subject to standard confidentiality provisions provides more protection than broadcast or published material. Written consent should be obtained and the circumstances in which the material will be used should be explained, with the option to rescind permission at any time.

Separate therapy record keeping

Where service failures have occurred, e.g. where serious incidents such as suicides or homicides have occurred, breakdowns in communication between agencies and individuals have been consistently described. Therefore, where individuals are referred to services and then to individual therapists, there have to be very good reasons for non-disclosure of important material in clinical records and even stronger justification for separation of records.

So, should therapy records be kept separately from other clinical records? This is diminishing as regular practice but the reasoning given for it has been that individual clients will not disclose sensitive personal information if it is included in records broadly open to people other than the therapist and their supervisor. Such an assertion can now reasonably be argued to be an over-generalisation as many therapists do now include their records in mental health systems and appear to be able to function effectively with clients accepting the assurances made. Whether they document every important detail is open to discussion and it is possible that some specific issues or events may be withheld. Sometimes, these can be personally sensitive, e.g. an extra-marital affair, but can be described in such a way in the records that it conveys the important aspects but not the detail. For example, documenting marital stress or simply relationship issues may be acceptable to the client and precise enough for the records.

Should mental health records be kept separately from other health and social care systems? This is much commoner practice for confidentiality and practical reasons. There have been examples where psychiatric records have been part of acute hospital systems where material related to contact with a mental health service has been accessed by general hospital staff and the client has become aware of this and distressed about it. This type of sharing may well become more standard practice – and occur with primary and social care. Where sharing occurs, this needs to be explained and permission to share needs to be agreed. In practice, computerised systems often have built-in safeguards on access to meet client wishes that can be explained to them. Systems are better at detecting breaches of procedure in accessing records than is the case with written records as each individual has their own identity and access level on modern systems. This does provide protection for most health systems as combined or closely linked systems become more available in the future.

Disclosure of records to clients and/or carers

In general terms, client records should be freely available to them and with their permission, to their carers. In practice, there may be material within an individual record, e.g. from others ('third parties'), for which separate permission needs to be sought prior to release or which needs to be withheld. This can delay access, although supervised access can speed this up. Frequently, the client simply wishes to see a specific part of their record and letting them look at it can be an appropriate approach to take. Carers may wish to see records when the individual is unable to consent to this occurring, and principles of assessing capacity and best interests then guide practice. Carers usually want information for valid purposes but caution is necessary because occasions can arise in matters of exploitation or for use in legal battles, e.g. over divorce or inheritance.

Procedures exist in most health systems to obtain photocopies of notes but these can be cumbersome and charges may consequently be made. Individual practitioners sharing records may lead to less bureaucracy but, nevertheless, need to be clear that they are acting in accordance with best practice in their organisation.

Complaints and investigations

Complaints are increasingly common and can mean concern about services is increasing but also that people are less likely to accept services with which they are not satisfied. Complaints can be very important in improving services and individual practice. Cooperation in dealing with them is essential – this may involve acting as investigator as well as being investigated. As crises can often be points of learning and change, complaints about your individual practice can act similarly. Sometimes, they can negatively affect relationships with clients but working them through will usually be appropriate and can often lead to more productive work and even a better, clearer, relationship for the future.

Would it be unethical to refuse to work with someone who complained about you? Probably – this would usually be the case if they were still prepared to work with you, although the organisation may decide otherwise. What if they were continually complaining? In this case, the relationship may have broken down to the point where neither can work with each other, but one of the benefits of supervision in either of these circumstances is being able to reflect on this with a supervisor and decide on the way forward.

Critical serious incidents can have an even greater effect, depending on their nature. These can rarely include serious harm to the client, including suicide, and even more rarely to others. These experiences can be personally devastating and seem like a profound criticism of your therapeutic practice and, e.g. where suicide occurs, of you as an individual. You will inevitably ponder and reconsider what happened in your last contacts and what you could have done differently. You may identify these and criticise yourself – and sometimes, sadly, be criticised – for these. We can only say that it happens to the best of us at some stage in our careers – and sometimes it happens whatever we do – because of the very nature of our profession, which is working with people who are distressed. Cooperation with investigations, including coroner's courts, is obviously appropriate and advice can be sought from different sources, e.g. managers, supervisors, colleagues or professional organisations. Do you contact any relatives? It is very important that their needs are considered. So, if you have been closely involved in care, contact with them can be supportive to them. But it is always important to take advice and others may have done so; reflecting on action with a team, a supervisor or a manager, can be most appropriate.

In summary, clients have a right to confidentiality and preserving this is an essential component of professional practice. But it is not unqualified – there are circumstances where breaches may be necessary. Above all, it is there in the individual's best interests and to preserve their autonomy – that will include ensuring optimal involvement of those who care and support them.

Activities

- Can you summarise the broad principles involved in working with families and carers where a patient does not give consent to share?
- Can you think of an example where this has worked well and perhaps another example where it has worked less well?

Further reading

Standards of practice for cognitive therapists, psychologists (UK) and nurses include specific guidance on confidentiality:

www.babcp.com/files/About/BABCP-Standards-of-Conduct-Performance-and-Ethics.pdf (accessed 19 September 2016).
www.bps.org.uk/system/files/documents/code_of_ethics_and_conduct.pdf (accessed 19 September 2016).
www.nmc.org.uk/globalassets/sitedocuments/nmc-publications/nmc-code.pdf (accessed 19 September 2016).

Specific guidance on confidentiality for psychiatrists, doctors and psychologists (USA):

www.apa.org/helpcenter/confidentiality.aspx (accessed 19 September 2016).
www.gmc-uk.org/guidance/ethical_guidance/confidentiality.asp (accessed 19 September 2016).
www.rcpsych.ac.uk/usefulresources/publications/collegereports/cr/cr160.aspx (accessed 19 September 2016).

6

PROFESSIONAL AND THERAPEUTIC COMPETENCE IN CBT

Learning outcomes

After reading this chapter and completing the activities at the end of it, you should be able to understand:

1. The values, principles and key ethical considerations around competence in CBT.
2. What constitutes 'professional duties'.
3. What is meant by 'competence' from a professional and legal perspective.
4. Professional codes and their role.
5. Virtue ethics as a way of addressing professional concerns.
6. Strategies for the enhancement of ethical practice.

Professionals have a privileged position in society and cognitive behavioural therapists are no different in this respect. Cognitive behavioural therapists carry considerable responsibility for delivering therapy of appropriate quality and for upholding the standards and good reputation of their practice.

In this chapter, the ethics of professional and therapeutic competence in cognitive behaviour therapy will be considered. The values and principles of CBT practice and the duties of the professional and the debates therein will be scoped and definitions and frameworks of competence reviewed. These frameworks will then be considered in light of legal and ethical definitions of competence and, finally, dilemmas in practice and frameworks for how to address these will be explored.

The values, principles and ethics relating to competence in CBT

Professionals are now working in an era of increasing demand, expectations and accountability from people who use services. Yet, whilst CB therapy is one of the most highly developed therapy approaches with regards to its theoretical, research base and standards for practice, it is much less developed in respect to its professional ethics (Bond and Dryden, 2012). Thus, a conceptual relationship change needs to occur in order to ensure that this over-generalisation of professional authority from a scientific domain with its focus on validation shifts to a field in tandem, with ethics being recognised with equal importance.

Despite its underdeveloped ethical basis, it can still be argued that CBT is implicitly a values-based approach to therapy. The overarching framework that guides CBT is made up of the principles and philosophy of the scientist–practitioner (Corrie et al., 2016). This scientific way of working helps the therapist to understand the clients' difficulties and needs through theoretical frameworks and research evidence in order to have a clear rationale for what they are doing and the choices they are making. It is a modality that is intended to help clients to take stock of the way in which they behave and the way in which they think about themselves and others, and to see whether there are alternative perspectives and actions that could be more useful to them. Thus, alongside this scientific approach to practice, it can be argued that good CB therapists also treat people as individuals and therapy as a co-constructed, individualised and relational process. This principle can be broken down into three further principles that can be used to underpin competent practice. One of the most important of these principles is that it is intended to be collaborative – the client is both viewed and encouraged to be a partner in the therapy process, with shared responsibility for the work. A second principle is that, although CBT is a structured therapy, it works best where the therapist uses a process of guided discovery in order that the client learns to understand themselves and why they think, feel and behave as they do. This leads to a third principle, which is that CBT should help clients learn skills that enable them to cope with their current difficulties and any future adversity in a more effective way in order to prevent future relapse (Roth and Pilling, 2008).

Ethical scenario

Ethyl was criticised by her supervisor for not providing an appropriate standard of practice to one of her clients with a post-traumatic stress disorder. Her specific concern was that Ethyl had carried out a reliving strategy to help her client process her trauma but had not undertaken a period of stabilisation first. Ethyl thought that she had acted appropriately, the client had coped well with the intervention and the outcome had been good. Ethyl believes that she has grounds to complain about the standard of supervision and support she is now receiving within the service.

Ethical questions

1. What is an appropriate standard of therapy?
2. How is an appropriate standard defined?
3. What does the law have to say on a standard of therapy?
4. In the above situation, who is right?
5. What are Ethyl's responsibilities in regards to her own competence?

Duties of the professional

A professional is a person who has completed specified training in order to undertake a specific activity and role in their profession. In addition, most professionals are subject to formal specified codes of conduct – e.g. of the American Psychological Association (APA), Academy of Cognitive Therapy (ACT), British Association for Behavioural and Cognitive Psychotherapies (BABCP) and the Australian Association for Cognitive and Behaviour Therapies (AACBT) – that enshrine rigorous ethical and moral obligations and standards of expected practice on its membership. It can also be argued that not all professions are equal as some serve particularly important and sensitive aspects of public interest and a general public good of society. Health professionals are usually thought of in this way. It is because of this public interest that health professionals governing councils have lay membership and, in many cases, lay people are in the majority on the council so as to ensure that society is protected.

Cognitive behavioural therapy, in the USA, UK and elsewhere, is complicated in respect to its professional status. CB therapists are not a homogenous group who perform all the same tasks, nor are they necessarily trained or even regulated in the same way. Most therapists have a core professional qualification in, for example, medicine, psychology or nursing or can demonstrate an equivalence to these professions, and are thus bound by their core professional standards and ethical codes of practice or conduct. They will then have done further postgraduate training and have applied for and been granted the status of accredited therapist. Accreditation in the UK is by the BABCP. Yet, not all people who practice cognitive behaviour therapy are accredited. Some deem themselves as competent or are broadly recognised as such due to their status in the field or their core professional training or experience through specialisation in this area. There are also now professionals working using modified or more limited versions of CBT, such as behavioural activation and problem-solving, for example psychological well-being practitioners working in the Improving Access to Psychological Therapies (IAPT) programmes in the UK and methods of modified accreditation are being developed for them with adherence to the ethics and values described in this book.

The field is also characterised by the diversity of the field itself, which encompasses several traditions and approaches such as behaviour therapists, cognitive therapists and rational emotive behaviour therapy or third wave therapies such as compassion-focused therapy, mindfulness-based cognitive therapy or acceptance and commitment therapy. A final issue relevant to competence is that therapists who have demonstrated an equivalence to a professional qualification through the BABCP and its Knowledge, Skills and Attitudes (KSA) process are not accountable for their practice to a professional body.

It is also important to note that BABCP, whilst badging itself as the lead body for CBT in the UK, is not as is sometimes thought a professional body. It is a multidisciplinary interest group for people involved in the practice and theory of behavioural and cognitive psychotherapy, with its aims as defined in the box below.

Aims of the British Association for Behavioural and Cognitive Psychotherapies

- Promote the development of the theory and practice of Behavioural and Cognitive Psychotherapies in all applicable settings in accordance with the Standards of Conduct, Performance and Ethics.
- Provide a forum for discussion of matters relevant to Behavioural and Cognitive Psychotherapies among members of all helping professions.
- Disseminate information about, set standards for and provide training in Behavioural and Cognitive Psychotherapies among members of all helping professions.

(Continued)

(Continued)

- Maintain standards for practitioners of Behavioural and Cognitive Psychotherapy by providing the opportunity for members who meet minimum criteria to become accredited.
- Represent the interests of behavioural and cognitive psychotherapists through liaison with public and professional bodies and other worldwide organisations with similar aims.
- Publish and circulate an academic journal, newsletter and other publications aimed at disseminating research and information about the applications of Behavioural and Cognitive Psychotherapies.
- Facilitate the formation of Geographical and Interest Groups in order to provide a local and special interest service to members.

Source: www.babcp.com/About/About.aspx (accessed 20 November 2015)

Professional codes

Professional codes can be a valuable source and key point of ethical guidance for practitioners and their employers. Such codes have usually been developed over many years, and have been through several consultation processes during that time, and they may well have been given legal clearance from the respective professional organisation's legal advisors. Thus, the codes often represent a longitudinal distillation of professional consensus of professional, ethical and legal principles. A code cannot, however, pre-empt every eventuality, but can be used as a guide or scope within which professionals can operate and are especially useful in clear or well-defined situations (Beauchamp and Childress, 2013). Nevertheless, as they only provide a general basis for professional behaviour and actions, they are not a substitute for reasoned ethical thinking and ethical awareness.

The professional code that governs the practice of members of the BABCP was originally developed in the early 1970s and, other than very minor changes, was only fully updated in 2008, and adopted at the annual general meeting in 2009, and published in its current form in 2010. The full document can be found on the BABCP website (www.babcp.com), and is titled 'Standards of Conduct, Performance and Ethics'. The BABCP professional code is rather unusual in that it focuses primarily on standards and, even more unusually, on performance. The document itself can be rather off-putting, potentially for both trainee and experienced therapists as it is structured around a series of imperatives. This can be considered a bit ironic for a therapeutic approach that considers client problems as the enacting of overly rigid beliefs and schema. The code has also come in for critical comment by Bond and Dryden (2012) for not setting out the ethical basis on which the standards that underpin it are based. Yet, a careful consideration of the BABCP Standards does indicate a set of implicit underpinning principles of 'do no harm' and 'fidelity' that will be discussed further below. It is also important to recognise that, whilst Bond and Dryden (ibid.) are critical, they are so from a constructive developmental perspective and explicitly suggest how the imbalance between the emphasis on science and ethics can be addressed. This they do through the provision of an ethical text that makes this case and provides guidance for the development of ethical awareness.

Competence, standards and decision-making

Ethics and the law are sometimes thought to be inextricably linked but there are basic distinctions. The law in its various forms is concerned with administration, judgement and regulation of the social, political and economic systems. Law, thus, has instrumental goals concerning the achievement of order through sets of rules. Ethics, on the other hand, concerns questions related to justice, truth and morality in local context-sensitive situations and governed by the interactions between two or more people (Komesaroff, 2001). It can also be argued that ethical obligations can exceed legal duties and, in some cases, the law can actually mandate unethical conduct. Examples include where a nation state has the death penalty on its statutes and a medical practitioner who has sworn the Hippocratic Oath is involved with an execution. Further, the reverse can also apply where a doctor or therapist is charged with allegedly illegal conduct and is then acquitted in a civil or criminal court, which does not necessarily mean that the professional involved acted ethically.

Competence is not a legal term but can be understood as the legal capacity to perform an act to the specified standard and to understand its impact and respond accordingly. The judiciary approach the matter of adequate standards of professionals, including counsellors and CB therapists, as exercising 'due care' or reasonable care or demonstrating reasonable skill (Bond, 2015).

This raises the question of what is a reasonable standard for a CB therapist and what are the therapist's professional obligations in this respect. Standards of care that do not concern a professional judgement are considered in the courts on the basis of common sense (or, as determined by the proverbial 'man on the Clapham omnibus'). Examples would be poor handwriting that led to a misinterpretation by another professional or not communicating that a client was suicidal or therapists who form a sexual relationship with a client. The other type of legal decision that the CB therapist may encounter concerns professional or clinical decision-making. This aspect of professional practice would not be within the court's notion of common sense. In these situations the court assesses the standards of care expected by reference to a reasonable body of practitioners in the field. What is noteworthy here is that this is a broad criterion, thought necessary as professional practice can be as much an art as a science and does permit differences of professional opinion. For example, professional difference might occur in the case of CBT, some therapists might choose exposure as the therapy of choice in panic, whilst another might use a combination of cognitive restructuring and behavioural experiments. In this example, there would be both a difference in theory and the actual choice of therapeutic strategy, yet both are likely to be regarded as 'reasonable'. The case law concerning what is an acceptable standard is based on the Bolam test of medical negligence (Bolam *v.* Friern Hospital Management Committee, 1957). The decisions made would also have to be reasonable and logical (Bolitho *v.* City and Hackney Health Authority, 1997).

Similarly, as suggested by Bond (2015), the exercise of demonstrating reasonable skill may in some circumstances be on the basis of the degree of risk involved in a professional decision. In other words, more might be reasonably expected of a practitioner who is working with an actively suicidal client or a client who is being subjected to domestic abuse or other trauma, compared to a situation where a therapist is working with a client with poor social skills, mild depression or anxiety.

There are also other situations where the decision as to the standard may vary. The degree or skill of the experienced therapist might be expected to be more than that of a newly qualified therapist or trainee in order to balance the disadvantage of professionals being in constant fear of legal action. However, the absolute minimal acceptable standard has to be established. This includes addressing any differences in levels of practice between non-professional staff, novices or trainees and expert practitioners (Newdick, 2005). This is often addressed by employing organisations by them defining the level of skill required to a professional job-role in the form of a job description, rather than the knowledge or skills of an individual who occupies such a role (Bond, 2015). In addition to this organisational strategy, oversight and supervision of practice policies and procedures are often mandated by the organisation and professional bodies in order to help maintain at least the minimum defined standard and to 'scaffold' the trainee at that minimum whilst they develop their competence and autonomy. These issues all apply to cognitive behavioural psychotherapists as much as they do to other professionals.

Ethical principles and competence

Competence is defined as the therapist delivering both the general and the specific knowledge and skills required to appropriately deliver CBT interventions that reflect the current research base (Muse and McManus, 2013). A CB therapist is expected to be competent in working with a wide variety of client difficulties from diverse backgrounds. They will also be expected to have the knowledge and skills to work and communicate well with other professionals and to work in a number of clinical settings. The therapist task is to develop therapeutic relationships, assess and conceptualise the client's difficulties using CB theory, draw up therapeutic plans, apply therapy techniques and use outcome measures to evaluate progress (Corrie et al., 2016).

All this work is also being carried out within an ethical framework that safeguards the interests of the client and the therapist to a degree that includes confidentiality with sufficiently maintained therapeutic boundaries. In order to deliver competent practice, professional ethics have been developed that are underpinned by a number of core principles (Beauchamp and Childress, 2013).

These include 'autonomy', which recognises that, in this context, CB therapists have certain rights to act freely and exercise choice in their professional practice. This is demonstrated most clearly as the therapist moves from being a novice with continuous supervisory oversight, to being an expert autonomous practitioner with total responsibility for assessment, through to discharge - sometimes, but not always, within the context of an interdisciplinary team (Milne, 2011; Corrie and Lane, 2015).

A second principle is 'fidelity', which is an ethical principle that encompasses competence and requires professionals to perform their duties in the way that is expected whilst being trustworthy and keeping any promises made during the therapeutic process. Broadly, this would mean being respectful to clients, ensuring competence in their duties and working to the professional codes and policies and procedures of their employer. Further, they would need to adhere to what is acceptable within society and the law.

A narrower perspective of fidelity is sometimes used in CBT, where a fidelity to the model of CBT is argued. 'Fidelity', in this context, is defined as therapy being delivered according to an explicit predefined protocol or guideline. The IAPT programme in England implicitly demonstrates such an ideal of fidelity. The goal of this unique and highly ambitions programme is to train thousands of therapists to apply CBT and other evidence-based therapies (EBTs) in primary care to the same standards as those achieved in controlled trials through following specified models and protocols of therapy. In order to underpin the practice, an important element of this programme was the identification of competencies that typified proficient CBT for clients with problems of depression and anxiety. Roth and Pilling (2008), in undertaking this work, devised a map of competences that provides clarification of the knowledge, skills and attitudes required of the cognitive behaviour therapist. These competencies were identified through a review of controlled trials, research synthesis and analysis of underpinning therapy manuals. However, despite this rigour and the openness of the process, the authors still argued that the competence framework should not be used prescriptively but instead be used in a flexible way to inform decision-making, therapeutic activities and assessment of therapist skills.

Within the Roth and Pilling framework, the competencies are organised around five domains, each of which comprises a range of activities that, in turn, consist of a set of specific skills. These are as follows (see also: www.ucl.ac.uk/CORE):

1. Generic (the so-called 'common factors' of effective therapy such as knowledge of mental health problems and the ability to form positive working alliances with clients).
2. Basic CBT competences (such as a working knowledge of common cognitive distortions, the ability to structure therapy and how to explain to clients the rationale for homework).
3. Specific behavioural and cognitive techniques (e.g. the principal methods and techniques that are employed in most CBT interventions such as exposure and response prevention and guided discovery).
4. Problem-specific competences (those CBT interventions and procedures adapted to specific disorders. The competence framework details these for specific phobias, social phobia, panic disorder, obsessive compulsive disorder, generalised anxiety disorder, post-traumatic stress disorder and depression).
5. Meta-competences (those 'higher-order' skills of thinking and procedural knowledge that enable a therapist to implement and adapt, pace and time specific interventions in response to client need).

A third core principle is 'beneficence', with its emphasis on doing good and the promotion of human welfare: the IAPT programme is an example of this, whereby the greatest good and improved psychological health is being sought from the limited resources that are available.

The fourth principle is 'non-maleficence': a CB therapist might use this principle in deciding whether to breech confidentiality in order to protect a client who has expressed suicidal ideas within therapy. A criticism of deontological and utilitarian ethics (as discussed elsewhere in this book and briefly here) is that they cannot always provide a totally satisfactory account of how one should 'be' as a professional or as a person more generally in society. It can be argued that CBT, like other talking-based therapies and the helping professions, is guided by decisions concerning 'doing the right thing' within the therapeutic process.

A fifth principal is 'justice', which concerns the obligation to treat all people equally and fairly, taking into account their own individual circumstances. In the CB context, this might mean affording a client additional therapy sessions when progress has been slow due to factors outside of the client's control or maybe just because their rate of improvement is generally slower than that of other clients.

Virtue ethics is an alternative branch of ethics that emphasises 'moral character', rather than focusing on the correct action, as is the case with consequentialist and non-consequentialist theories of ethics. The underpinning notion that guides virtue ethics is that the right thing to do in a given situation is what a virtuous person would do in those circumstances. Thus, professionals would not seek to achieve a desired outcome and, unlike in duty-based ethics, a prescribed moral rule would not be followed (Ellis, 2015). Virtue ethics instead focuses on the development of the self to be a good person. It is this emphasis on character that distinguishes virtue ethics from the other branches of ethics and makes this area of ethics potentially of importance in underpinning therapy that is relationally and developmentally orientated as is the case in CB therapy. Thus, virtue could become a central construct within CBT as an underpinning ethical philosophy that brings together a number of areas of practice and science within the field. These could include areas such as the development of positive health and human growth, therapy as the basis for promotion of a healthy character and community well-being. These go alongside the focus on resilience and meanings and the development of wisdom within life (Sandage and Hill, 2001). These notions could also be criticised from a post-modern perspective. It can certainly be argued that the language of virtue ethics might undermine the science that has been so successful in the development of CBT. Programmes such IAPT or managed care systems, with their functional emphasis, may also be at odds with virtue ethics. These stress a reduction in symptoms, rather than human growth and the facilitation of meaningful and moral lives and worldviews (ibid.).

Example of the ethics of competency in CBT supervision

John is a qualified accredited CB therapist who has been practising therapy for 20 years. He has some standing in the field, he is involved with the

(Continued)

(Continued)

professional body, doing committee work, and he works both in the NHS and in private practice at the weekends and on occasional evenings. During supervision, it has become increasingly apparent that John has not really been engaging with his continuing professional development (CPD) beyond superficial attendance at events. He often cancels supervision, which has become rather sporadic. Observation of his practice suggests good therapeutic relationships but with an overly didactic approach, which is more instructional than collaborative/Socratic with an approach very reliant on behavioural change strategies.

Ethical analysis

The above is a good example of a therapist who is perhaps going through the motions, could not be described as being a dangerous therapist in the short term but whose clients may not be benefiting fully from the CB therapeutic approach. The failings from the client's perspective might be in respect to learning how to become their own therapist, thus increasing the likelihood of relapse and the scope of strategies used might also limit their recovery. Thus, from a general ethical perspective, whilst not seeking to cause harm, John might be doing so through his omissions. More specifically, he is not upholding fidelity and from a virtue ethics perspective, it can also be argued that John is no longer seeking to develop his 'good professional character' and is thus no longer striving to make virtuous decisions. His repeated cancellations of supervision and poor engagement with CPD would be considered a breach of acceptable standards as defined by his code of practice.

Implications and actions

As a supervisor, the CB therapist would also have a number of ethical and professional obligations. Similar to practice, they would be held accountable for their standard of practice – in this case, their standard of supervision. In the above case of John, there would be an ethical imperative to help him recognise the apparent deficits in his practice. A possible virtuous approach to this would consist of trying to understand John's situation, and being considerate and respectful towards him. However, this would need to be in balance with a similar consideration to the clients for whom John is responsible. This balance of considerations to what is right and proper would suggest that John's professional practice would need to be addressed from a developmental perspective. However, if he does not address these problems in a professional and timely way, then a 'do no harm' perspective on ethics might have to be adopted by the supervisor – in this case, the problem being drawn to the attention of the manger to whom John is professionally accountable.

Maintenance and enhancement of competence

Continuing the principle of ethics into the enhancement and maintenance of competence as an indication of the competence of the CB therapist is where they are able to recognise the limits of their practice and either seek further training or supervision or make appropriate referrals. It is also important that CB therapists are able to recognise their own personal issues and work in order to ensure that they do not become confused with those presented by the client. This is always important but particularly so when working with complex and vulnerable individuals. It is also important that therapists are able to manage their own stress and also withdraw from practice if their own functioning is affected due to personal or emotional difficulties, physical illness or other concerns. Supervision can also provide the oversight to help CB therapists to recognise and manage these situations and, in some situations, personal therapy might be helpful in this process (Milne, 2009).

Professional development and accreditation

In order to maintain and enhance competence in the CB therapist, the BABCP has developed a system of accreditation and reaccreditation of practitioners and also maintain a listing of all therapists who have been assessed as meeting the required standards (www.babcp.com). This process was developed and implemented in the early 1990s. Accreditation lasts for five years and on application/reapplication, a portfolio of evidence must be submitted for review. Accreditation proves that a CB therapist has followed a specific accredited programme of study, has a specified period of professional practice and experience and has committed to meeting the criteria for accreditation. It also shows that they work to the BABCP standards and competencies learned in training. In addition, accreditation shows commitment to the high standards that are required in order to maintain their accredited status through continually developing their skills through supervision, continued professional development and reflective practices.

In summary, in this chapter it has been argued that there needs to be a balance between the science of practice and its ethical basis. In this way, professional accountable practice can continue to develop within the CB field. Competence in itself is not a legal term: expected standards are what the law is concerned with and what underpins professional practice and decision-making. In recent years, the CB field has made considerable progress in defining its competencies – at least in broad terms through the IAPT programme. Competency can be considered from a number of ethical perspectives. This includes consequentialist and non-consequentialist perspectives as well as a virtue ethics perspective. However, it remains with the professional as a therapist or a supervisor to maintain at least the minimum level of expected practice: to understand what this minimum is and to take corrective action if this is compromised.

Activities

- Give thought to your own level of competency. What do you consider to be your weakest area of practice? This might be a relational issue or it might be working with a particular client group or it might be about professional communication.
- Ask yourself and discuss with your supervisor(s) what would be the minimum acceptable standard of therapeutic work and how you are meeting (or not meeting) this standard.
- Read over the Roth and Pilling (2008) competencies, consider your own development as an ethical practitioner and develop an action plan for the next 12 months.

Further reading

Bond, T. (2015) *Standards and Ethics for Counselling in Action* (4th edn). London: Sage.

This book is a superb comprehensive counselling text, which draws together the author's many years of experience in researching and writing about ethics in counselling and psychotherapy.

Bond, T. and Dryden, W. (2012). 'Ethical principles for CBT practitioners', in W. Dryden and R. Branch (eds), *The CBT Handbook*. London: Sage.

This chapter provides a state-of-the-art analysis of ethics in CBT. It is a thought-provoking chapter that also gives the reader a framework for ethical decision-making.

7

RESEARCH AND EVIDENCE

Learning outcomes

After reading this chapter and completing the activities at the end of it, you should be able to understand:

1. Why assessing the evidence base for practice is an ethical issue.
2. How to gain knowledge and skill in assessing evidence.
3. The strengths and limitations of currently used research methodologies.
4. The difference between audit, service evaluation and research.
5. The role of evidence-based guidelines.

Consideration of the evidence base for practice is necessary because:

- Claims made need to be justified.
- Therapies offered should be effective or at least have a reasonable chance of being so.
- The use of public or private money needs to be justifiable.
- Practitioners can then be appropriately trained and continue to develop their skills.

Research and evaluation

As described in Chapter 1, there has been a strong emphasis in CB therapy on research and the evaluation of specific interventions since the founding of behaviour and cognitive therapies (Hawton et al., 1989). It is frequently argued that engagement in decisions about the best use of resources and use of the evidence to decide on the appropriateness of an intervention and to support the use of a clinical intervention, is an ethical approach to scientifically underpinned modern practice. Advocates of this way of thinking about practice would argue that, if public or private funds are expended on therapy, then that therapy should be demonstrably effective and evidence supporting its benefits and risks should be made available to clinicians and service users. The further argument would be that the intervention ought to be cost-effective.

Additionally, where therapies are under development and thus the evidence is either not currently available or robust enough to consider it as evidence-based, it can be argued that it is incumbent upon those using the emerging interventions to evaluate and support research into them. However, many clinicians would not see themselves as researchers nor would they feel that they have the skills to perform research. If so, the degree of innovation that they might apply in their practice would need to be carefully considered. In practice, each individual presents a unique set of life experiences and perspectives and, so, every consultation is a novel experience that requires flexibility and responsiveness by the therapist. However, where this moves outside of the adaptation of recognised and evidence-based techniques, there are ethical considerations as to whether these go beyond good practice.

In this chapter, we will consider the validity of these arguments, along with the issues of research engagement within the context of developed and developing health care systems from an ethical and values perspective.

The scientist–practitioner

A scientist–practitioner approach to practice provides the CB therapist with a framework for making the best use of evidence in practice (Corrie and Lane, 2010). The scientist–practitioner would accept the principles that underpin evidence-based practice, defined as: 'the process of systematically finding, appraising, and using contemporaneous research findings as the basis for clinical decisions' (EBMWG, 1992: 2420). As well as the distillation and consideration of research studies, a scientific approach would also be used at the individual level. A hypothesis is formed as to what is maintaining the client's difficulties and these are tested and refined throughout the therapeutic process.

We would concur that this is a useful way of approaching practice but it is not without its dangers. It could be considered, for example, as an approach that psychopathologises people who are then experimented upon. Yet, this is not how we would conceptualise practice and this is where values are important.

The client is a unique individual, with therapy being a collaboratively constructed and personally experienced relational process between two individuals with ongoing evaluation as part of this process that provides systems of checks and feedback on progress. Thus, it provides information on which decisions can jointly be made. Basic evaluation using available outcome measures is possible in our view with any of the broad mental health conditions, even if this simply involves before-and-after comparison. The selection of outcome measures is an important consideration and, whilst services or the therapist often define these decisions themselves, involving the client in this can also be important in determining what is an important outcome and thus what ought to be measured. Measures at the individual level are usually best if they are client- or patient-rated where possible because this allows a degree of independence - although this may supplement clinician-rated tools that can provide other perspectives, e.g. in relation to areas where individual perspectives may be affected such as assessment of personal substance use or psychotic symptoms. Importantly, ratings of the therapeutic relationship are also available - both patient- and therapist-rated, which can again be a valuable form of feedback.

Therapy itself also involves testing hypotheses by setting experiments (Bennett-Levy et al., 2004) - often behavioural in type - and drawing conclusions that can shape future coping strategies and directly challenge dysfunctional beliefs. These can involve exercises to explore or even challenge beliefs about experiences, e.g. fears that the individual will not cope with going out of the house or with meeting specific people or that others may say negative things about them. Again, careful evaluation of these exercises is essential to ensure maximum learning and minimise unnecessary stress.

It is also important to recognise that interventions, including psychological ones, can have unexpected or unwanted side effects or consequences and, whilst these may not generally be as potentially harmful and irreversible as occurs in the use of chemical substances, they can lead to distress, disability and, in the most extreme circumstances, harm to self or others. These can occur because of the reactivation of suppressed events in a manner that leads to destabilisation or affects beliefs about the self or others. As an example, in an early CBT study of anxiety and depression (Kingdon et al., 1986) a depressed patient engaging in CBT seemed to be making substantial improvements but as her mood lifted, she developed a hypomanic episode that eventually required hospitalisation. She did eventually make a full recovery and whilst it is possible that this episode would have occurred whether or not she had been receiving CBT, the similarity to the effect of antidepressant medication in inducing hypomania was noted and its potential as a side effect of therapy. Certainly, lesser effects where therapy has caused distress are well described by patients with the range of therapies and it is incumbent upon therapists to minimise these. This is particularly the case as outlined above with the use of novel techniques that are untested.

Ethical scenario

Jeremy, a CB therapist, was referred a male Indian client, who was psychotic with depression and anxiety problems. He was coping reasonably well with the help of his family, who were all well educated and affluent and keen to be involved. He was not taking any illicit substances but he was refusing all antipsychotic medication and both the client and his family had read about the side effects of the medication and they had been advised of a recent study comparing antipsychotic medication and psychological therapy, suggesting that for some people antipsychotic medication might not be needed. The client's parents had also read about the recovery movement, both in the UK and worldwide, and were keen to help their son to become involved with this as well. The client was less sure about this but was influenced by his parents and the views of other family members.

Ethical questions

1. How ethical is an evidence-based approach to CB practice?
2. What is a CB therapist's role in appraising an evidence base?
3. How might the evidence in this complex situation be appraised?
4. How might any divergence of opinion between the therapist, the evidence base, the client and the family be managed?

Principles of evidence-based practice

The scientist–practitioner approach is part of the evidence-based practice movement within professional practice. This involves consulting a range of qualitative and quantitative research. Qualitative work might include case studies that have become increasingly refined and provide a richness and depth that quantitative studies can lack. However, there has been a strong emphasis on using randomised controlled studies and specific outcome measures, often purpose-built for specific conditions. Exponents of evidence-based practice refer to 'hierarchies of evidence'. This is shown in Figure 7.1. This has been the subject of significant critical debate as it implies that some evidence forms of evidence, such as randomised controlled trials, has more value than other forms of evidence, such as qualitative phenomenological studies of peoples' experiences of using services. To reconcile this, we simply argue that rigour is important, no matter what form the research takes, no form of research is superior to another but the evidence that ought to be considered is the one that best addresses the question being asked. So, a randomised controlled trial (RCT) would not, for example, answer a question about the experience of therapy but a phenomenological study most certainly could.

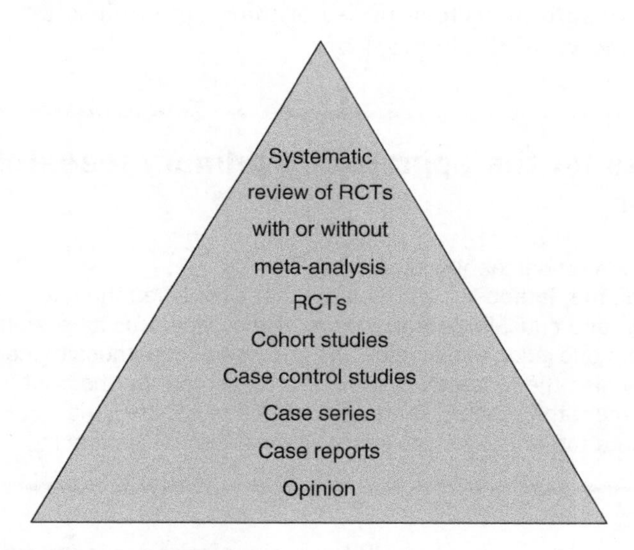

Figure 7.1 Hierarchy of evidence

This evidence base for CBT has been painstakingly developed over the past 40 years and now there are over 1000 RCTs into its use for a very wide range of conditions. These include depression, where CBT was first described and where the first trials were initiated, anxiety disorders and also bipolar disorder and psychosis ('schizophrenia'). There has also been work on mechanisms to inform understanding of conditions and therapies. Despite this valuable research, discussions about evidence-based practice still engender both negative and positive reactions from clinicians and academics.

How do we assess evidence?

Evidence-based medicine is a multistep process. The ability to use critical assessment is now something that has become part of most training courses and accreditation processes. Despite the multitude of articles reviewing the evidence base and guidelines based on it, the individual practitioner will still be confronted with circumstances, regarding which they will need to make a judgement about the value of interventions. This may be because the combination of problems or the situation presenting is unusual and there is no strictly relevant guidance, or because a relevant intervention has not been tested but seems to be a pragmatic way forward.

The CB therapist can incorporate evidence into their practices in one of three distinct ways. The first of these, and perhaps the best but also most time-consuming, is to appraise primary research sources using the process as shown in the box below.

Process for the appraisal of primary research sources

1. Devise a researchable question.
2. Search the databases for research that addresses the question.
3. Obtain and critically appraise each of the papers using a standardised pro forma to guide the process and give some robustness to the process.
4. Synthesise the research by making a judgement on the best approach.
5. Implement the research findings with the client or client group.
6. Evaluate the effectiveness of the intervention or approach.

The second approach that the CB therapist might use is potentially more rapid and involves restricting the search to sources that have already undergone critical appraisal by others. This is a common approach and would involve using evidence-based guidelines or evidence. Such evidence is becoming much more readily available, with recommendations being made in many clinical guidelines internationally - e.g. NICE, PORT, APA - and is supported by professional and client groups. These can provide valuable assistance but, by their nature, consider client groups in general and cannot take into account all the individual factors that a practitioner has to consider, e.g. age, ethnicity, previous therapy and other treatment (see full discussion later). Finally, there is an opinion approach, where the views of respected leaders in the field are followed or guidance is used from a more experienced CB therapist through discussions in supervision. Each of these processes for working with the evidence have a number of advantages and disadvantages. To make the best use of an evidence-based approach will require using each of these approaches and will mean moving back and forth between them, depending on whether the problem is familiar or rare for the CB therapist or a more controversial area of practice. However, when it comes to using techniques in clinical practice, it is a consideration of 'what works for whom' (Roth and Fonagy, 2010) now that, in our view, really needs to inform practitioners.

Criticisms of evidence-based practice

Some of the criticisms of evidence-based practice relate to the limitations of some of the research methods or approaches themselves. RCTs, seen by many as the gold standard for working out if an intervention is effective or not, are quite difficult to carry out in psychotherapeutic work. Many conditions have lengthy histories and studies have taken place over 6–9 months, with follow-up periods extending to five years. Therapy is also constrained by the nature of clinical trials and might not match well with the complexity of cases seen by CB therapists in their own therapy settings – but this can lead to more rigorous assessment of fidelity and training. Thus, ethically, the onus does remain with the CB therapist to weigh up the importance and relevance of evidence. That may also vary in its methodological quality, and issues such as whether trials are truly blind, follow intention-to-treat principles, and are methodological with sound randomisation. Allegiance, personal bias and disclosure of factors relevant to studies are also influential and need to be considered.

Paradoxically, a further criticism of research trials is that the therapy is expert and thus 'too good' and so not sustainable in clinical practice – although, even here, attempts have been made to replicate results in 'gold standard RCTs' in clinical practice (e.g. Turkington et al., 2006). There has also been a development of clinical outcome measurement in practice – led by the IAPT services in the UK. This has also led to targets being set for achievement in terms of recovery that does raise issues around the practicalities of this and also whether there are ethical issues consequent upon it. For example, once outcome measurement is being used to set targets, methods of 'gaming' to meet the target, without necessarily providing the service or desired effects, arise. This has been an issue in target setting in health care universally and is now potentially occurring in therapeutic settings. This becomes a particular issue where funding is attached – as so, too, will happen with the international aspiration to develop 'payment-by-results' systems. There is certainly an ethical issue around the distortion, if not frank deceitfulness, in achieving targets but also around whether targets are in fact achievable and the ethics of setting these targets.

Further issues have arisen around the 'production-line' approach to therapy and the dangers of lacking an individually tailored approach. Formulation is a key part of CBT and is designed to provide a focus on individual need, but therapies have often been tested - and sometimes - constrained by diagnoses and specific inclusion and exclusion criteria. Generalisability can be an important issue - comorbidity is a feature of conditions, although, arguably, some of this is due to a lack of psychosocial input into the classification process, e.g. drugs or trauma and psychosis.

There are also important considerations specifically related to the psychological therapies field. This often involves conditions that can be quite variable in presentation and severity. Much work has been done to develop homogeneous concepts and client groupings, especially through the *DSM* and *ICD* diagnostic process. Nevertheless, depression or psychosis remain relatively broad concepts, essentially syndromes, with differing individuals presenting a range of diverse symptoms as exemplified from some work that we did on CBT in China (see the box below).

Differences in presentation of psychosis

In work that we did on CBT in China, the population with psychosis who we were meeting differed significantly from those in the UK (Li et al., 2015): non-opiate substance misuse, e.g. of cannabis or cocaine, and childhood sexual abuse (whether actually present or not) were very rarely encountered in therapy, in marked contrast to experience in the UK. So, the population with psychosis differed and thus results of intervention for psychosis in the UK could not be confidently predicted to also occur in China. Aggregation of studies into meta-analyses can completely miss this as an issue. Therefore, it might be considered an ethical violation to apply CBT in this context without thought to such differences and how the overall approach might need to be changed.

It can also be argued that interventions can be very heterogeneous; a chemical can be directly replicated, although how it is delivered can have a major effect on its efficacy, e.g. long-term injectable or short-term by mouth. There can be some differences in metabolism in different races but these are relatively unusual and adjustment of dosage can usually be used to compensate. However, a psychological treatment can be described but, the more specific the description and protocol adhered to, the less individualised the approach will be – this can be accounted for in the manualisation of therapies to some degree or in assessment of outcome. Nevertheless, there are personal characteristics on both therapist and client sides that complicate and reduce homogeneity.

The evidence base has to be viewed from a broad perspective: meta-analyses and randomised controlled trials can be valuable in assessing defined interventions delivered over relatively short periods of time. Problems that endure and are multiple, involving comorbidities, may also require longitudinal descriptions and qualitative studies of interventions and services. The length of studies should be influenced, if not determined, by the length of treatment. An intervention for six weeks that seems to show an improvement in symptoms may be of little relevance to a disorder which is then known to continue for many years – unless it is curative, and even then assessment of relapse should occur. The ideal study would continue for the life-course of a disorder – this is relatively easy for a brief episode of a condition such as pneumonia but not for depression or psychosis when in many cases may last for years.

Management considerations include practicalities such as whether social issues, e.g. homelessness or risk, take precedence over therapies or choices or whether there are sufficient trained and motivated staff to provide an intervention. Cultural factors influence not only the uptake of health care, but also its delivery and impact (e.g. Black and Minority Ethnic (BME) groups, organisational practices and care delivery). Cost affects the prioritisation of what can be provided: 'Values-Based Commissioning' relates to the right care, reducing variability, eliminating waste and decommissioning interventions of limited clinical value (www.rightcare.nhs.uk).

Preferences, choice and service user involvement in evidence-based practice and research

Choice may also influence outcome. Patient preference studies have been done to take this into account. More patients prefer talking treatments to medication, for example, which may influence outcome – it may be that an individual would prefer a moderate effect from a therapy than a greater effect from medication because of their feeling of being more empowered and in control of a talking treatment. Side effects may also contribute to such a decision. The outcomes measured need to be relevant to those experiencing the problems, and symptoms may not be as important as functioning or quality of life or a sense of empowerment and control over your life. It can even be 'how much trouble I cause to others'. Simple outcomes, e.g. eradication of infection, can be appropriately assessed using the hierarchy - remission of depression and psychosis are more difficult because some degree of sadness responsive to events is normal and, indeed, adaptive as, too, can some degree of suspiciousness and confusion about the intentions of others.

There are, therefore, a number of different components to any evaluation of therapy that affect its relevance to the person for whom it is being proposed. The concept of triangulation of data is a very useful one in trying to ensure that outcomes are valid. Comparison can be made between clinician rating of outcome with patient rating and measure of their experience - which may be qualitative rather than quantitative. If all three aspects agree, the result of the evaluation will be unequivocal. Where they do not agree, the discrepancies can be explored and taken into account in further treatment.

The therapist has to weigh up whether evidence that is recommended by meta-analyses is relevant and more appropriate for an individual than evidence from long-term uncontrolled studies or expert opinion. Services have been developed to try to structure this decision-making - for example, the IAPT services use inclusion criteria to select people with similar symptoms, applies a range of low-intensity and then high-intensity interventions (including, but not only, CBT) and measures outcomes in terms of symptoms, functioning and recovery. Figures for recovery are now at 45 per cent, rising towards 50 per cent, with meaningful improvement at 60–70 per cent. However, there remain many people who either do not engage with or respond to first-line interventions that may need other approaches. Levels of evidence for these approaches - CBT and other psychological modalities or social interventions - may be less but sufficient to consider.

Practice is balanced by service user and carer experience and perspective, clinical expertise, cultural factors, management and cost considerations. So, the evidence may be neutral but the interpretation of it may not. It is subject to individual and collective value judgements that need to be made explicit in order to understand their influence. Collaboration with the service user around these issues is essential. Service users and carers both provide expertise-by-experience that can, and has been, systematically collected. Service user and carer perspectives can be useful in assessing acceptability and feasibility of treatment options; they frequently coincide but occasionally conflict; and both are often quite different from staff opinion. All contribute to values-based practice.

There are practical and value considerations in relation to whether to involve a client in research. Unfortunately, in practice, therapists are often reluctant to get involved in research or even support their clients becoming involved by discussing options with them and referring them. There are practical considerations in that such discussion takes time, although studies frequently supply referrer and patient information leaflets to make this as simple and brief as possible. There may also be concerns about the time required to discuss referrals with the research team and assist with locating clients and introducing them. Where studies expect even more involvement, such as a formal process of consent for participation this can go beyond the capacity of therapists – so, most well-designed studies ask for the minimum that ethics committees require for this purpose.

However, the advantages of participation in research are considerable for the client and therapist. Clients in studies have better outcomes generally, whether in treatment or in control groups, which may be because of the increased contact they receive and the monitoring that may detect early problems or even allow some brief exploration of them. The client also gains if a therapy or procedure is successful and they are in the treatment group. If clients are not in the treatment group, then they are likely to be early recipients of the successful therapy because therapists trained in the techniques are usually available and will train other local therapists after the study is completed. Studies may be observational or exploratory, rather than therapeutic, but can still have the benefit accruing from the extra monitoring offered.

The therapist gains from the involvement with a research team and frequently opportunities arise to learn or assist with the development of evolving therapies. It can also mean that their client is offered more time and contact supplementing their work. There is the possibility that involvement complicates therapy but this seems relatively unusual.

Doing research

We will not be describing the detailed process of doing research but there are key ethical considerations that need to be considered.

All research involving human subjects requires permission from an established ethics committee. Universities will oversee such research where conducted under their auspices ('sponsorship'). They will have ethics processes that usually involves a research and development department with a multidisciplinary group who review applications and make recommendations. These recommendations will be mandatory before studies are allowed to proceed. Such university ethics committees oversee research into subjects who are not patients within the health service. Those who are will require consideration in the UK by independent research ethics committees organised nationally (www.hra.

nhs.uk/about-the-hra/our-committees/research-ethics-committees-recs/). In other countries, such committees tend to be established and run by hospital authorities but work to similar principles:

> The ethics committee is an independent body in a member state of the European Union, consisting of healthcare professionals and non-medical members, whose responsibility is to protect the rights, safety and well being of human subjects involved in a clinical trial and to provide public assurance of that protection, by, among other things, expressing an opinion on the clinical trial protocol, the suitability of the investigators involved in the trial and the adequacy of facilities, and on the methods and documents to be used to inform trial subjects and obtain their informed consent. (Directive 2001/20/EC)

Key issues are information and consent. Informed consent is dealt with in Chapter 2. Information needs to be full and complete, written clearly and understandably. In the UK, committees now frequently ask for the person responsible for the care of the person, often but not always a doctor or therapist, to approach the patient in the first instance in order to independently ensure that they are agreeable to discuss the relevant research with the clinical team. Consent to approach the individuals by the person responsible may be sufficient for someone who is not a member of the research team, e.g. from the research office of a hospital or NHS Trust, to make the initial approach but the principle is to ensure that there is no coercion.

Research, audit and service evaluation

The distinction between research, audit and service evaluation is arbitrary but important as it determines whether studies require ethical approval or not (NHRA, 2007).

Service evaluations are used as management tools on a very regular basis but tend to use high-level information that does not identify individual clients. They are used to examine the effects of service changes and to see whether they have led to improvements or deterioration or had unexpected effects. The methodologies used are not always robust and, in particular, they may not account for the many factors influencing services. Whilst trying to control such factors is usually not feasible, the interpretation of results needs to be considered so as to avoid false conclusions being drawn. Nevertheless, despite limitations, it is necessary to evaluate changes and this is too frequently ignored. Good practice should be disseminated but demonstrating that innovation is just that and that it is progressing beyond previous services can be difficult. Changing one part of a system can lead to unwanted effects on other parts, even if it is simply that staff time is reduced or management attention diverted.

Audits examine practice in relation to established standards that have been drawn up prior to the evaluation. These may be by national bodies, e.g. Royal Colleges or Associations of Psychologists, or other professional groups or using guidelines that have been established by expert groups, e.g. NICE. They may also be standards described in journals that are adopted by services for implementation, e.g. standard of letters to GPs and clients. The audit involves a check on a sample, either random or purposive – that is established for the purpose of adequately covering a range of, for example, situations, and groups of clients and staff. After an audit has been completed, results should be produced, interpreted and disseminated. The audit cycle involves going back and redoing the audit to see whether and where improvements have occurred. Single audits without re-auditing have much less impact on practice. Audits can be done by the individual on their own practice and can be valuable but is enhanced if there is independent collection of data and scrutiny.

Research is new work developing or testing specific hypotheses in order to increase knowledge. It will often involve gathering additional data that is routinely collected and may involve treatments or investigations that are not used in normal circumstances. Where there is doubt, the NHS Health Research Authority in the UK or bodies such as the local Institution Ethics Committee in many countries or National Institute of Mental Health in the USA can be contacted to assist in determining whether a project is research, evaluation or audit. University Ethics Committees can also provide similar guidance or signpost to the national body.

Role of clinical guidelines, especially NICE and PORT

Clinical guidelines have become increasingly important and useful in practice. In the past, diagnosis has been considered a medical responsibility but in modern services, where many patients are not seen by doctors, especially when referred for psychological interventions, there is a need for a system of allocation to guide practice. Monitoring organisations such as the Care Quality Commission in the UK, now require the use of clinical guidelines, such as those produced by the National Institute of Clinical Excellence. The guidelines used in mental health, have been developed to cover broad categories and allocation to these categories is necessary to inform good practice. Where there are doubts about allocation, medical opinion can be sought from family doctors or psychiatrists. In the UK, *New Ways of Working for Psychiatrists* was developed in 2005 (Department of Health, 2005) with this multidisciplinary context in mind. However, the guideline groupings are relatively self-evident and it is arguable whether sub-categories in *ICD-10* and *DSM-5* add much to them. The major ones are:

- Psychosis and schizophrenia
- Psychosis with substance misuse
- Common mental disorders (with specific guidelines for Anxiety, Depression, OCD and PTSD)
- Eating disorders
- Personality disorders (including 'borderline')
- Bipolar disorder
- Eating disorders
- Substance misuse

There is also specific guidance on areas such as self-harm and managing aggression.

Such guidelines represent expert consensus opinion on the areas described and include collaboration with, and guidance written for, patients and carers. They therefore carry significant weight as individual practitioners will not have the breadth of knowledge and expertise that these groups have, and so would not be expected to know all the evidence covered by the guidelines but need to be able to action the recommendations.

In practice, there are some provisos:

- Individual patients may not fit neatly into the categories selected by the guidelines.
- They may have a number of problems/diagnoses that inter-relate.
- Individual circumstances will differ.
- However hard they may try to be comprehensive, guidelines cannot cover every eventuality.
- Guidelines get out of date.

Nevertheless, if a guideline is not followed, the practitioner needs to be able to justify why not and should document these reasons. Where things go wrong, it is important to have the reasons for the divergence from the guidelines available - and, in any case, considered and documented reasoning can ensure that the divergence is for justifiable reasons and not just because the therapist disagrees with the guideline group.

Activities

- Consider a situation where you have used an intervention that is not evidence-based and weigh up your reasons for using it (discuss with colleagues or a supervisor if you have difficulty in identifying such a situation).
- Think of a project that you have been involved with and weigh up the arguments for it being a service delivery, audit or research project.

Further reading

Roth, A. and Fonagy, P. (2010) *What Works for Whom? A Critical Review of Psychotherapy* (2nd edn). New York: Guildford Press.

8

THE ETHICS OF USING A CBT APPROACH

Learning outcomes

After reading this chapter and completing the activities at the end of it, you should be able to:

1. Describe how a cognitive behavioural approach (or similar concept) differs from individual therapy.
2. Critically discuss the ethics issues in delivering a cognitive behavioural approach.
3. Generate service solutions to this ethical dilemma in terms of developing an appropriate empirical approach to treatment.
4. Consider how the training is equipping the trainee to deliver CBT approaches and what competencies will still need work post-training.
5. Critically evaluate how services can best serve the population, and what are the ethical issues inherent in service design.

The many forms of cognitive and behavioural therapies are diverse but with both discrete and overlapping theoretical rationales.

This chapter examines the use of CBT approaches delivered by staff who are not formally trained in psychological interventions. It explores the ethical tensions around using such approaches and proposes a way of resolving these issues.

The ethics of training front-line staff to use psychological formulation and change approaches should be considered when these methods have been generated to be used primarily by those with a professional or accredited training. Professional and accreditation board codes of practice (e.g. the American Psychological Association, British Psychological Society and British Association for Counselling and Psychotherapy) all stress 'beneficence' as essential to psychological therapy practice. Thus, it is incumbent on all professionals who operate according to these codes to ensure that the work that they do to enable others is also conducted according to this maxim, as far as they are able. So, whatever we do as trainers must be in the best interests of the client.

Cognitive behaviour therapy and its variants share a number of fundamental aims, notably those of collaboration, empiricism and formulation in ways designed to be understandable by clients and their support staff as well as therapists themselves. These pose fundamental ethics issues, both positive and of concern.

First, the ease of understanding inherent in the delivery of cognitive and behavioural therapies enables individuals to believe that they may be receiving or practicing a formal psychological therapy, despite not having received formal training. Second, people may behave unethically in terms of causing distress to others unnecessarily or without a clear aim in mind. A fundamental question here is whether CBT can be delivered as an 'approach' or whether a formal, theoretically driven and evaluated method of delivery is necessary. This inherent tension may be addressed by ensuring clarity of the consuming population and evidence base supporting delivery for that population and clarity in the mechanism of change. These are issues that may be addressed most usefully with an empirical method.

The highly collaborative nature of cognitive and behavioural therapies may mean that attempts to reduce the inherent power differential between therapist and client may be more successful than other therapies (although it is acknowledged that it can never be entirely eradicated, as will be discussed later).

Ease of delivery

There are a number of theoretical approaches in cognitive and behavioural therapies, ranging in terms of complexity and empirical standing. Some, such as Relational Frame Theory (RFT) (Hayes, 2004), are fairly complex and fine-grained and underpinned by highly reduced concepts. Others, such as Ellis's cognitive model (Ellis, 2003), are relatively high-level models that do not attempt to describe a cognitive reality but, rather, provide an extremely useful clinical heuristic, making intuitive sense but lacking a granular theoretical approach. Behavioural theory has on one level an intuitive simplicity that is easily transmitted (e.g. Skinner, 1963), but can be utilised in the service of more complex theoretical frameworks (again, e.g. RFT; Hayes, 2004).

In many senses, cognitive and behavioural therapies are designed to be 'common-sense' therapies in their delivery, in that the clinical principles are made as simple as possible to enable clients who may be suffering from cognitive and emotional difficulties to understand them to a point where they can engage in often very difficult behavioural change. Of course, these 'simple' clinical methods are increasingly underpinned by robust cognitive and behavioural science that is not necessarily shared with the client as part of a clinical intervention. One of the key skills in CBT practice is ensuring that sometimes complex theory is translated into practice in an acceptable and understandable and, therefore, effective way. The therapist may understand many complexities around the nature of the problem (within a particular theoretical framework), but limits the 'teaching' of these complexities to those which are useful to a client at a particular point in therapy, in terms of their understanding of, and engagement in, change. Therefore, a key advantage of cognitive and behavioural methods is that they may be communicated in many ways and on many levels, with increasing complexity as necessitated by patient understanding and therapeutic process.

The ease of understanding and use of common-sense concepts enables therapeutic techniques to be used out of the context of a formal therapy, often called a 'CBT approach', or sometimes 'cognitive behavioural coaching' (or, less usefully, 'CBT-lite'!). Although there are many advantages in enabling staff in many organisations who are not formally trained to deliver psychological therapies to deliver CBT-informed interventions, there are a number of ethical issues to consider, two of the most significant being whether we should engage in supporting a 'CBT approach' at all, given the effect this may have on formally delivered therapies in an austere health environment; and, second, the issues around the delineation between an 'approach' and formal therapy given may drift, one into the other.

CBT approach

Should we do it at all? An ethics dialectic

The dilemma is a simple one: should we make what we know available to as many people as possible within a restricted budget through providing basic training in an approach? Or should we ensure that existing funding goes to the interventions that we know are effective, ensuring continued quality of delivery and reducing the temptation to invest in a 'cheap alternative', which threatens effectiveness? There is emerging evidence of a downward trend in effectiveness of CBT with depression, which may or may not be due to dilution of technique (Johnsen and Friborg, 2015). This issue has been rehearsed in many fora, with apparently no resolution.

One side of the debate may be articulated thus. If we train people to deliver CBT approaches as psychological interventions, we are contributing to the failure and ultimate demise of CBT as an effective intervention. A hypothesised mechanism would be reduced commissioning (funding) of the intervention, particularly in times of austerity and funding cuts. CBT is understood to be an effective intervention with a rich evidence base in terms of theory and outcome, recognised by many organisations, including NICE. This 'brand' may be misused by people purporting to offer such interventions to appeal to commissioners of services who may or may not understand the intricacies of how an evidence base is earned. Financial directors, whose jobs may rely on driving down costs, may pressure commissioners to fund cheap options that have an appearance of effectiveness. Thus, unless the service has a good, theoretically sound mechanism, enabling effective, measurable change, the evidence base is threatened. If this process continues at multiple levels in multiple services, CBT becomes another 'fad' – passing fashion – that ultimately disappears.

Of course, this global conclusion becomes less likely as measured effectiveness has been built into the culture of the use of the intervention and national services, such as IAPT in England, have continuous evaluation and development built in. However, it may be that in certain areas where money is scarce, provision of effective CBT may be threatened.

The other side of the dialectic may be expressed as follows. CBT and its variants are known to be effective for many populations of people who are unlikely to receive individual or group interventions provided by a formally trained therapist, e.g. marginalised populations, those abusing drugs and/or alcohol, many with chronic physical health problems and especially the developing world. It therefore could be argued that an intervention known to be effective is being withheld from such populations, an issue, were it to be a pharmacological solution, that would receive a great deal of press attention. It therefore becomes incumbent upon the CBT workforce to make such provision, in whichever way funds allow. The most sustainable way of doing this is to train those already working in the field who have existing expertise with the population of people with whom they work (e.g. nurses, hostel workers, case managers, probation workers). Thus, a set of ways of thinking and interventions are made possible that otherwise would have been denied underserved populations.

So, the ethics issue may be framed as a question of providing a possibly sub-standard psychological intervention on the basis of cost, versus providing at least some aspect of an evidence-based intervention to people in need who otherwise would not receive it.

A solution to this ethics dialectic may be, of course, to ensure that all interventions, however diluted, are evaluated in terms of both outcome and change mechanisms. This is, of course, an essential process in establishing the validity of a new or adapted intervention in order that a new literature may be generated. The Medical Research Council (MRC) guidelines on such issues can be extremely helpful at such times (Craig et al., 2013). If we find the interventions to be effective, arguably effort should be put into developing them without threatening the evidence base. If they are not effective, commissioners may be dissuaded from funding cheap but ineffective interventions. But research studies take many years to prepare, obtain funding, recruit, complete and disseminate and, in the meantime, consideration of how much extrapolation from existing evidence can be used.

The investigation of change mechanisms is often neglected in favour of more crude 'does it work or not' research questions. But understanding why something is effective or not is in the longer term as important if we are to evolve therapies in terms of understanding components which should be maintained or dropped. Additionally, the categorical language of 'working or not working' should also be adapted to express how useful an intervention is in terms of specified outcomes.

Therapy vs approach

Delivery of cognitive and behavioural therapies can be seen to be on a continuum in terms of technical expertise and use of theory, practical skills, etc. This is to some extent exemplified by levels of stepped care used in England by the IAPT programme, in which high-intensity therapy is delivered on an individual basis according to a formulation-driven approach, whereas for others online and telephone support may be appropriate. A growing literature on a CBT approach describes clinicians, e.g. nurses (Moss-Morris et al., 2013) and other support workers, working within a psychological framework, but not formally delivering therapy (e.g. psychologically informed environments; Keats et al., 2011). These approaches can be extremely useful in making evidence-based principles and practice available to a much wider population than would be able to access formally delivered psychological therapies. This is particularly true for populations excluded from health and social care, e.g. rough sleepers, who are primarily supported by charity staff not formally trained in psychological thinking.

However, there are problems inherent with this practice. Although it could be argued that it is best to make use of evidence-based interventions based on empirically sound theoretical frameworks in this way, the evidence may not necessarily be generalisable to the use of the 'approach'. Second, many people may claim to use such an evidence-based approach without any kind of adherence. Third, there are commercial implications in claiming the CBT 'brand' as something that is practiced. And, fourth, and perhaps most importantly, it is vital to understand the difference between the therapy and an approach.

Inherent in many therapies is the assumption that work at emotional and cognitive levels will require expression and experience of those emotions and articulation of fundamental ways of thinking. For many people without adequate emotion coping mechanisms, perhaps associated with early abuse and trauma, the unmanaged discussion of such issues may be highly traumatic, although this has to be balanced against past and present experiences of not being allowed to discuss vitally important issues. It is reasonable to differentiate between asking about childhood trauma that should be part of any mental health and therapeutic assessment and then providing the right support and expertise to allow the person to fully and effectively discuss these experiences. The latter does not necessarily involve highly trained psychotherapists but agencies such as Rape Crisis have demonstrated that their skilled, trained and compassionate staff can offer effective and supportive services.

Accredited therapy programmes enable the learning of important emotion work skills through teaching and experience. Such emotions may be manifest when disclosing or reliving difficult experiences, or perhaps as a result of acknowledging core beliefs, lack of behaviour in the service of values, etc. Helping clients manage such cognitions and resulting emotions, and emotion expression, in itself is a key set of skills often requiring a great deal of practice within an appropriate model. Within a formal therapeutic situation, when using trauma-focused cognitive therapy (T-FCT) or DBT, emotion-regulation skills would be taught first, in order that the client will be able to engage in such difficult discussions using less harmful coping strategies. Engaging in such work without such learning may result in emotional expression that may lead to problematic behaviours, e.g. self-harming, drug and alcohol use and possibly suicidal ideation or behaviour. Those working outside of a formally supervised therapy with people suffering such emotion regulation difficulties may drift away from an 'approach' into a more intrusive therapy process if they do not fully understand the difference between the two – i.e. they may be engaging people in discussion of issues which elicit significant emotional responses without the practice framework or skills to manage those emotions within a session or across sessions.

Other factors are also important to bear in mind, e.g. other environmental stresses, management of a session so as not to engage in the most distressing work just before the end, ensuring a trusting relationship, etc. Many of the clinical decisions within such work would be governed in the main by training and experience; a short course would not generally equip a person to deal with such issues without risking unmanaged distress.

However, there are many situations in which staff working with people who have suffered trauma are in residential or other situations in which staff have not been trained to deal with trauma (e.g. homelessness hostels). In such situations, it would be unlikely that staff without formal training would never hear descriptions of such experience, and would, of course, not be likely to try and close down such a conversation. In these cases, most natural instincts would be to listen and validate the narrative and emotions, relying on the individual to manage their own disclosure (i.e. limiting it if too distressing), with gentle prompts to do so from the staff. This is distinct from trying to actively manage distress and engage in purposeful enquiry about the experience or try and work on some form of change.

This is not to say that disclosure of traumatic experience is inherently dangerous. Many support workers listen to such experience regularly without adverse effects on their clients. Indeed, some clients may find it useful to discuss such issues and it would be poor practice to stop a discussion and invalidate the individual based on perceived expertise. Just listening can be the most useful thing to do. Indeed, Marsha Linehan (1993) usefully breaks down validation processes into six steps:

1. Actively listening: Showing that you are genuinely interested in what the person is saying.
2. Reflection: Basic reflection and paraphrasing of what has been said.
3. 'Mind reading': Articulating unexpressed emotions or thoughts, showing that you have understood the implications of what is being said.
4. Validation in terms of the past: Showing that you understand current events, behaviours, emotions, etc. in terms of the client's past experience.
5. Validation in terms of the present: Showing that you understand current events, etc. in terms of the current environmental context.
6. Radical genuineness: A high-risk, high-gain strategy in which the therapist offers honest feedback about, e.g., the effect of behaviours on others, including themselves. Only done within a trusting, predictable relationship.

In practice, the first three levels are the most useful in thinking about responding to narratives about trauma, but within some good-quality keyworking relationships, it may be ethical to use level 4. Level 6 may be used naturally with some clients, often in the context of humour but, without considering the consequences, it could be very damaging. It may be appropriate, but should be consciously considered in terms of the experience of the client.

Anecdotally, when asked at the beginning of CBT/DBT workshops, many staff do express the fear that they will be expected to be 'therapists'. A discussion about what they would and would not be expected to do is usually helpful here, making clear the kinds of behaviours that they would engage in (validation) and those that they would not (active exploration and change). It has been found useful, therefore, to ensure that the training in this issue focuses on effective validation and the building of a trusting relationship.

These are issues perhaps best considered within an ethics framework. The argument made above may pertain, i.e. that many people, e.g. populations of people excluded from health care, are being denied access to an intervention with a known evidence base, assuming that a CBT approach is available. But, on the other hand, the issue of the limits of a therapeutic intervention not being observed by non-practitioners is a significant one. The ethics of not providing an intervention should be tensioned against the dangers of non-expert provision.

This ethics dilemma may be resolved by ensuring the delineation between a CBT approach and CBT therapy in terms of what the support worker does, and ensuring adequate training and ongoing reflective practice.

The delineation may not be an easy one. When does good listening become 'therapy'? What active interventions constitute good, common-sense behaviour change and what constitutes formal psychological interventions? Ethically, it becomes important to try to articulate this definition so as to minimise the possibility of damage done as the CBT approach becomes more popular, and ensure adequate training and supervision (or reflective practice) for those involved.

A principle that may be helpful centres on the emotions elicited by interventions. Within a therapeutic intervention, we may expect to elicit an emotional response and enable the individual to work to manage the emotions as well as their precursors or causes. The language about emotion regulation is articulated particularly well with the DBT framework. This requires knowledge of such skills as grounding techniques, distraction and cognitive work centred around emotions, as well as experience of their practice and reflections on when they have been effective and when they have not. These specific skills, although deceptively simple to describe, should always be practiced by a qualified person.

Likewise, enquiry and discussion about fundamental ways of thinking (e.g. core beliefs in CBT, values work in AaCT) may be problematic if the client has a strong emotional response.

A therapeutic approach vs a therapy

A way of expressing the line between a therapeutic approach and therapy may therefore be around intentional use of questioning skills to elicit fundamental emotions and cognitions. A CBT approach would not do this but, for example, would be around articulating thoughts about specific incidents or events, and understanding environmental triggers for particular behaviours, perhaps mediated by thoughts.

In conclusion, we can ensure that we are training ethically by ensuring that: the contents of our training are intended to benefit clients; the people we train are clear about the difference between therapy and human, empathic interaction; and that we think carefully about what people are actually going to do differently as a result of our training. This then poses questions that may be answered empirically.

Training non-clinical staff

If we take seriously the ethics issue of training staff not familiar with psychological concepts in a CBT approach, but also that we may resolve this by evaluating any such interventions in terms of mechanisms of change and outcomes, we must answer two empirical questions. First, we need to address the issue of the effectiveness of the training, i.e. has any training resulted in changes in staff knowledge and behaviour consistent with the appropriate use of a CBT approach? Second, does any new set of skills (behaviour change) adopted by the trained staff result in change for the people with whom they are working?

Is staff training effective in the acquisition of skills?

In order for staff training to be effective and therefore ethical, it needs to be as simple as possible and appeal to good pedagogical principles. Ethical training goes beyond the issue of dealing with traumatic experience. If we are going to teach staff to use psychological therapeutic techniques to engage clients in the process of change, we need to be careful about what these techniques are, and about the consequences of their use.

One approach to this is to teach skills that enable staff to deal with 'here-and-now' issues, making use of formulation and change techniques which are just beyond common sense, i.e. they are not much of a stretch from what people do naturally. This is sometimes referred to as movement from unconscious competence to conscious competence, i.e. being able to articulate what you are doing and the effect that you want it to have. CBT, being a common-sense therapy, has many such techniques available.

One such framework is 'graded hierarchies', i.e. the setting-up of a difficult task by describing a number of steps to achieve that task, and the imagined anxiety associated with engaging with the task. Many staff members are already familiar with the concept, but often do not enable the client to define each step themselves, describe each step and emotions in detail, or keep a written record to revisit. When engaging clients in change, it is most likely to appeal to an ethics code if staff members ensure that the client designs their own interventions and goals as much as possible.

The premise here is to keep all techniques, whether they are formulation or change techniques, simple and easy to learn, for both staff and client. It is also imperative to work as hard as possible to enable staff to become as confident as possible when learning new skills. 'Drilling' (repeated practice of new skills) is a useful educational strategy, but this cannot substitute for repeated, supportive reflective practice as a way of enabling experiential learning through a learning cycle (Kolb, 2014) and the effective acquisition of those new skills. Arguably, an ethics issue, therefore, is to use pedagogical good practice to increase the likelihood of effectiveness. Learning cycles are essential in this, i.e. they are a significant aspect of the effective development of new skills – it is arguable, therefore, that training workshops which do not facilitate ongoing reflective practice in the service of skills acquisition represent a threat to ethical practice.

Training should be assessed in some way as an evaluation of effectiveness. Assessing by observation whether the skills taught are being practised most directly does this. There are other outcomes which may also be important, for example how effective staff believe themselves to be in effecting change, burnout, etc., which may have an effect on organisational effectiveness.

Is the training effective in terms of client work?

The second empirical question is the more important, i.e. do any changes in knowledge and behaviour have a discernible effect on client outcomes? This is the fundamental effectiveness question, i.e. is a CBT approach effective on whatever treatment variables are important for that population. A number of trials have been able to assess these, finding mixed results with different populations defined often by psychiatric diagnosis (e.g. personality disorder). An important aspect of such research is to be able to assess adherence to whatever the CBT approach has specified as good practice, in order that staff behaviours can be tied to cognitive, emotional and behavioural change.

Conclusion

- Cognitive and behavioural therapies are designed to be easily transmitted to clients, despite often having complex, empirically evaluated theories.
- This ease enables staff not trained in psychological approaches to learn formulation and practice techniques. Such staff may work in services serving underserved populations who would not normally receive psychological input.
- The affordability of non-clinical staff offering evidence-based interventions may be appealing to commissioners, meaning that qualified posts may be reduced and effective treatments not provided.
- This poses an ethical dilemma: should cheap services be provided to underserved populations that may reduce the evidence base and cause distress due to poor training?
- This ethics dialectic may be resolved by ensuring an evidence-generating approach to evaluate both training and practice.
- A range of approaches can ensure that if approaches provided by less well-trained staff are unsuccessful, individuals can receive therapy from more highly trained staff, with increasing levels of expertise provided through direct intervention and supervision.

Activities

- Consider whether your service is clear about where formal therapy or a CBT approach is being used, and who is delivering those interventions:
  - Are people appropriately qualified to deliver the intervention you intend?
  - Is a CBT approach being used when formal therapy is expected?
  - Are there any financial considerations that are driving an 'approach' being labelled as 'therapy'?
- Consider the empirical basis of the interventions being used in your service:

  - Is there a formal evidence base?
  - Are there opportunities to contribute to such an evidence base, no matter how small? E.g. service evaluation, case studies.
  - How can your service generate data that would inform commissioning processes?

- As a trainee, consider the competencies that you are learning:
  - Will these competencies enable you to immediately enable others in teams to make use of CBT skills?
  - Will you be a competent supervisor? Educator? Evaluator of supervisee's work?
  - What will your ongoing training needs be in this respect? Do you have a plan to address these needs post-qualification?

Further reading

Keats, H., Maguire, N., Johnson, R., and Cockersell, P. (2011) *Psychologically Informed Services for Homeless People: Good Practice Guide*. Available at: http://eprints.soton.ac.uk/340022/1/Good%20practice%20guide%20-%20%20Psychologically%20informed%20services%20for%20homeless%20people%20.pdf (accessed 1 April 2016).

9

SPECIFIC POPULATIONS

Learning outcomes

After reading this chapter and completing the activities at the end of it, you should be able to:

1. Understand the relation between culture and psychopathology.
2. Understand the need to culturally adapt CBT to facilitate engagement and improve outcomes in patients.
3. Recognise challenges and opportunities in adaptations of therapy that impact on treatment.
4. Be aware of social considerations, societal pressures and potential coercion.
5. Understand the nature of ethical issues with excluded populations.
6. Work with the issues around capacity in people with learning difficulties.
7. Recognise how ethical principles and values relate to therapeutic work with clients who are living with a chronic medical condition.
8. Understand the values, principles and key ethical considerations in using CBT with suicidal clients and in suicide prevention.
9. Be able to consider the choice between respecting the client's autonomy and the commitment to do 'good' through attempting to help a client to maintain their own life.
10. Use strategies for the prevention of suicide through the enhancement of appropriate ethical and clinical practice from a CB perspective.

Cultural issues

Cultural adaptation is a major issue with all therapies and simply transplanting interventions to different cultures has been a major concern – 'Eurocentric' therapy imposed on other cultures without adaptation can potentially do great harm or, at best, be a misuse of resources and not draw from cultural strengths. However, work that we and others have carried out has shown that achieving such adaptation can be done effectively (Rathod et al., 2015). This involves examining philosophical, theoretical, practical and technical considerations in relation to the person's culture, family and individual beliefs and norms. Different therapies approach self-disclosure, mentioned previously, in diverse ways (ibid.). Its use is seemingly more welcome with some cultures than with others, e.g. Black African-Caribbean than South-East Asian, but always within ethical and boundary issues. Family involvement is also integral to work with many cultures, in some contrast to Western culture where family have become less central to individuals' interactions. Rationality, in terms of logical discourse, seems a universal phenomenon in relation to therapy but cultural beliefs, both spiritual and religious, can seem less understandable to therapists from other cultures whilst being perfectly functional.

Ethical scenario

Farooq, aged 42, has been brought to your clinic by his family and appears very depressed and developmentally delayed. Communication is difficult – family members are trying to help you understand what has been happening but the story is confusing. You are not sure how well Farooq understands what you are asking him and it is not clear whether this is due to his understanding of English or his symptoms of depression.

Ethical questions

1. How should you proceed?
2. Do you need to make any adaptations to how you use CBT in relation to his cultural background?
3. If so, what changes would be appropriate?

According to the Health and Social Care Information Centre (HSCIC), people from minority ethnic groups are more likely to be coerced into treatment. 53.9 per cent of the Black and Black British inpatients spent time compulsorily detained in hospital compared with 31.8 per cent of inpatients overall. The rate of admissions for the Black and Black British groups was 170 per cent greater than the rate for all ethnic groups (2004–09 figures). Of the total number of patients, 8.4 per cent spent time as an inpatient, compared to 19.3 per cent for the Black and Black British groups (Health and Social Care Information Centre, 2009).

The over-representation of these groups in the more intense and coercive forms of care may be attributed to their non-engagement with services until a point of crisis. They also had higher rates of access to all services, including those delivered in the community (ibid.). They are also less likely to have their social and psychological needs addressed within the care planning process (Bhui, 2002) and may have poorer outcomes, e.g. of schizophrenia (Bhugra et al., 1997).

We found in our 'Insight Study' (Rathod et al., 2015) a significantly lower change in insight when comparing the White group to the the Black Caribbean group ($p = 0.004$; CI = – 4.14 to – 0.766) and Black African ($p = 0.020$, CI = 0.532, 6.142), and significantly higher dropout rates in the Black African and African-Caribbean groups (54 per cent; $p < 0.001$). Dropouts had a higher insight score in the African-Caribbean population. This was despite the therapist for most of the Black group coming from a Black African background.

Culture significantly impacts all aspects of mental health – commencement of problems, psychopathology, course, treatment approaches and outcomes. Incidence and prevalence varies across the world (Selten et al., 1997) and within countries (Kirkbride et al., 2012). This may be because of genetic differences but is more likely because of environmental and social factors, e.g. perinatal care, mothering styles, family expectations and policy, e.g. the one-child policy in China, trauma, family support which may be comparatively protective, views and use of hallucinogenic substances, cultural beliefs, grief, guilt and shame.

Presentations of mental health problems, e.g. depression and psychosis, in developing countries and different cultures (Rathod et al., 2015) can be more acute, have more florid positive symptoms, more catatonia with a shorter duration and more emphasis on physical symptoms than in Western societies such as Europe or North America. Content of hallucinations and delusions can be culturally influenced – for example, in India, it has been reported that delusional content may have more prominence of religious and supernatural delusions and delusions of possession can be prominent in rural settings where clients can describe being possessed by a goddess. In South Asian Muslims, religious themes are common and so, too, are conspiracy and supernatural causes. In China, themes include possession of the ancestors by spirits, conspiracy theories and erotomania.

So, if cultures differ in their presentation of conditions, do interventions, specifically CBT, therefore need to be adapted to different cultures? It can be argued that CBT is intrinsically adaptable as it is individually focused, collaborative, responsive to feedback and formulation based. But there are issues that distinguish between cultures, e.g. depth of family involvement or a collaborative versus authoritative stance, and understanding these can make that adaptation effective.

Culturally Adapted Interventions can be effective (Griner and Smith, 2006; Wykes et al., 2008). Challenges include: cultural competence of the cultural adaptation team; surface structure adaptations (observable aspects) and deep structure adaptations (health behaviours) (Resnicow et al., 2000); conceptualisation of culture in the design of an adapted EBT – cultural relevance; accommodation of wide within-group cultural variation; balancing fidelity to model to effects of adaptation; risks of not delivering adapted therapy; engagement issues – poor therapeutic alliance; obstacles in the change process; poor outcomes; poor experience; inequality of access.

CBT is a pragmatic, collaborative, and relational approach that utilises conceptual frameworks that are primarily consistent with Western philosophies. It can however be adapted philosophically with culture being used as a strength and emphasis on 'learning from diversity' with a recovery focus. Behavioural components of such adaptations can be easier to use with interpreters. This assertion is supported by CBT-based therapies being used successfully in low- and middle-income countries (Patel et al., 2007; Rojas et al., 2007). A cognitive behavioural therapy-based intervention provided by trained community health workers has also been shown to effectively treat perinatal depression and improve infant outcomes, according to a cluster-randomised trial conducted in rural Pakistan (Rahman et al., 2008).

Thus CBT seems to be acceptable if adapted to incorporate or address culture, acculturation, attributions to illness, help-seeking behaviours, and barriers to accessing CBT.

A useful framework has been provided by Tseng et al. (2005):

- Philosophical orientation
- Practical considerations
- Theoretical modifications
- Technical adjustments

Philosophical orientation involves consideration of differences in the cultural background that exists between patient and therapist, differences in general philosophy and values that will be affected by the level of acculturation. Culture affects an individual's basic view of and attitude towards human beings, society and the meaning of life, e.g.: more passive and accepting as against striving and assertive; beliefs and attributions to illness, e.g. depression or psychosis, as originating from supernatural, natural or medical-psychological reasons. Cultural orientations towards psychotherapy vary in terms of the understanding and expectation of therapy that is shaped by views, beliefs and experiences that impact on help-seeking behaviour, knowledge and barriers in accessing therapy.

Possible barriers to therapy include lack of knowledge of access and referral processes, shame and stigma, perceptions that the therapist does not understand cultural background, language/terminology/interpreters and attributions as described. Practical considerations include the effects of economic conditions, immigration policies and health systems and the reputation of local units, funding arrangements and racism within services.

Technical adjustments needed to adapt include: considerations of setting and environment of therapy; therapeutic relationship - society defines the therapist–client relationship and differs from a culture that stresses authority or democracy; and choice of therapy - this can differ among cultures - as Western therapy values the rational, cognitive approach to understanding the nature and cause of problems and how to deal with them. Eastern therapies stress the importance of actual experience without cognitive understanding. CBT can bridge these considerations, especially by involving mindfulness/acceptance and commitment approaches. Family structures and goals may mean that families are much more involved in therapy than occurs with Western patients and increased consideration of the role of religion is needed. Gender issues vary across cultures, e.g. in relation to acceptability of male therapists with female clients and vice versa. Self disclosure expectations can also differ: small elements of self-disclosure and warmth can build trust and also give the feeling of being respected as equals and is very acceptable with some cultures but much less so with others who expect the authority figure (the therapist) to be more aloof and distant. The role of the extended family, community and 'elders', including religious elders, e.g. priests, needs consideration.

Social aspects

Ethical scenario

You have just seen an advert for a job in your local newspaper to work as a therapist at a local employment centre. It pays very well and you have the right qualifications for it – and you are looking for a change from your current position. You find out that it is part of a pilot scheme being funded by government.

Ethical questions

1. Are there any potential ethical issues in applying for the job?
2. Are there any practical issues that you need to consider in accepting the post?
3. How could you reassure yourself about these?

More broadly, psychotherapies, and particularly CBT, have been strongly criticised as ignoring or avoiding social issues. Essentially, therapists are castigated for taking the position that: 'it's not what happens to you (e.g. abuse/social deprivation), it's how you think about it that matters'. This can be construed at one extreme as meaning that CBT is taking a position that poverty, inequality and injustice may frame how people experience distress but alleviating or coping with it involves internal cognitive behavioural approaches.

The implication is that political and social changes are not relevant to the therapist. These issues are political as opposed to ethical and moral and such issues are for governments, albeit through democratic processes, to deal with. So, CBT does not specifically engage with these issues, although Beck has produced general views on these broader areas. However, it does take the position that individuals are affected by their environment and do respond to adversity in a variety of ways. Their perspective affects these and CBT enhances those ways of responding. It also does not ignore societal adversities and injustices that lead to distress and disability. It may be fair to say that these wider issues have not been addressed by the professional CBT organisations, but it can be countered that it would be wrong – and might affect charitable status – if they were to do so. Individual therapists, however, have the right and duty to express their views and take actions as they see fit in relation to perceived injustice. It is also very important that they ensure that discrimination does not occur between groups in the availability and quality of therapy, for example for those who are homeless, lesbian, gay and transsexual people and those from Black and minority ethnic groups (see earlier).

Therapists can be criticised for offering therapy only to those who are able to pay for it and not to more down-trodden and poorer clients. Health systems vary considerably and this becomes more of an issue in those where coverage is incomplete and mental health facilities, especially psychological therapies, are unavailable. However, there can also be a selection bias by therapists – even in systems like the NHS – towards those, 'more like us', from less-deprived backgrounds, more similar to the therapist and with less complex needs and likely to recover more quickly – and so may be considered more rewarding to work with.

Power dynamics

The importance of power and how CBT addresses it has been described as potentially leading to such problems and therefore there is a need for therapists to give it serious consideration (Proctor, 2008). As Adshead (personal communication) has described how each therapy model proposes and individual therapists believe a client's life can be improved is a matter of ethics and value judgements. Role power is that which emanates from the therapist–client position, with the client seeking help and then paying for it, personally or through insurance/taxation, and the client therefore being in a relatively disempowered position to that of the therapist, who has skills, knowledge and competencies that they do not possess. 'Societal' power is also a factor as gender, age and class often favour the therapist. 'Historical' power is also described as relevant by Proctor (2008) – the client often brings experiences of powerlessness in previous relationships to the therapeutic situation.

Each of these aspects need to be understood and considered when the therapist is attempting to form a relationship that strives towards mutual respect and equality. This is enhanced if the personal power that the client has in relation to their knowledge of themselves and of the services and therapies that they have encountered, is taken into consideration – the expression 'expert-by-experience' encompasses this. Payment for services can also be viewed as a part of this dynamic – the client as 'customer' with a right to consideration, politeness and a high-quality and effective service.

CBT has also been criticised as being based on principles of modernism and the rationality of science, with an emphasis on psychoeducational approaches, although the collaborative nature of this is stressed. It has been suggested that some 'third wave' therapies are more relationship- and emotion-focused, although the centrality of emotion in CBT goes back to the early works of Aaron Beck. Proctor (2008) has also commented on CBT having: 'normalising principles on which the "right" or "helpful" way to think are based. The focus on "realism" can be used to discount the feelings or views of the client, who can be accused of being prey to "cognitive distortions"' (2014: 56–7). This is an inherent problem in any therapy – that the therapist's view of what is right may contrast with the client's and, indeed, with that of the individual's culture or society. There is some similarity with similar arguments made about other therapies where interpretations are made which, if not accepted, can then be taken to indicate that the person is 'in denial'.

Supervision is important to support ethical practice, through discussion and reflection, and to ensure that the therapist's agenda does not impinge on the relationship – fulfilling their needs, rather than those of patient, or even being distorted by their interests, beliefs about causation of symptoms or other biases. There remains the potential for collusion between supervisor and therapist with CBT as with other models. This may be more the case for CBT as self-awareness is not as explicit in the model or stressed as much in training, although it is not disregarded. The concept that complete neutrality or objectivity is, by the nature of human experience, not possible is clearly accepted and the importance of taking this into consideration in therapy interactions is emphasised.

CBT and coercion

A major concern, that has arisen as evidence of effectiveness has emerged and the availability of CBT developed, is that people can be required to accept it as being in their own and society's best interests. At its worst extreme, there have been suggestions that if people do not accept treatment that can benefit them, then they are not deserving of welfare or sickness benefits and these should be progressively withdrawn.

Psycho-compulsion,

> defined as the imposition of psychological explanations for unemployment, together with mandatory activities intended to modify beliefs, attitude, disposition or personality, has become a more and more central feature of activating the unemployed and hence of people's experience of unemployment. (Friedli and Stearn, 2015: 42)

The argument is made that, whilst the individual has rights to refuse treatment, the state, and consequently taxpayers, should not have to support individuals who refuse to accept help which would reduce or stop their reliance on such support. Added to this, may be the point that it can be seen as in the individual's best interest to seek help and through compulsion to do so, this is motivating and subsequently benefiting them.

This argument is also used in relation to the Criminal Justice Services. The offender may be offered treatment as an alternative to prison or fines or be allowed greater freedoms if they cooperate with treatment. This can be implicit in parole conditions or tribunal decisions imposed in the context of an individual accepting their culpability for a crime and consequently attending for treatment and cooperating with it.

If the individual has reason not to accept treatment - e.g. that they find it too stressful or that it brings back troubling memories, or through poor motivation as in persistent depression and psychosis - then there seems little case to support ethically penalising that person for not collaborating in psychological treatment. However, where there is no such objection, the argument is more difficult to sustain.

This has been the subject of a statement by the joint psychotherapy and psychological associations (reproduced in full below). It sets out clear concerns and guidance but does leave open the possibility of changes in the future in this position, e.g. after the pilot studies suggested by the British government have been completed. This is, therefore, likely to be a continuing debate and the ethical issues involved have not been fully resolved at the time of writing.

Joint statement on government 'therapists in jobcentres' plans

In recent months, the British Association for Behavioural and Cognitive Psychotherapies, British Association for Counselling and Psychotherapy, British Psychoanalytic Council, British Psychological Society and UK Council for Psychotherapy have met with officials from the government's new Joint Health and Work Unit to scrutinise government plans to help jobcentre clients who experience mental ill health.

Last year, concerns were raised in the media when the government stated its intention to co-locate therapists in jobcentres. These concerns were principally that:

- The underpinning rationale was not for improving health, but rather for ideological purposes.
- Employment was being considered as a clinical outcome.
- People would be coerced into therapy or face sanctions on their unemployment benefit payments.
- People would have to access therapy in an unsuitable therapeutic environment.
- There would be a lack of privacy in a jobcentre environment.

In August 2015, we took the decision to engage with the Department for Work and Pensions, to ascertain the facts and to try to scrutinise and, if necessary, to influence plans. Our priority is patient or client health and well-being and the need to examine the underlying socio-economic causes of people suffering from mental ill health, rather than stigmatise people suffering from mental ill health who happened to be unemployed.

We have relayed the above concerns and more to officials based at the Department and have additionally met with staff working in a jobcentre evaluating the feasibility of one of the proposed government approaches. We have asked many questions, drilling down into the minutiae of the government plans, and advocating above all that:

- Plans must be aimed at improving mental health and well-being rather than as a means of getting people back to work.
- There must be no conditionality or associated sanction on unemployment benefit.
- Clients must be treated compassionately.

- Clients must have their privacy respected.
- Client choice must be central to the method and location of delivery of therapy.

We have been consistently advised that the government has:

- Ruled out any use of coercion or sanctions in relation to therapy.
- Opted to pursue a small-scale co-location feasibility trial which, importantly, will thoroughly evaluate privacy issues and mental health outcomes comparative to those achieved by therapy in other settings.

In addition, following our discussions, the government has agreed to also trial a number of alternatives, such as providing jobcentre clients with access to therapy in alternative community based, non-jobcentre settings.

We are acutely aware of the sensitivities around this issue and will continue to engage with the Joint Work and Health Unit to critically examine their ongoing work, to ensure that the full range of potential co-location options trialled are in the best interests of clients, and that the evaluations will be thorough and robust enough to pick up on all of our areas of concern. We are particularly aware that for the government plans to be ethical, employment must at no time be seen as a clinical outcome, staff must not be involved in coercion, and client attendance must not be mandatory.

Source: *CBT Today* (2016: 8)

Activities

- What constitutes an ethically appropriate environment to offer therapy?
- Do you agree that 'employment must at no time be viewed as a clinical outcome', as stated in the joint statement?
- Are there any circumstances in which it would be reasonable for 'client attendance [at therapy] to be mandatory'?
- Is it ever reasonable to offer a client therapy as part of a package of care, acceptance of which constitutes:
    - A condition of receiving a full payment of benefits.
    - An alternative to imprisonment or other detention?

Chronic medical conditions

The number of people living with a chronic medical condition is increasing, in fact it has been suggested that we now live in a 'remission society', where an important question is: 'how to live a good life whilst living with a medical condition' (Frank, 2013: 156). This said, being diagnosed with a chronic medical illness such as multiple sclerosis, fibromyalgia or cardiac disease can be devastating and life-changing. Indeed, research indicates that depression and anxiety are common in patients with a chronic medical condition, having a serious negative effect on quality of life (Yohannes et al., 2010). Life can become unpredictable because bodily disturbances occur unexpectedly, whilst anticipating their path or duration is difficult, if not impossible. Moreover, some medical conditions, such as myalgic encephalopathy/chronic fatigue syndrome (ME/CFS), a particularly complex condition with no clear biological marker, can lead to people with this condition feeling stigmatised and marginalised in society (Asbring, 2001).

While people with a chronic medical condition are faced with changes at a physical level, where the body is no longer able to carry out the individual's intentions or fulfil their goals, they might also experience biographical disturbance. The individual's sense of self, who they are, can become fragile for some time because functioning and social relationships change and, in addition, employment is difficult to sustain. It is not surprising then that a complexity of emotions may be experienced. Edwards et al. (2007), for example, found that some people with ME/CFS felt anger towards health professionals, had feelings of being let down, and emotional pain associated with having a sense of loss of identity. Hence, it is quite foreseeable that a diminishing sense of self-worth or self-esteem might follow.

Ethical scenario

Kate is a CB therapist working for an organisation that provides CBT for the NHS. The organisation has a long waiting list of clients requiring CBT. Jill, a 39-year-old woman, sought CBT for depression. Jill was diagnosed with ME/CFS four years earlier. She is no longer employed and lives alone; her long-term partner left her eight months ago. Jill's ME/CFS symptoms fluctuate and are unpredictable. On what she described as a 'bad day', she finds it difficult to do most things and sleeps most of the time. On a good day, she is able to function fairly well. Jill attended an NHS ME/CFS service two years ago and found it helpful. Jill said that she understood the importance of pacing and tried to do this even on a bad day, but it was difficult, as she felt so tired. Recently, her mood had dropped and she just wanted to feel better about herself; that it was worth getting up in the morning. Kate felt that she could help Jill with her depression, however Kate was concerned that Jill might miss appointments due to the unpredictable nature of the ME/CFS symptoms.

Ethical questions

1. How can Kate ensure that Jill receives the treatment for her depression, given the unpredictable nature of Jill's symptoms and the waiting list for CBT at her organisation?
2. How does your solution fit with being non-discriminatory, and adhere to the ethical principle of justice?

Therapeutic work

Unquestionably, CB therapists endeavour to demonstrate respect for their clients, consistent with the BABCP's Code (Section 1.2) and the APS (2007) (General Principle A). However, it must be remembered that the client with a chronic medical illness who enters the therapy room will have had a lot of communication with the medical service, where their symptoms were the predominant focus. For some, this might not have been a positive experience (Edwards et al., 2007) and might have left them feeling somewhat invalidated. Although, of course, the client's physical symptoms are important, it is essential that the CB therapist listens to the client's illness journey. It is recommended that the therapist responds to the individual as a 'whole person', adopting a 'person-centred approach' (Gatchel et al., 2007). By shifting the focus from the symptoms to the client's experience and feelings, it helps communicate respect for and acceptance of the client. From an ethical position, this is in keeping with the principle of beneficence; whilst it also helps validate the client's experience, it also enhances the therapeutic engagement process, and therefore progresses the client's well-being. This approach is also confluent with aspects of Deontology (see Chapter 1), which emphasises treating people as 'an end in themselves'. This can be interpreted to mean that in the case of people with a chronic medical condition, avoiding treating the client as a set of symptoms demonstrates a commitment to work with the person in their entirety.

The client with a chronic illness will probably have over the years accumulated a lot of medical knowledge, and will potentially know far more about their condition than the therapist does. Given this, it is important that the therapist is honest and transparent about the extent of their knowledge of the client's medical condition. This is consistent with the BABCP's requirement for the therapist to work with honesty and integrity (Section 14) and the APS Code of Ethics (General Principle C). By being transparent about the level of understanding that the therapist has, it can demonstrate respect for the client whilst encouraging collaboration, as information is shared. Fundamentally, though, it promotes trust, which is an essential ingredient in the development of the therapeutic relationship. Moreover, being trustworthy is the essence of the ethical principle of fidelity.

During the assessment, adopting a biopsychosocial model is appropriate. Increasingly, research highlights the benefit of employing this model when working with chronic medical conditions (Gatchel et al., 2007). It is therefore congruent with the BABCP requirements that, as a therapist: 'You must maintain high standards of assessment and practice' (Section 2). The Chronic Illness Coping Model (CICM) (Macdonald and Stalmeisters, 2015), as an example, adopts a biopsychosocial approach and takes into account the client's social context, support and resilience and draws links with bodily systems, thus helping to formulate an understanding of how the client copes with their illness. Arguably, such models take an ethical position in that they help to paint a broader picture of the client's situation, by combining internal factors with external factors that may be impinging and shaping the illness experience. Developing an understanding of these areas goes some way towards appreciating the boundaries of the client's autonomy.

Given that biographical disruption can occur when living with a chronic medical illness, and that autonomy can be reduced, the therapists endeavour to ensure that the client's voice is heard, that their autonomy is respected becomes significant. Understanding the client's lived experience and helping the client to articulate their needs goes someway towards strengthening the client's autonomy. However, the therapist also needs to consider whether the service that they are offering or the therapy room that they are using might be limiting the client's autonomy in any way. Attention is drawn to this in the APS Code of Ethics, which states:

> Psychologists acknowledge people's right to be treated fairly without discrimination or favouritism and they endeavour to ensure that all people have reasonable and fair access to psychological services and share the benefits that the practice of psychology can offer. (Section A, p. 11)

With this in mind, consideration needs to be given as to how to support any physical limitations that the client might experience, in order to make sure that they are not excluded from participating in therapy. Questioning how the therapy room and treatment might be adapted to meet these needs is necessary. For instance, some clients with chronic pain may need to take breaks and move around. They might need firm supportive chairs. Moreover, it is not uncommon for people with ME/CFS to experience concentration and memory problems and/or be light- or noise-sensitive. Although addressing these points may be seen as common sense to some extent, they make a difference and help ensure that people with a chronic illness can engage and are included in therapy. Being sensitive to such needs goes some way towards ensuring equality, avoids discrimination and adheres to the principle of justice, which as the APS Code of Ethics points out, involves having *'a high regard for the diversity and uniqueness of people'* (Section A, p. 11, emphasis added).

Finally, it is not difficult to imagine that some people with chronic illness find it difficult to come terms with the changes they experience and might encounter despair. Certainly, it has been reported that one in ten suicides is linked to chronic or terminal illness (Ramesh, 2011). Feelings of helplessness and hopelessness can surface as physical health fluctuates and deteriorates. It is imperative that at such times the therapist working with a client with these feelings seeks clinical supervision as soon as possible after the session (on the suicidal client, see later in this chapter). It is also important that the therapist is aware of their employing organisation's policies in such circumstances, particularly in relation to breaching confidentiality. Moreover, pre-empting such situations and considering what actions they might take can lead to 'an informed, reasonable and professional judgment' (BABCP: 5). Notably, working through the 'Verb' ethical decision-making model (see Conclusion) can help the therapist feel more confident about the actions they might take in such circumstances.

Activities

- Reflect on your views about ME/CFS, a chronic illness with no clear biological marker. Consider why some people with this condition might feel marginalised.
- Consider how you might have to adapt your practice for someone who has chronic obstructive pulmonary disease (COPD), in order to increase the client's autonomy and participation in the therapy room.

Excluded populations and people with learning difficulties

The ethics of treating people with complex difficulties are often not considered in great detail. It is often supposed that, assuming the client is willing, therapy is inherently a good thing, managing difficulties as part of the therapeutic process.

However, there are ethics issues to consider in this process that may be expressed as a resolvable dialectic. Two populations are discussed below, illustrating how the ethics of treatment are often taken for granted. The issues faced by these populations, although different, do highlight some ethical principles that should be considered.

Homelessness

A significant and growing body of evidence now indicates that many, if not most people, who are rough sleeping or live in hostels have suffered childhood abuse and neglect. Thus, although societal problems are also implicated, many behaviours implicated in becoming and staying homeless may be explained in terms of the mental health issues associated with such early abuse. There is a growing evidence base around cognitive and behavioural therapies in treating such issues (e.g. self-harming behaviours, emotion regulation) in psychiatric populations, which may indicate the usefulness of psychological treatments. Early feasibility research provides further evidence of this (Maguire et al., forthcoming).

There are, however, ethical reasons not to engage in some types of therapeutic approach (in addition to those discussed elsewhere about the use of CBT by non-experts). A significant proportion of the homeless population use drugs and alcohol that are behaviours that serve functions of emotion regulation and withdrawal avoidance. It may be argued that chronic use may incapacitate the individual, rendering their informed consent to therapeutic interventions inadequate. It may also be that when under the influence of alcohol or other substances, the individual may not be in full control of what they choose to disclose, resulting in discussions that the client may not be able to manage emotionally. Standard techniques used to help people ground themselves or manage emotions may be rendered ineffective due to the impaired ability of the client to think, listen, etc.

The other side of this dialectic concerns the inclusion imperative for populations of people who are, for many structural and individual reasons, excluded from health care and an opportunity for recovery. This argument may be that it is essential to provide psychological interventions to such populations through a planned strategic approach to engaging such people, ensuring that inclusion or exclusion criteria and structural barriers that we may apply in mental health settings do not inhibit the provision of treatment. For example, in the provision of psychological therapies in hospital environments requiring travel, appointment administration may provide insurmountable blocks for homeless people (no access to personal transport or funds for public transport; difficulties in using public transport; addresses held by hospitals that are out of date; no reliable way of receiving post). If there is an adequate indicative evidence base to justify provision, we need to work to overcome other barriers.

Exclusion criteria are often around current drug and alcohol use. The rationale is often that the client needs to commit to non-use, and current use would impair the effectiveness of the therapy. For many substances, this latter point would appear to be true, e.g. alcohol, cannabis, stimulants. However, the clinical evidence for some drugs, e.g. heroin, seems less clear. Clients will often report feeling entirely functional a short period after having used the drug. These exclusion criteria are often cited as mechanisms of exclusion for people with complex problems, alongside those structural issues described above. At the extreme, these criteria could be argued to enable stretched services to manage the 'treatable population' numbers and therefore caseloads and waiting lists. It is more difficult to engage people from excluded populations and the complex issues that they suffer may involve more complicated and lengthy psychological treatments.

The argument, therefore, is whether or not it is ethical to try to engage people suffering complex mental health, substance abuse, relationship and social issues in therapeutic processes. There are a number of treatment and mental health issues that might suggest that it is not ethical (effectiveness, emotion regulation, regularity of intervention, etc.), but given that this population is by definition excluded, they will probably remain so if we continue to act according to these criteria. The ethical dialectic is that, on the one hand, we should do what we can to enable excluded populations with mental health problems to make use of evidence-based psychological therapies; whereas, on the other hand, there are issues for this population that might make it unethical to use such methods.

If we are to serve the whole of society as health care providers, we need to adapt our methods to ensure that we do include such populations whilst providing psychological therapies ethically. Principles of ethical treatment involve ensuring that consent to treat and ongoing treatment are enabled when the person is most likely to be at their best in this regard. Clinically, we have found that the first couple of hours in the morning are best before any substance has been ingested or at least only that needed to stop withdrawal symptoms. We have also found contracting to be important, with both sides committing to achievable delivery methods and the contract being regularly reviewed. Consent should be an ongoing topic; given capacity issues (as well as a demonstrated incidence of undiagnosed cognitive dysfunction), it cannot be assumed. Sessions need to be carefully managed, and if the therapist has any doubts about a client's capacity to work with emotions or manage what they are saying in a session, it should be discontinued or a different, more practical tone, should be taken, followed, at an appropriate time, by a review of the contract. These techniques are familiar to therapists treating, e.g. self-harming and suicidal behaviours, so they are not untested.

The important point here is that, by expressing such treatment issues as ethics problems, it forces us as therapists to think very carefully about how we use our skills, and about how our existing methods may need to be adapted for particular populations.

Adults with learning disabilities

There is a small but growing evidence on treating people with learning disabilities using CBT methods (Willner et al., 2013). Two basic forms of intervention are used: CBT techniques delivered by non-expert staff (as discussed elsewhere); and direct cognitive and behavioural work provided by trained staff. Whatever the intervention, the issue of capacity cannot be ignored. Although there is some excellent guidance on physical and medical treatments for these people (e.g. National Patient Safety Agency, 2004), very little exists for psychological treatments and almost none specifically for cognitive and behavioural therapies, which tend to be structured in approach.

Interventions with people with learning disabilities are often around challenging behaviours (e.g. self-harming, aggression, sexual inappropriateness), with many other challenging behaviours that involve introversion, isolation, etc. being missed. This is often due to the view taken by staff or parents about which issues interfere with functioning most. Thus, it may be that psychological interventions are being used, not because the person has themself indicated distress, but that others around them want a particular behaviour to diminish. Although it is, of course, accepted that therapeutic interventions ultimately must have the health and well-being of the client in mind, it may be that important ethics issues are not fully articulated in the rush to treatment, however well intentioned.

For example, functional analysis of behaviours may highlight particular triggers or functions of a behaviour; the treatment, as for many others, may be differential reinforcement of an alternative more functional behaviour. However, where this population is disadvantaged is that their understanding of the process, particularly removal of an identified, problematic reinforcer, may be highly limited and therefore stressful. The extra stresses involved in psychological interventions are well documented, but the demonstrably limited capacity to understand and agree to these, for many people with learning disabilities, places this firmly within the ethics discourse. The National Patient Safety Agency (NPSA) recommends that the decision on whether or not to treat should be made through a formal multidisciplinary process, although it is not specified what this may be. Common practice in routine psychological care is simply to make a recommendation for treatment, perhaps this being discussed by key workers for that person. It is essential that when the person cannot consent formally, that all is done to enable a detailed discussion of the possible downside. This is in all likelihood done but, as yet, there appears no guarantee that these issues are considered as ethics issues.

In summary, for both of these populations of people, there are issues of access to CBT and then consent to make use of it, for different reasons. Such consent issues should be considered through an ethics lens, which may then inform consideration of treatment and the nature of the treatment itself. Given the marginalised nature of both of these populations, it is imperative that these issues are considered carefully alongside the adaptions to therapy that increase likelihood of effectiveness.

Suicide and suicide prevention in CBT

CB therapists, no matter where they work, will at some point encounter clients with a history of suicide attempts, are reporting suicidal ideation (thoughts) or have a high and immediate risk of suicide. The latter is sometimes referred to in professional practice as the client being 'actively suicidal'.

Suicide for the therapist and teams with whom they are working presents a very dramatic, highly anxiety-provoking and, as a consequence, demanding practice situation. In this context, and within their wider professional practice, the CB therapists may also encounter the direct experience of needing to support families after a family member has killed themselves.

Estimates put suicide in 2008 at 782,000 worldwide, which, according to the World Health Organization's own estimates, is about 1.4 per cent of total worldwide mortality. The suicide rate for the world as a whole is thus estimated at 11.6 per 100,000 inhabitants. The male-to-female ratio of suicide is estimated to be significantly higher for males than for females (Värnik 2012).

In the UK, 6045 people aged 15 and over committed suicide in 2011, i.e. 11.8 incidences per 100,000 people, which is about 1 per cent of all UK deaths. Almost three-quarters of suicides were of men. In addition, in more deprived areas, suicide rates are almost double those found in more affluent areas (Brock et al., 2006). It is also estimated that unsuccessful suicides outnumber successful ones by tenfold.

The success of CB therapy over the last 40 years and its extension into other areas where the risk of suicide is high, such as severe depression, psychosis and bipolar disorders, makes the ability to assess the risk of suicide and prevent or manage it a core CBT competency. These issues of suicide assessment and management are an integral part of most mental health professionals' core professional training, but usually not part of their CBT training. The BABCP, European Association for Behavioural and Cognitive Therapies (EABCT), Academy of Cognitive Therapy (ACT) and the Australian Association for Cognitive and Behaviour Therapy (AACBT), all assume that a therapist will be professionally qualified and have subsequently undertaken specialist CBT training. In the UK, some CB therapists have equivalence to a core professional qualification (see Chapter 7 for a further discussion of this). Thus, it is possible that knowledge and skills in the assessment and management of suicide and ethical decision-making may vary from profession to profession.

Ethical scenario

John was seeing a CB therapist for panic with agoraphobia that he had coped with for many years. He was also under the care of a psychiatrist in outpatients. He had coped through a very over-dependent reliance on his wife, Sarah. Sarah had been diagnosed 12 months ago with a terminal illness and had only 3–6 months to live. John was extremely distressed by the situation, to the extent that he was constantly in tears during therapy sessions. His extreme distress was not limited to therapy sessions. Everyday, he would contact a friend or family member to try to talk about his own problems and with not being able to cope with Sarah's terminal care. This was to the extent that they were rejecting him, refusing to take his calls and avoiding any face-to-face contact. John was now isolated, restricted in his movements and alone. John was also explicit that he intended to take his own life after Sarah died and that he did not wish to continue to live his life without her. He intended to do this through hanging himself. He was very clear that this would be in the garage and that he had everything he would need to do this and it would be on the day of his wife's death. This appeared to be a reasoned decision. He was not clinically depressed. His rationale for taking his own life was: (i) not being able to manage his panic and agoraphobia; (ii) being unable to cope with the distress of his loss; (iii) he expected a poor quality of life in the future. John was also explicit in that he did not want his suicidal intent to be communicated to other professionals, family members or his wife.

Ethical questions

1. Should the CB therapist continue to see John to try to help him cope and overcome his agoraphobia and panic and help him to develop more helpful coping strategies?
2. What aspects should the therapist be considering in supervision?
3. What are the risks posed to the therapist and the employing organisation by the above scenario?
4. What should the therapist be communicating and to whom in this scenario?
5. Does the CB therapist have the right to communicate John's suicidal intent?
6. Does John have a right to privacy regarding his intent?
7. Does John have the right to take his own life?

The values and principles of suicide and suicide prevention

Suicide is rarely about wanting to die but is a desire to no longer live with current life circumstances. It can also take the form of passive suicide, when the individual might refuse lifesaving intervention; or active, when people seek out a lethal method to take their own life.

Suicide differs significantly from other practice dilemmas in a number of important ways. Most people at some point in their lives are likely to consider suicide at low points in their lives or during particularly distressing times such as divorce or bereavement. CB therapists are no exception to these life circumstances and therefore to these thoughts. Thus, it can be hard for CB therapists to take a balanced and objective view, especially if they are in a state of distress themselves for any reason. The CB therapist may also be exposed to the unfortunate context of working within a risk adverse organisation that may have a blame-based culture. This can lead to pressure to emphasise being safe and protective of the individual client – and of the therapist's job circumstances and their organisation's reputation, as opposed to respecting individual autonomy. There is also the further issue of the understandable pressure from the family to do something in the context of a threatened suicide. Any one of these scenarios holds the possibility that the CB therapist's own danger and self-preservation schema will be activated. This activation of the therapist's own schema may result in behaviour that is unduly paternalistic, and risk averse or result in an uncompassionate and or detached response to the client, when what is really needed by the client in such a desperate situation is humane understanding and rational balanced evaluation of the client's situation and the risk to themselves.

Suicide also differs in a further important way from other types of CB ethical decision-making in that the main considerations are to collaborate around consideration of the right means to a given end that are shared between the CB therapist and the client. Suicide, however, focuses on the end itself, about which the therapist and client are likely to hold opposing dichotomous views. In addition, unlike most other ethical situations, the outcome of suicide is final and irreversible. Suicide also differs in that the question is not about living a more fruitful or perhaps virtuous life but about whether to continue to live at all.

Suicide and suicide prevention are difficult problems to work with as the problem is fundamentally beyond a disagreement in therapy goals. Thus, given the opposing beliefs that may be held between the CB therapist and their suicidal client, the task extends beyond the application of strategies of coping and into the realm of trying to change the client's most basic desires and attitudes to life. Most people share this value of life, its sanctity. Sanctity of life is also enshrined in some religious and cultural ideals as well as underpinning professional values and debates. Thus, some CB therapists may find particular challenges in working with actively suicidal clients (Bond, 2015). This is because, for some CB therapists, a violation of the sanctity of life might be experienced as an assault on the therapist's deeply held personal or religious convictions. Some CB therapists may even find that the thought of suicide triggers anxiety or even feelings of disgust. The challenge for CB therapists who strongly hold these beliefs is how to manage them within a therapeutic context in order that the focus remains on the client's needs, rather than being dictated by the beliefs of the CB therapist.

Duties of the professional in respect to suicide and suicide prevention

Deontology or duty-based ethics (as discussed in Chapter 1) concerns the actions taken or not taken (omissions) that brings about specific consequences. Emmanuel Kant is credited with the initial development of deontological ethics (Ellis, 2015). In respect to suicide and suicide prevention, the application of a duty indicates defined rules for professional practice that are based on what a rational CB therapist would decide through a reasoned approach (Beauchamp and Childress, 2013).

On the face of it, such an approach would be considered to fit well with many of the ideas that underpin CBT, with its emphasis on rational appraisal of thoughts and beliefs and the development of therapy protocols and guidelines. This is not as simple as it may seem because it is not always clear in complex clinical situations what the rules are or when they might be applied when this involves many parties such as other professionals, family and the client themselves. Indeed, what might a rational rule for suicide prevention actually look like in such circumstances; or even what would constitute a rational appraisal, given the considerable uncertainty present? For example, deontological ethics ('best interests') might lead the CB therapist to follow a universal rule that they must protect the client and prevent the suicide at all costs, but yet other universal professional duties such as reducing suffering might then be violated for example in end-of-life situations.

The picture is still further complicated as the evidence base for specific interventions to prevent suicide prevention at both societal and individual levels indicates a limited overall impact on suicidal rates. This limited impact applies within society and across cultural boundaries, so, even if the rule is to protect at all costs, it is difficult to see how this duty can actually be discharged. Deontological ethics also has the problem of how the rules are developed and who develops them. Client-based rules might well be very different to CB therapist-based rules and, in such a situation, whose rules should apply?

Finally, the law in many cases is underpinned by the ethical principle of autonomy, and the right of the competent person - and in the absence of a mental illness - to make decisions about their own body and to end their own life actively through, for example, a planned suicide or through the refusal of life-saving treatment (Bond, 2015).

Suicide and autonomy

Autonomy in ethics is about being free to make decisions and choose a course of action. As briefly discussed earlier in this chapter, in the UK (within its various jurisdictions) and in similar jurisdictions worldwide, an ethic of respect for adult autonomy is favoured in law (Komesaroff, 2001; Bond and Dryden, 2012). This has a number of important implications for the CB therapist who is working with actual or potentially suicidal clients.

The principle of autonomy would always require the CB therapist to take into account the decisions of the client with respect to their therapy and their own bodies. Thus, autonomy is about the individual's right to self-determination. The BABCP, in its Standards of Conduct, Performance and Ethics, implicitly refer to autonomy in Standard 10: 'You must get informed consent to give treatment (except in an emergency)' (p. 11).

The issue of consent is a fundamental issue under the Human Rights Act, in that treatment cannot be given to a patient or client unless the person has given a valid authorisation (although exceptional circumstances do exist, see Chapter 2). If treatment were to be given without consent, the CB therapist would likely be open to an action for battery. The professional involved would also likely be in breach of Article 3 of the Human Rights Act on the basis of having wilfully participated in giving degrading treatment (Wilkinson and Caulfield, 2000; Newdick, 2005).

In order to be valid the CB therapist must ensure that any consent being given meets three requirements:

1. The consent needs to be freely given (thus, without coercion).
2. The client would need to be given sufficient information on which to base the decision (positive and negative effects of the information, including any side effects).
3. That the consent is given by someone with the mental capacity to make a reasoned decision.

In applying the above requirements alongside the principle of autonomy to suicide, a number of issues arise. First, at end stages of life, in the face of pain and suffering, a patient or client may elect to take their own life through refusal of treatment or of food and fluids or they may take a more active form in order to relieve their suffering through, perhaps, an overdose of medication. The CB therapist is only likely to encounter end-of-life suicide dilemmas such as these situations on a regular basis if working as part of a multidisciplinary team in a physical or palliative health care setting.

A more frequent scenario that the CB therapist is likely to encounter is when working with a client who reports suicidal thoughts. Bond (2015) argues that, in respect to working with suicidal clients, the principle of autonomy and the law can help the therapist to respond appropriately. It is important for the CB therapist to recognise that just by expressing a wish to die through suicide does not mean that someone is mentally disordered and is lacking in capacity. The legal system does generally support an adult's right to make informed decisions if they are not mentally disordered, detained under a Mental Health Act or suffering from a physical illness that would interfere with decision-making processes. The situation is more complicated in respect to children and young people regarding when they might be deemed to be responsible and have capacity (see Bond, 2015).

In respect to the CB therapist's responsibilities, the therapist will have to assess the needs of the client and risk of suicide. The National Institute for Health and Care Excellence (NICE) have established guidance in this respect (see the box adjacent for details).

Self-harm in over-8s: long-term management

Full guideline available from: National Institute for Health and Care Excellence, Level 1A, City Tower, Piccadilly Plaza, Manchester, M1 4BT.

National Institute for Health and Care Excellence (2011) *Self-harm in over-8s: long-term management*. London: National Institute for Health and Care Excellence. Available at: https://www.nice.org.uk/guidance/cg133 (accessed December 2016).

Source: www.guidelines.co.uk/nice/self-harm (accessed 13 April 2016).

It can be argued that the success of CBT is achieved through the fundamental underpinning values of a shared approach and mutually agreed goals within the context of a collaborative relationship. Yet, as introduced above, this may be absent or lacking in some way when working with a suicidal client (Corrie et al., 2016). Thus, the scenario of clients wanting to take their own life and of being unable to discuss this openly with the CB therapist, sets up an acute ethical dilemma. Do you respect the client's autonomy or try to do something to save the person's life?

Legally, within a UK context, assisting someone to take their own life is an offence. It is not, however, an offence to attempt suicide. So, the CB therapist would risk prosecution if they actively encouraged or supported a client's suicide. It is common practice in CB therapy to use interventions such as a cost-and-benefit analysis. This technique helps clients to weigh up the possible advantages and disadvantages of a course of action. Yet, in this situation, might this be considered an encouraging act of supporting a suicide? This could particularly be the case if an unbalanced negative picture was built up – there are circumstances where there can appear to be overwhelming reasons for committing suicide but a skilled therapist will be able to draw out counter-balancing reasons for living.

It is clear that assisting a suicide is an offence, but would it be ethical not to intervene? If the CB therapist did nothing in the context of a client who had capacity to make such a decision and they were not being coerced, then it can be argued that this would be ethical on the grounds of respecting autonomy. Yet, would this be an appropriate professional course of action or morally the right approach to take? In order to address this, it is also important as part of the assessment and management process to at least initially discuss any concerns with the client themselves. Talking about suicide is highly personal and distressing and, for some, an indication of a personal flaw or failure. This, coupled with suicide being a taboo subject in society, leads many people to fear burdening others with their problems or for some individuals also a fear of being rejected.

The shared approach might also be impeded on the additional grounds that discussions about suicide can, in addition, be anxiety-provoking for therapists but also for fear of being criticised or being disciplined by employers or even the possibility of having to defend their actions at a coroner's hearing if the client were to take their own life. Some CB therapists may be wary of discussing suicide with their clients through an erroneous belief that the very act of discussing suicide may make it more likely. Thus, both of these influences can lead to a negative cycle of avoiding discussing or adequately addressing the issue. It is our view, through experience and the evidence, that many suicidal clients often report what a huge relief it is to be able to talk about what they are experiencing in a non-judging supportive environment.

Thus, it is important to discuss suicide with all clients at initial CB assessment and at other points in the therapy process where this is relevant to do so. It is not an issue that can or should be avoided. In situations where suicide intent is communicated by the client within a confidential setting, the question for the CB therapist to consider is whether they have grounds to breach the therapist–client confidentiality. The grounds for doing so would be if the assessment indicated that capacity to make an informed decision was compromised or if the initial contract with the client had made clear that, in such circumstances, the therapist was retaining a right to breach in life-threatening situations to self or others. At the very least, the therapist should be documenting that a discussion around confidentiality has occurred and the exceptions made explicit to the client (see Chapter 5). Some therapists, on the grounds of good communication and defensive reasons, use a written contract for this purpose. This is to ensure that there is written evidence of what was agreed between the therapist and client for the therapist's own security. In a situation where limits to confidentiality have not been agreed from the outset and the therapist breached, they might be open to a legal action and possibly a complaint to the CB therapist's professional body (Bond, 2015).

Another contested area is whether the CB therapist should try to intervene therapeutically when a client is suicidal. In the context of a mental disorder, the answer would almost always favour intervening. Alongside therapy and other treatments for the mental disorder, risk management would be appropriate through the development of coping and suicide prevention plans. Such an agreement, which can be verbal or written, can prove invaluable in preventing suicide. Such plans explicitly state what the client will do in terms of seeking help if they become actively suicidal.

A more difficult dilemma occurs in the relatively common situation of when the client has capacity and is thus making a fully informed decision to take their life. The problem here is that to attempt an intervention would violate the clients' autonomy. Some therapists in this situation would always attempt an intervention, on the grounds that they would construct a wish to take one's own life as a mental disorder. This reasoning, as discussed earlier, cannot necessarily be justified and would take the view that they must respect the client's decision and autonomy, even if disagreeing with the decision. Therefore, a simply always correct 'off-the-peg' decision cannot be made here. The solution might be an open discussion with the client. Perhaps agreeing to disagree over the client's decisions and trying to persuade the client at least to attempt to make changes through therapy and other forms of support. It might be possible at least to agree a period of time for this work to take place. To breach and inform others of the intended suicide would, as discussed above, need to rely on the contract agreed at the outset. Additional protection might also be available to the CB therapist who has to comply with specific organisational requirements (Ellis, 2015). It will almost always be better to err on the side of trying to save a life than in letting it be lost. Certainly, no individual practitioner should be making such decisions without consultation with supervisors and peers.

Where risk appears imminent or is seriously threatened, the involvement of mental health services in assessing and managing risk is indicated. Assessment of capacity is not straightforward where someone is considering suicide – it is rare that they are not depressed and this can affect their capacity to make rational decisions. It is possible for the therapist to be persuaded that someone's life is so negative that suicide is a rational response and that the individual has capacity, but this is such an emotive and difficult assessment to make that no therapist should be making it alone. Mental health services regularly make such assessments and will do so at the request of most accredited therapists (although possibly involving the individual's family doctor). They may then be able to provide increased support and monitoring for the individual and their family. They may make a formal assessment under mental health legislation and this can occur in most countries as risk to self will be clearly present. Treatment and detention in hospital under compulsion is a last resort but can be the least restrictive intervention to preserve life and provide support and treatment for depression or other mental health problems. If someone has communicated that they wish to die, intervention and reassessment will always be appropriate – the very fact that the communication has been made usually indicates ambivalence and is certainly signalling an opportunity for intervention. An example of applying ethical models and problem-solving to suicide/suicide prevention can be found in the Conclusion chapter.

Suicide and its prevention are a therapeutic challenge for the CB therapist. It is common in everyday practice to encounter clients who are considering suicide or are actively suicidal. Whilst there is a wealth of research on suicide and its prevention, current prevention strategies are limited in what they can achieve. The main ethical consideration in ethical thinking for suicide is how far to accept the ethical principle of autonomy. Further to this are considerations of how or whether to work with someone who is suicidal and how to handle considerations of confidentiality, communication, risk assessment and management. The CB therapist's own values and beliefs systems are also an important consideration. Such difficult decisions should, however, never be taken in isolation.

Activities

- Consider your own value base with respect to suicide. Is suicide ever acceptable? Or is it the ultimate expression of self-determination. Now think about how this might influence your reactions to your clients and your decision-making processes.
- Consider your professional own personal support, including supervision for working with suicidal clients, and how adequate this is for you within your own work environment.

Further reading

Bond, T. (2015) *Standards and Ethics for Counselling in Action* (4th edn). London: Sage.

This book is a superb comprehensive counselling text, which draws together the author's many years of experience in researching and writing about ethics in counselling and psychotherapy.

Cutcliffe, R.R., Santos, J., Links, P.S. et al. (2016) *International Handbook of Clinical Suicide Research Paperback*. London: Routledge.

This excellent authorative text includes a contemporary analysis of research with and about survivors of suicide and indigenous populations from a number of professional perspectives.

Kingdon, D. and Finn, M. (2012) *Tackling Mental Health Crises*. Hove: Routledge.

Text-based, using cognitive behavioural principles for working with people in crisis.

Rathod, S., Kingdon, D., Pinninti, N., Turkington, D. and Phiri, P. (2015) *Cultural Adaptation of CBT for Serious Mental Illness*. Chichester: Wiley.

This book gives details of principles and practice of cultural adaptation of CBT.

CONCLUSION: ETHICAL DECISION-MAKING

We have covered a lot of areas as the book has progressed and now want to pull these together in a way that allows them to be applied in day-to-day situations.

Any therapist can become anxious and worried when faced with an ethical dilemma, whether they are a novice or experienced. Moreover, the therapist needs to be able to justify the action they take because this is a professional responsibility. Approaching an ethical dilemma in a systematic manner can help clarify thinking and help to reduce anxiety. Practice for therapists in working through ethical scenarios needs to be part of their continued professional development. Clinical supervision – both individual and group – is a useful place to do this. Although no two ethical dilemmas will be exactly the same, being familiar with the process of ethical decision-making is without doubt valuable.

Using an ethical decision-making model or framework can help in this decision-making process. The rights and wrongs of behaviour are complex and the process of ethical decision-making reflects this. However, using an ethical decision-making model can help anchor the ethical decision-maker when they feel lost, concerned and drifting. The model that we have put forward is that of the Verb Model of Ethical Decision Making (Figure 10.1). We have called it the 'Verb Model' in order to emphasise that ethical decision-making is very much a 'doing' activity, 'doing nothing' – 'ignoring dilemmas' – *is not an option*, although there may be times when whether to act or not is a decision that has to be taken. It is a model that can reflect the complexity of the systems that the CB therapist works in. It takes into account legal and organisational requirements, whilst also being sensitive to the therapist and the client's value system.

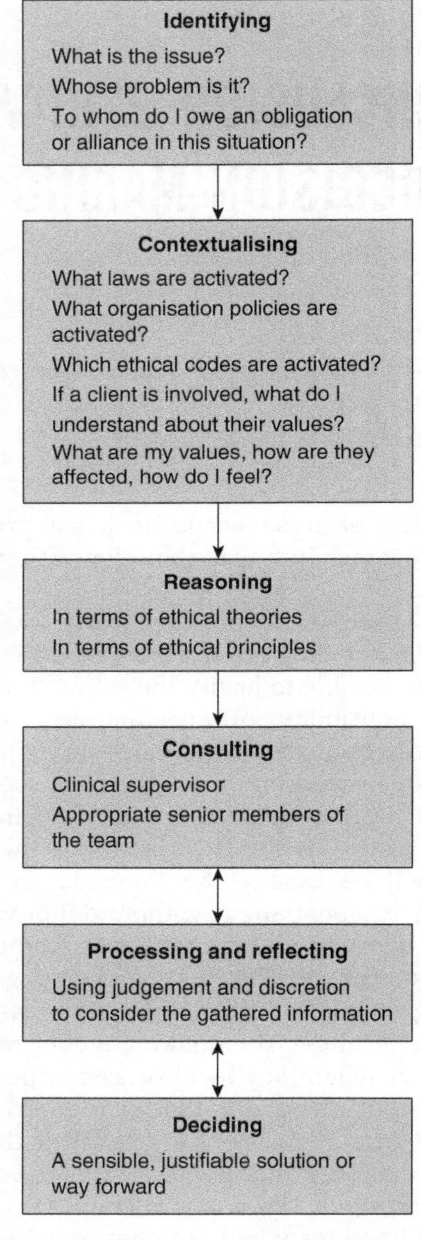

Figure 10.1 The Verb Model of Ethical Decision Making

Six stages are identified to work through:

- Identifying
- Contextualising
- Reasoning
- Consulting
- Processing and reflecting
- Deciding

Again, each of the stages are labelled as verbs in order to stress the need to be doing - taking action. Questions are posed to the therapist to reflect upon at the Identifying and Contextualising stages. At the Reasoning stage, the therapist is asked to consider how the dilemma might sit with the ethical theories, for instance Deontology and Utilitarianism (see Chapter 1) or practical applications, for instance, safeguarding. Reflect on such questions as:

- Are the persons involved being treated as a means to an end, or as an end in themselves?
- Could following a particular action be transferred to other situations or not, is that important?
- What are the long-term and short-term consequences for all those involved?
- What ethical principles are activated?
- Do the principles compete?
- Which principle appears to be the most significant in this situation?

The last three stages of the model are very much aimed to be interactive, where additional support to clarify thinking is sought before deciding on an action. Discussing the issues with clinical supervisors and/or senior members of staff is appropriate, mindful, too, that they will have boundaries relating to confidentiality that they will have to adhere to.

Examples of worked scenarios

We have worked through a few scenarios to help you understand the process. However, although we have tried to rationalise the ethical decision-making process by providing a framework for ethical decision-making, it is necessary to remember that this process is informed by values, and values are subjective. Therefore, the importance of discussing ideas with other professionals is essential in order to work out what the values leading the decision are. This said, in life-threatening situations, a rapid response will be necessary.

Additionally, the necessity for clear contracting is highlighted in the scenarios. It is important to consider how we contract, as previously questioned, are clients really in a position to fully digest the contract at the beginning of therapy? As we are all probably aware, it is easy to agree to things or not read the small print when we really want something, or are not fully ourselves. What can we do to ensure that clients understand the contract? Also, how frequently should we remind our clients of this contract, given that as the therapeutic relationship develops, clients tend to feel more comfortable disclosing significant information, information that could have serious consequences?

As you read through the worked scenarios, consider how your values might influence the decision-making process and how well your therapist–client contract would support you if faced with the ethical dilemmas. Remember too, that no two ethical dilemmas are ever the same, and that our worked examples here are no substitute for seeking appropriate legal advice.

Scenario 1

You work for an organisation that delivers CBT. The organisation has a long waiting list for clients seeking CBT. You discover that a colleague, another accredited CBT therapist, who is off work with stress, is currently seeing private clients. There is no doubt that this is happening. What do you do?

Identifying

What is the issue? Whistle-blowing.

Whose problem is it? The therapist that discovers the problem, the 'sick' therapist and the organisation.

To whom do I owe an obligation or alliance in this situation? The organisation, colleagues and clients on the waiting list.

Contextualising

What laws are activated? Money has been gained by deception from the employer, therefore gross misconduct has occurred. As the law works in the public interest, the therapist is unlikely to be prosecuted, but could be cautioned, if the employer pursues the care.

What organisation policies are activated? Potentially, the contract of employment.

Which ethical codes are activated? The BABCP section 1.5 code states:

> The safety of service users and others must come before any personal or professional loyalties at all times. As soon as you become aware of a situation that puts a service user or someone else in danger, you should discuss the matter with your clinical supervisor, a senior colleague or another appropriate person.
>
> You must behave with honesty and integrity and make sure that your behaviour does not damage the public's confidence in you or your profession.
>
> You must limit your work or stop practising if your performance or judgement is affected by your health.

Although the clients may not be put in danger, the therapist's capacity to help clients may be limited due to her illness. Is the sick therapist acting with honesty and integrity?

If a client is involved, what do I understand about their values? Unknown.

What are my values, how are they affected, how do I feel? Honesty and trust are important to the therapist. With a strong work ethic, it is difficult to see colleagues work hard and the waiting list continue to grow.

Reasoning

Whistle-blowing

In terms of ethical theories:

- Deontology: We have a duty to be honest and act with integrity, this can become a universal law.
- Consequentialism: Consider short-term and long-term consequences of whistle-blowing – the sick therapist might get the help she needs or conversely be disciplined. If she returns to work, interpersonal problems may develop. However, if she returns to work, the waiting list might reduce in size. If she is really sick and gets the help that she needs, clients would no longer be put at risk from any inappropriate decisions that she might make as a result of her own health issues.

In terms of ethical principles:

- Autonomy: Whistle-blowing without informing the 'sick therapist' does not respect her autonomy.
- Beneficence: By whistle-blowing, the organisation will be able to sort out staffing – it could also mean less pressure on staff and more

clients might be seen. Moreover, if the 'sick therapist' is ill, she might get appropriate support. Current private clients may be directed to another therapist, who is in a better place to help them.
- Non-maleficence: The 'sick therapist' might be disciplined for breaching standards and regulations, therefore harm might come to her. If the therapist returns to work, there might be an atmosphere, particularly if she has been disciplined. The private clients whom the therapist is currently seeing might not be receiving the help they need because of the therapist's own problem, harm may ensue.
- Fidelity: Trust has been brought into question by the 'sick therapist's' action. However, by whistle-blowing, the sick therapist or colleagues might not trust the 'whistle-blower' again.
- Justice: Only private clients are being treated by the sick therapist not the ones on the waiting list of the therapist's organisation – is this fair or correct?

Consulting (clinical supervisor or appropriate senior members of team)

The BABCP code notes that it is necessary to inform a supervisor if clients are put in danger, however the extent to which the clients are put in danger by this therapist is not clear.

In this case, the clinical supervisor or a senior member might be duty-bound to inform management, because of this, moving to the processing and reflecting stage of the framework first might be helpful.

Processing and reflecting (using the judgement and discretion to consider the gathered information)

Whistle-blowing in this situation fits with the therapist's value of honesty. However, the 'sick therapist' might be disciplined if she is found to be dishonest. Causing others grief is difficult: the sick therapist is already off with stress and, if this is genuine, reporting her could cause her more stress. It is not uncommon for individuals to 'turn a blind eye' to such activity and, indeed, there may be colleagues who are also aware of what is happening, and doing just that. However, if she is sick, she might get extra support.

Here, then, the principles of beneficence and non-maleficence compete. However, clients may be put at risk because of the therapist's potentially poor judgement. The BABCP code is supportive in this case.

Deciding (a sensible, justifiable solution or way forward)

After working through this process, the therapist felt comfortable that the best way forward was to disclose this information to her supervisor. The therapist felt that she could justify the actions using the ethical principles and felt supported by the BABCP code of practice.

After discussion with the supervisor, the approach agreed is that the therapist informs her colleague, the sick therapist, that she is aware of the situation and allows the 'sick therapist' to report her situation to their employer. However, assurance is sought that this will happen and the colleague is made aware that if this does not happen, the therapist would feel obligated to report it.

Scenario 2

You work as a CBT therapist with a local charity that supports homeless people into secure accommodation. You work for an NHS Trust, with the charity buying out two days a week of your time for providing therapeutic support in a small hostel. Your supervision arrangement is within the Trust.

You have been asked to see a resident who is under threat of eviction having made threats to kill another resident after drinking heavily. The hostel staff believe that you may be able to enable him to deal with this issue, to the extent that they can rescind the notice to quit. He is still drunk when you see him. You have a good relationship with him but are aware that he can become quite emotional, to the extent that he may self-harm. You have no immediate supervision available. Although this is your regular day with the charity, the session would be unplanned and is unscheduled.

What do you do?

Identifying

What is the issue? The resident will be evicted if he doesn't report some sort of insight into his actions to hostel staff. They have asked you to intervene as you have a good relationship. However, a psychological intervention may cause unmanageable emotions and further behavioural issues.

Whose problem is it? The resident. They may be evicted or become more emotionally unstable.

To whom do I owe an obligation or alliance in this situation? The individual, in terms of reducing the chance of eviction and rough sleeping with those inherent risks.

Contextualising

What laws are activated? None.

Which organisation policies are activated? The risk policy of the charity, which stipulates criteria for eviction. Practice organisation risk policy.

Which ethical codes are activated? No formal ethical code, but two questions around values are informed by the National Institute for Health and Care Excellence (2012).

If a client is involved, what do I understand about their values? They do wish to engage in change in behaviour and are very aware of the link between drinking and problematic behaviours.

What are my values, how are they affected, how do I feel? Support to marginalised people is important, enabling them to make changes in behaviour to reduce the possibilities of them sleeping rough, thereby putting themselves at more risk and contributing to negative psychological and emotional processes. Change and support in difficult circumstances are therefore important.

Reasoning

In terms of ethical theories:

- Beneficence: We must always act in the best interests of the client. The BABCP ethics guidelines stipulate this and that you must always get informed consent for treatment (except in an emergency). Arguably, this person may not be in a position to give informed consent, given their heavy drinking, but likewise it may be considered some form of emergency even if it is not an acute medical one. The ethics issue here is that we may need to sacrifice structures and informed consent to serve and avoid the greater harm of rough sleeping.
- Deontology: We have a duty to act in the client's interest at all times. One action, to engage the client, may result in increased predisposition to self-harm and emotion dysregulation. It is also acting outside the structures of the agreed therapy, unless ad hoc time has been agreed in advance (e.g. DBT coaching).
- Consequentialism: There are possible consequences for either course of action. If the therapist refuses to see the client because it is not a scheduled appointment, then the chances of eviction are high, meaning possible serious risk to the client (overdose, self-harm, assault, etc.). However, if the therapist agrees to see the client, it may be difficult to avoid an emotional exchange that

results in little behaviour change due to alcohol use and emotional dysregulation. The urge to self-harm may increase. It may be that engagement is warranted, on a coaching, problem-solving level (e.g. DBT coaching), being careful not to invalidate or perhaps become dragged into an emotionally charged and uncontrolled exchange. This method would be best served if it was initially set up as part of the contracting process.

In terms of ethical principles:
The health of the client should always be paramount:

- Beneficence: Either option is arguably in the best interests of the client. One has short-term costs but possible longer-term gains; the other has longer-term costs.
- Non-maleficence: It would be important, if the intervention were to be engaged, that it should be conducted in a way that minimised emotion regulation for the client.
- Fidelity: There is a departure from standard practice, both in terms of the structure of the therapy and the interventions used. The charity may start to do this more often, i.e. engage the therapist in ad hoc interventions, having been reinforced for this.
- Justice: Arguably, social justice is being served by adapting protocols that were not designed for this group of people. It may serve as a useful case study if successful.

Consulting (clinical supervisor or appropriate senior members of team)

In this case, the supervisor was not available. However, it would be important to discuss the case at the earliest convenience to work out expert value-driven interventions with a clear rationale for departing from protocol.

Processing and reflecting (using the judgement and discretion to consider the gathered information)

The information would probably point to a need to predict such issues at the beginning of therapy. DBT proposes a useful model of coaching which is entirely problem-solving in nature and asks the person to reflect on the skills that have been taught so far in therapy. This would need to be considered as part of a review process, possibly with all clients who may risk eviction to the street. Work would also need to be done with the charity workers on how they refer for such 'emergency' interventions.

Deciding (a sensible, justifiable solution or way forward)

It would seem that a DBT-style ad hoc, but limited, coaching intervention may be the most appropriate. It addresses the need for an intervention, whilst minimising the risks of emotion dysregulation, although this would have to be skilfully done. It may be useful for staff to receive training in DBT-style coaching sessions, maintaining fidelity to a model.

Charity staff could also be taught to understand the function of such behaviours. The risk policies could be adapted to include 'cool-off' periods in safe environments whilst individuals recover the capacity for thinking through these issues.

Scenario 3

You are working in an organisation that delivers high-intensity CBT. One of your clients, a 30-year-old woman reveals that she was sexually abused as a child by her stepfather. Her mother and stepfather no longer live together, in fact she has no idea where he lives now. She has never told anyone about this before. She does not want you to let anyone know.

Identifying

What is the issue? Breaching client confidentiality. Safeguarding children.

Whose problem is it? The therapist, the client and the organisation.

To whom do I owe an obligation or alliance in this situation? The client, the organisation, the profession and, potentially, children who might come to harm.

Contextualising

What laws are activated? Whilst there is no mandatory duty to breach confidentiality here, the organisation has opted into the 'Working Together' framework and adopted their abuse reporting procedures.

What organisation policies are activated? Potentially, contract of employment related to sharing information in relation to the Working Together framework.

Which ethical codes are activated? The BABCP code states in sections 1.1 and 1.3 that:

- You are personally responsible for making sure that you promote and protect the best interests of your service users. You must respect and take account of these factors when providing care or a service, and must not abuse the relationship you have with a service user, sexually, emotionally, financially or in other ways.
- You must not do anything or fail to do anything, or allow someone else to do anything that you have good reason to believe will put the health or safety of a service user or others in danger. This includes both your own actions and those of other people. You should take appropriate action to protect the rights of children and vulnerable adults if you believe they are at risk, including following national and local policies.

If a client is involved, what do I understand about their values? Trust is an important issue for this client.

What are my values, how are they affected, how do I feel? Trust and honesty are important. Breaching confidentiality here feels uncomfortable as the client has clearly asked not to share the information about abuse.

Reasoning

Breaching client confidentiality. Safeguarding children:

In terms of ethical theories:

- Deontology: We have a duty to be honest and act with integrity. Also, we have a duty to protect children. These can become universal laws.
- Consequentialism: Consider short-term and long-term consequences of breaching confidentiality. If details were passed on, the client might have to look at issues that she had tried to avoid for some time, she might have to face the perpetrator. In the long term, though, this might help her resolve this issue:
    - The perpetrator may continue abusing others.
    - The therapist: Would be complying with her organisation's policy and her professional requirements. However, she might lose the trust of her client, and therefore the opportunity to help the client would be lost. The client may consider that therapists cannot be trusted and therefore terminate therapy and not seek further therapy.

In terms of ethical principles:

- Autonomy: By breaching confidentiality the client's wish for non-disclosure and thus autonomy will not be respected.

- Beneficence: By breaching confidentiality, the therapist will be adhering to her organisation's policies. Other children might be protected.
- Non-maleficence: The therapeutic relationship might be harmed. The client might lose trust in therapy. The client may have to look at issues that she might not be ready to explore.
- Fidelity: The extent to which the client can trust the therapist and any future therapists might be questioned.
- Justice: The boundaries of breaching confidentiality are explained to all clients.

Consulting (clinical supervisor or appropriate senior members of team)

The clinical supervisor pointed out that as part of the contracting agreement, it is made clear to all clients prior to starting therapy when breaching confidentiality is necessary. This is one of those situations. However, it also noted that at the start of therapy, clients may be so desperate to start therapy and/or do not think clearly, that they might agree to a contract that they have not fully absorbed, and therefore might not understand its implications.

Processing and reflecting (using judgement and discretion to consider the gathered information)

Breaching confidentiality does not sit comfortably with the therapist's values, particularly as the client has asked for confidentiality to be kept. Respecting the client's autonomy is important and trust is fundamental to the therapeutic progress. The client has identified her need for therapy and this may stop her from getting her needs met. However, it appears that the perpetrator is still alive and might be abusing others, therefore harm might come to them. By breaching confidentiality in this situation, the therapist would be adhering to her employment contract, however deontology points out that it is important not to treat people as a means to an end. It could be argued that breaching confidentiality may result in the perpetrator being brought to justice, and thus potentially preventing harm to others, however it is questioned at what cost to this particular client.

The BABCP code of ethics is not explicit in the specific situation of historic abuse, however it is clear about preventing harm from happening to others.

Deciding (a sensible, justifiable solution or way forward)

After working through this process, the therapist felt comfortable that the best way forward was to remind the client of their original contract regarding breaching confidentiality. The need to disclose this information to the person in the agency that deals with safeguarding, because of the potential serious harm to others, was explained. The therapist also reinforced that she understood the importance of trust and that she sincerely wanted to help the client work through her issues.

Scenario 4

You are working in a primary care setting with a severely depressed client who is not improving with CBT. He informs you that he is suicidal and has plans to take an overdose within the next few days. He has gathered together a large volume of painkillers. He expresses a profound sense of hopelessness and his score on the Beck Depression Inventory is 46. He asks you not to tell anybody that he is suicidal so that he can be at peace, he sees no other options. He has told you he is suicidal simply to say goodbye. What do you do?

Identifying

What is the issue? The client is at serious and immediate risk of suicide, within the context of a formally diagnosed mental health disorder.

Whose problem is it? The therapist.

To whom do I owe an obligation or alliance in this situation? In this case, an obligation to protect the client and respond, accordingly.

Contextualising

What laws are activated? Whilst the client would be acting within the law by taking his own life (Suicide Act 1961), this would be in the context of a person whose capacity to make such a decision is compromised by their mental disorder of severe depression (Mental Capacity Act 2005).

What organisation policies are activated? Possibly contract of employment policies.

Which ethical codes are activated? Section 1.5 of the BABCP code states that:

> You must protect service users or others if you believe that any situation puts them in danger. This includes the conduct, performance or health of a colleague. The safety of service users and others must come before any personal or professional loyalties at all times.

> As soon as you become aware of a situation that puts a service user or someone else in danger, you should discuss the matter with your clinical supervisor, a senior colleague or another appropriate person.

If a client is involved what do I understand about their values? Respects authority. Does not want to be a burden.

What are my values, how are they affected, how do I feel? Respecting the client's autonomy is important, however this is based on their ability to make an informed, rational decision.

Reasoning

In terms of ethical theories:

- Deontology: We have a duty to behave in a manner that develops trust and not to violate relationships, this could become a universal law. However, we have a duty to protect vulnerable clients, to help keep them safe.
- Consequentialism: If no action is taken, the client will not survive. By taking action, the client may get the help he needs and eventually his depression should lift.

In terms of ethical principles:

- Autonomy: Respecting the client's wishes means he won't survive.
- Beneficence: By breaching confidentiality, eventually his mood may improve and his quality of life may improve.
- Non-maleficence: By doing nothing, harm will happen to the client.
- Fidelity: By breaching confidentiality, trust will be breached, but this could be repaired in time.
- Justice: You would treat anyone in such a situation, experiencing mental illness, in the same way.

Consulting (clinical supervisor or appropriate senior members of team)

This is a life-threatening situation and thus requires a rapid response.

Processing and reflecting (using the judgement and discretion to consider the gathered information)

Rapid response is needed, that places client safety as the main consideration. The issue is serious and immediate.

Deciding (a sensible, justifiable solution or way forward)

The decision is to inform the client that confidentiality will need to be breached and an ambulance arranged to take them to the local Accident and Emergency Department (A&E) for assessment. It is agency policy to engage the emergency services in this way. The client is also informed that his family doctor will be contacted, so that his doctor is aware of the active suicidal status.

The client is reminded that this was discussed at the contracting phase of therapy. This information is shared in an empathic manner, and it is stressed that the client might think differently if he was not depressed and that, with the right treatment, he can still recover from his depression.

Reluctantly, the client agrees to comply with the assessment through A&E. Later that day, communication is received that the client has been admitted to the local mental health unit under the Mental Health Act for assessment purposes.

At the contracting phase of therapy, the client had been informed that in such situations, confidentiality would be breached. Although, even if this had not been done, a breach would be justified. The client's capacity is compromised and thus the principle of autonomy does not apply. In this situation, the therapist, in order to do no harm, must act in a paternalistic way to protect the client and ensure their welfare.

This is a medical emergency situation and no matter what the setting is, decisive and rapid action is necessary. Where possible, there is a need also to explain this decision to the client and try to engage them in the process.

Scenario 5

You work as a private therapist in a small town. A former client keeps requesting to be your friend on social media. She left therapy six months ago. The issues you worked with related to her low self-esteem and social anxiety. You developed a very good therapeutic relationship with her. You recall that rejection had been a significant theme in her life. What do you do?

Identifying

What is the issue? Boundary crossing.

Whose problem is it? The therapist.

To whom do I owe an obligation or alliance in this situation? The former client and the profession.

Reasoning

Boundary crossing

In terms of ethical theories:

- Deontology: We have a duty to behave in a manner that develops trust and not to violate relationships – this could become a universal law.
- Consequentialism: Consider short-term and long-term consequences of boundary crossing. By becoming a friend on social media, the client may feel validated in the short term, however once a boundary is crossed, the relationship could not return to a therapeutic one. Therefore, she would lose future therapeutic benefits of this relationship. Short- and long-term consequences for the therapist: the therapist could lose a sense of privacy, but gain a friend, however she is content with the friends she has.

In terms of ethical principles:

- Autonomy: By making the client a 'friend' she would be respecting the client's wishes.
- Beneficence: The client's self-esteem may be increased.
- Non-maleficence: Boundary crossing can be problematic. The therapist might feel her privacy is reduced as the boundary between work and her private life cross over. If the therapist does not make the client a friend, the client may feel rejected.
- Fidelity: The literature suggests that dual relationships can lead to problems that can lead to a reduction of trust in the profession.
- Justice: All clients are made aware of the therapists' boundaries around the therapeutic relationship at the start of therapy, thus promoting fairness and equality.

Contextualising

What laws are activated? None.

Which organisation policies are activated? None.

Which ethical codes are activated? The BABCP code states that you must keep high standards of personal conduct. Section 4.1 of the BABCP codes states that:

> You must keep high standards of personal conduct, as well as professional conduct. You should be aware that poor conduct outside of your professional life may still affect someone's confidence in you and your profession.

If a client is involved, what do I understand about their values? Respects authority and tends to put other people first.

What are my values, how are they affected, how do I feel? Treating people equally and with respect is important. This situation compromises the therapist's values of keeping work life and private life separate.

Consulting (clinical supervisor or appropriate senior members of team)

The supervisor and therapist considered the situation chiefly in terms of beneficence and non-maleficence. Attention was drawn to the therapeutic contract that had omitted boundaries in relation to social media.

Processing and reflecting (using the judgement and discretion to consider the gathered information)

Maintaining clear boundaries enables separation of the therapist's private and professional life. It potentially keeps the client and therapist safe, as well as the reputation of the profession. Conversely, the client's self-esteem might be negatively affected and she might feel rejected, therefore the principle of non-maleficence would be compromised.

Although the BABCP code does not give clear guidelines regarding boundary crossing, they do support keeping high standards of personal conduct.

Deciding (a sensible, justifiable solution or way forward)

After working through this process, the therapist felt comfortable that the best way forward was to remind the client of the contract agreement, in which it was discussed what would happen if they saw each other outside of therapy. This was included in the contract as the therapist worked in a small town and was aware that she might bump into clients and former clients. However, it had not covered social media specifically.

The client was again made aware that the contract reinforced the need for clear boundaries and is employed with all clients, it thus adheres to the ethical principles of justice and fidelity. Also, the client will be told that having clear boundaries meant that she would be able to return to therapy with the therapist if she ever felt the need to. The therapist emphasised that she valued the work they had done together.

Additionally, the therapist amended her contract to include social media as well.

Practice scenarios

Now, have a go at working through the ethical dilemmas below. Remember that it is important to explore them with others in order to discover how your own values might be influencing the decision-making process.

Scenario A

A friend tells you that one of his friends, John, is very distressed. John has developed a close relationship with his therapist, May, whilst he was in therapy with her. John started seeing the therapist socially, however once the relationship became intimate, therapy stopped. The therapist moved in with John and lived with him for approximately a year. The therapist ended the relationship a few weeks ago and sharply moved out. John is devastated. Your friend is shocked by May's behaviour, describing it as 'selfish'. How do you react?

Scenario B

You are an accredited CBT therapist. One of the CBT students in your organisation with whom you are friendly needs to complete a case study. It is her final case study, however, she forgot to obtain written consent from the client to record the session. She tells you that she doesn't have another recording that she can use, and that she can't contact the client. She privately tells you that she intends to forge the client's signature; she says that the university won't find out. What do you do?

Scenario C

John, aged 34, has misused alcohol for many years but tells you that he is prepared to detox. However, he says that when he has done so in the past, memories of adverse childhood experiences come back that he can't deal with. What do you advise him to do? What do you do?

Scenario D

Brian is a patient whom you have known for many years and have a good relationship with. He tells you that he has broken the joystick for his games console. You have a spare one at home and tell him that you will bring it in for him next time you meet. Are there any ethical considerations that you need to take into account? What if instead of giving it to him, you offered to sell it to him for a small fee?

Scenario E

Jenny has been seeing you for almost six months and has had 18 sessions of therapy. She has made slow but steady progress. Both of you think that she would benefit from continuing past the 20 sessions that you are allowed to offer her by your agency. What are the ethical issues involved? How can you resolve them? What do you say to her?

Scenario F

You work in a community team and have received a referral for a sex worker who has suffered multiple traumatic events in the last three weeks and has overdosed on paracetamol once. She refuses to be admitted and criteria for sectioning aren't met. She has found CBT input helpful in the past and has asked for someone to see her. She lives in a homeless hostel, where there is a private room available. She won't come to the team base and has no other mental health support other than sporadic use of a GP working in a homeless health care team. As an accredited CBT therapist, what do you do?

Scenario G

You have received a referral for a man with moderate learning disabilities who is reported as having problems with anger, sometimes lashing out at other service users. He doesn't seem to understand why he is being taken to his room at such times and seems frustrated and anxious when this happens. Staff can seem to find no trigger for his outbursts, having already had some input from psychology. He is wary of professionals since the time of a set of difficult medical interventions. What do you do?

Ethically developing as a CB therapist

Finally, as part of their professional training and specialist training in CBT, therapists will have considered the ethical basis for practice.

Yet, this formative training, no matter how well it has been internalised through deep learning strategies from a rigorous education curriculum, can endure without continuous professional development. Thus, it falls to the clinician to take responsibility for their own learning and development to revisit and reconsider the ethics and values of their work. This, in our view, is necessary in order to refresh, reconsider and revitalise ethical knowledge and skills. By doing so, the CB therapist will be able to continue to apply this knowledge in a reasoned way to everyday and increasingly complex ethical situations and dilemmas. Yet, the field of cognitive behaviour therapy – as we have discussed throughout this book – has been relatively slow to develop its ethical underpinnings whilst is strives to develop its evidence base. This is understandable in the context of policy-makers demanding evidence before they support service commissioning. Increasingly, then, it now falls to each of us to take responsibility for our own ethical learning and development so as to ensure that our knowledge and skills remain fit for purpose for the benefit of our clients (Corrie et al., 2016). It is hoped that this book will assist the trainee therapist and experienced therapist with this process.

In order to conclude this text in a form that can be used for self-directed or curriculum learning, we recognise the value of using 'reflective tools' that have been extensively developed, described and used in their own work by Sarah Corrie and David Lane (Lane and Corrie, 2006, 2012; Corrie and Lane, 2010, 2015). Essentially, reflective tools, much like the therapy process of CB therapy, are based on a series of guided questions that relate to the different ideas covered in this book as well as the debates drawn from professional practice and the wider literature (Corrie et al., 2016).

We recommend that you revisit the reflective tool and questions therein from time to time with colleagues, supervisors and trainers and with clients themselves. You can creatively open up your ideas and ethical reasoning to others for constructive discussion, debate and feedback, thus turning them into a form that has implications for your future values-based and ethical CB practice.

Your reflective tool

This reflective tool has been partly reproduced and partly adapted from Corrie, Townend and Cockx (2016) with permission:

1. Spend some time reflecting on what drew you initially to becoming a CB therapist and the values you now hold as a therapist? What

are the factors from your personal and professional history that have shaped your values and how you approach ethical issues and dilemmas? Use the following questions to guide you:

(a) What (or whom) has been most influential in shaping your values as a CB therapist?
(b) What do you consider to be your most important values and why are they so important to you?
(c) What have been the major ethical challenges that you have faced in your work as a CB therapist? How have you attempted to manage these and what have you learned from them?
(d) In terms of values and ethics, what learning have you gained from formal training, experience and your colleagues?

List any insights below:

____

____

____

____

____

2a. Reflect on your practice in relation to human and legal 'rights' (recap on Chapters 1 and 2 if you need to refresh your memory on any of the key points discussed). Having done so, consider your responses to the following questions:

(a) Do you have a preferred set or bill of rights that you try to uphold in your therapy? If so, what is it and why is it preferred?

- To what extent is your practice based on the rights of the client?
- To what extent does your place of work influence how you enact those rights?

(b) Review the rights in Chapter 1 and the rights that underpin ethical codes in Chapter 1. Which rights are incorporated into your professional practice? Are there any areas that would be useful to think about and develop more fully?

List any insights below:

____

____

____

____

____

2b. Having responded to the questions in 2a above, and having reflected on the content of Chapter 1, what do you now know about your current level of capability and skill in the area of incorporation of rights and values into your practice?

(a) What are your strengths/areas where you do best?
(b) What are your current limitations/areas where you are least effective?
(c) Which specific areas would it make most sense to work on for the immediate future?

List your responses below:

____

____

____

____

____

3a. Reflect on your usual approach to ethical dilemmas (recap on the second part of Chapters 1 and 2 if you need to refresh your memory, and other chapters for specific applications on any of the key points discussed). Having done so, consider your responses to the following questions:

(a) How or do you use deontological, consequential or virtue ethics in your practice?
(b) Are there any typical problems, challenges or ethical dilemmas that you regularly encounter in your CB practice?
(c) When attempting to reason through ethical problems, do you have a preferred way of understanding or formulating the issue?
(d) For irregular ethical issues, whom can you discuss these with, how well developed is the support available to you? Are you able to approach the problem together?

(e) Does the ethical problem-solving process outlined in this chapter help you to solve regular and novel ethical problems?

List any insights below:

___

___

___

___

___

3b. Having responded to the questions in 3a above, and having reflected on the content of the different chapters, what do you now know about your current level of capability and skill in the area of using ethical theories to help you make reasoned professional decisions?

(a) What are your strengths/areas where you do best?
(b) What are your current limitations/areas where you are least effective?
(c) Which specific areas would it make most sense to work on for the immediate future?

List your responses below:

___

___

___

___

___

4. Having read this book, what do you now know about the values, ethical frameworks and ethical reasoning that underpins your professional practice in CBT? How ethical is your practice?

(a) What are your strengths/areas where you do best?
(b) What are your current limitations/areas where more attention to values or ethics would help you to become more effective?
(c) Which specific areas would it make most sense to work on for the immediate future?

In considering each of the above, spend some time reflecting on your responses and what you feel comfortable with and if anything has made you feel uncomfortable. This process is intended to help you to fully appreciate the implications for your work and professional practice. Is there anything that you would like to change in your CBT practice for the immediate future? Are there any learning needs which reading this book or engaging with these questions have alerted you to that you need to follow up on (e.g. with your supervisor, line manager etc.)?

List your responses below:

____

____

____

____

____

5. Based on all of the above, what future direction do you wish your value and ethically based CBT-related professional development to take and what resources do you need to help you get there?
   (a) What supervision arrangements might need to be in place to help you take these next steps?
   (b) What training courses or workshops might be needed to top up your knowledge and skills?
   (c) What further reading is necessary?
   (d) Are there other forms of self-directed learning that might be beneficial?

List your responses below:

____

____

____

____

____

Concluding remarks

In this chapter, we employed the Verb Model to explore ethical dilemmas through a set of worked scenarios (with further examples to try) and a reflective tool to examine your own ethics and values. We have tried to emphasise that the ethical decision-making process is subjective whilst being based on statute, guidance and reasoning, and that because of this, discussing each dilemma with other professionals is essential. Not only should you be able to justify your decision, but it is necessary, too, that you feel as comfortable as possible with the decision made - you and your client will live with it.

REFERENCES

Adshead, G. (2015) Personal communication.

Alford, B.A. and Beck, A.T. (1997) *The Integrative Power of Cognitive Therapy*. New York: Guilford Press.

American Psychiatric Association (2013) *Diagnostic and Statistical Manual of Mental Disorders (DSM)*. Arlington, VA: American Psychiatric Publishing.

American Psychological Association (APA) (2007) 'APS Code of Ethics'. Available at: www.apa.org/ethics/code/index.aspx (accessed 18 September 2016).

Asbring, P. (2001) 'Chronic illness: A disruption in life: identity-transformation among women with chronic fatigue syndrome and fibromyalgia', *Journal of Advanced Nursing*, 34(3): 312–19.

Australian Psychological Society (APS) (2007) *Code of Ethics*. Available at: www.psychology.org.au (accessed 18 September 2016).

Barnes, F. and Murdin, L. (2001) *Values and Ethics in the Practice of Psychotherapy and Counselling*. Buckingham: Open University Press.

Barnett, J.E., Wise, E.H., Johnson-Greene, D. and Bucky, S.F. (2007) 'Informed consent: Too much of a good thing or not enough?', *Professional Psychology: Research and Practice*, 38(2): 179a.

Bateman, A.W. and Fonagy, P. (2012) *Handbook of Mentalizing in Mental Health Practice*. Arlington, VA: American Psychiatric Publications.

Beauchamp, T.L. and Childress, J.F. (2013) *Principles of Biomedical Ethics*. New York: Oxford University Press.

Beck, A.T. (1963) 'Thinking and depression: I. Idiosyncratic content and cognitive distortions', *Archives of General Psychiatry*, 9(4): 324.

Beck, A.T., Rush, J., Shaw, B.F. and Emery, G. (1979) *Cognitive Therapy of Depression*. New York: Guilford Press.

Beck, A.T. (1979) *Cognitive Therapy and the Emotional Disorders*. London: Penguin.

Begley, A. (2005) 'Practising virtue: A challenge to the view that a virtue-centred approach to ethics lacks practical content', *Nursing Ethics*, 12(6): 622–37.

Bennett-Levy, J., Butler, G., Fennell, M., Hackman, A., Mueller, M. and Westbrook, D. (eds) (2004) *Oxford Guide to Behavioural Experiments in Cognitive Therapy*. Oxford: Oxford University Press.

Bhugra, D., Leff, J., Mallett, R., Der, G., Corridan, B. and Rudge, S. (1997) 'Incidence and outcome of schizophrenia in whites, African-Caribbeans and Asians in London', *Psychological Medicine*, 27(4): 791–8.

Bhui, K. (ed.) (2002) *Racism and Mental Health*. London: Jessica Kingsley.

Blease, C.R. (2015) 'Talking more about talking cures: Cognitive behavioural therapy and informed consent', *Journal of Medical Ethics*, 41(9): 750–5.

Bolam *v.* Friern Hospital Management Committee (1957) 2 ALL ER 118, 122.

Bolitho *v.* City & Hackney Health Authority (1997) 3 WLR 1151.

Bond, T. (2015) *Standards and Ethics for Counselling in Action* (4th edn). London: Sage.

Bond, T. and Dryden, W. (2012) 'Ethical principles for CBT practitioners', in W. Dryden and R. Branch (eds), *The CBT Handbook*. London: Sage.

Brewin, C. (2003) *PTSD: Malady or Myth?* New Haven, CT: Yale University Press.

British Association for Behavioural and Cognitive Psychotherapies (BABCP) (2010) *Standard of Conduct, Performance, and Ethics in the Practice of Behavioural and Cognitive Psychotherapies*. Available at: www.babcp.com/Files/About/conduct--ethics.pdf (accessed 18 September 2016).

British Psychological Society (2009) *Code of Ethics and Conduct*. Leicester: British Psychological Society.

Brittle, R. (2004) 'Managing the needs of people who have a learning disability', *Nursing Times*, 100(10): 28–9.

Brock, A., Baker, A., Griffiths, C., Jackson, G., Fegan, G. and Marshall, D. (2006) 'Suicide trends and geographical variations in the United Kingdom, 1991–2004', *Health Statistics Quarterly*, 31(6): 6–22.

Cambridge Dictionary (2015) Available at: dictionary.cambridge.org/dictionary/english/ (accessed 18 September 2016).

CBT Today (2016) 'Joint statement on government "therapists in jobcentres" plans', *CBT Today*, 44(2): 8.

Children Act (1989) Available at: www.legislation.gov.uk/ukpga/1989/41/contents (accessed 18 June 2016).

Cochrane Collaboration (2006) *Cochrane Handbook for Systematic Reviews of Interventions 4.2.*6. Available at: http://community.cochrane.org/sites/default/files/uploads/Handbook4.2.6Sep2006.pdf (accessed 4 January 2016).

Corey, G. (2009) *Theory and Practice of Counselling and Psychotherapy* (8th edn). Salem, OR: Thomson, Brookes/Cole.

Corrie, S. and Lane, D.A. (2010) *Constructing Stories, Telling Tales: A Guide to Formulation in Applied Psychology*. London: Karnac Books.

Corrie, S. and Lane, D.A. (2015) *CBT Supervision*. London: Sage.

Corrie, S.T., Townend, M. and Cockx, A. (2016) *Assessment and Case Formulation in Cognitive Behavioural Therapy*. London: Sage.

Council of Europe (CoE) (2004) Committee of Ministers Recommendation on Human Rights and Psychiatry (11). Strasbourg: CoE.

Craig, P., Dieppe, P., Macintyre, S., Michie, S., Nazareth, I. and Petticrew, M. (2013) 'Developing and evaluating complex interventions: The new Medical Research Council guidance', *International Journal of Nursing Studies*, 50: 587–92.

Cutcliffe, R.R., Santos, J., Links, P.S., Zaheer, J., Harder, H.G., Campbell, F., McCormick, R., Harder, K., Bergmans, Y. and Eynan, R. (eds) (2016) *International Handbook of Clinical Suicide Research Paperback*. London: Routledge.

Dalal, F. (2014) 'Ethics versus compliance: The institution, ethical psychotherapy practice (and me)', *Group Analysis*, 47(1): 62–81.

Daubert *v.* Merrell Dow Pharmaceuticals, Inc. (1993) (92–102), 509 U.S. 579.

Davidson, K. and Townend, M. (2016) 'A case study of borderline personality disorder', in S. Corrie, M. Townend and A. Cockx (eds), *Assessment and Case Formulation in Cognitive Behavioural Therapy*. London: Sage.

Department of Health (DH) (2005) *New Ways of Working for Psychiatrists: Enhancing Effective, Person-Centred Services Through New Ways of Working in Multidisciplinary, Multiagency Contexts*. London: Department of Health.

Department of Health (DH) (2009) *Reference Guide to Consent for Examination or Treatment* (2nd edn). London: COI for Department of Health.

Dryden, W. and Branch, R. (2012) *The CBT Handbook*. London: Sage.

Dunn, P. (2000) *No Secrets: Guidance on Developing and Implementing Multi-agency Policies and Procedures to Protect Vulnerable Adults from Abuse*. London: Department of Health.

Economic and Social Research Council (ESRC) (2015) *Shaping Society*. Available at: www.esrc.ac.uk/ (accessed 18 September 2016).

Edwards, C.R., Thompson, A.R. and Blair, A. (2007) 'An "overwhelming illness": Women's experiences of learning to live with chronic fatigue syndrome/myalgic encephalomyelitis', *Journal of Health Psychology*, 12(2): 203–14.

Ellis, A. (1962) *Reason and Emotion in Psychotherapy*. Oxford: Lyle Stuart.

Ellis, A. (2003) 'Similarities and differences between rational emotive behavior therapy and cognitive therapy', *Journal of Cognitive Psychotherapy*, 17(3): 225–40.

Ellis, P. (2014) *Understanding Ethics for Nursing Students*. London: Learning Matters.

Ellis, P. (2015) *Ethics for Nursing*. London: Sage.

European Parliament (2001) 'Directive 2001/20/EC of the European Parliament and of the Council on the approximation of the laws, regulations and administrative provisions of the Member States relating to the implementation of good clinical practice in the conduct of clinical trials on medicinal products for human use'. Available at: http://eur-lex.europa.eu/LexUriServ/LexUriServ.do?uri=OJ:L:2001:121:0034:0044:en:PDF (accessed 4 January 2016).

Evidence-Based Medicine Working Group (EBMWG) (1992) 'A new approach to teaching the practice of medicine', *Journal of the American Medical Association*, 268: 2420–5.

Feltham, C. (2007) 'Ethical agonising', *Therapy Today*, 18(7). Available at: www.therapytoday.net/article/show/742/ethical-agonising (accessed 18 September 2016).

Francis, P.C. and Dugger, S.M. (2014) 'Professionalism, ethics, and value-based conflicts in counseling: An introduction to the special section', *Journal of Counseling & Development*, 92(2): 131–4.

Frank, A.W. (2013) *The Wounded Storyteller: Body, Illness, and Ethics*. Chicago, IL: University of Chicago Press.

Friedli, L. and Stearn, R. (2015) 'Positive affect as coercive strategy: Conditionality, activation and the role of psychology in UK government workfare programmes', *Medical Humanities*, 41: 40–7.

Gabriel, L. (2005) *Speaking the Unspeakable: The Ethics of Dual Relationships in Counselling and Psychotherapy*. Abingdon: Routledge.

Gatchel, R.J., Peng, Y.B., Peters, M.L., Fuchs, P.N. and Turk, D.C. (2007) 'The biopsychosocial approach to chronic pain: Scientific advances and future directions', *Psychological Bulletin*, 133(4): 581–624.

Gibson, M.F. (2012) 'Opening up: Therapist self-disclosure in theory, research, and practice', *Clinical Social Work Journal*, 40(3): 287–96.

Gilbert, P. and Leahy, R.L. (2007) *The Therapeutic Relationship in the Cognitive Behavioral Psychotherapies*. Hove: Routledge.

Grant, A., Townend, M., Mulhern, R. and Short, N. (2010) *Cognitive Behavioural Therapy in Mental Health Care*. London: Sage.

Griner, D. and Smith, T.B. (2006) 'Culturally adapted mental health intervention: A meta-analytic review', *Psychotherapy: Theory, Research, Practice, Training*, 43(4): 531.

Gutheil, T. and Brodsky, A. (2008) *Preventing Boundary Violations in Clinical Practice*. New York: Guilford Press.

Hall, R.C. and Hall, R.C. (2012) 'Compensation neurosis: A too quickly forgotten concept?', *Journal of the American Academy of Psychiatry and the Law Online*, 40(3): 390–8.

Hawton, K.E., Salkovskis, P.M., Kirk, J.E. and Clark, D.M. (1989) *Cognitive Behaviour Therapy for Psychiatric Problems: A Practical Guide*. Oxford: Oxford University Press.

Hayes, S.C. (2004) 'Acceptance and commitment therapy, relational frame theory, and the third wave of behavioral and cognitive therapies', *Behavior Therapy*, 35(4): 639–65.

Hayes, S.C., Strosahl, K.D. and Wilson, K.G. (1999) *Acceptance and Commitment Therapy: An Experiential Approach to Behavior Change*. New York: Guilford Press.

Health and Social Care Act 2012. Available from: www.legislation.gov.uk/ukpga/2012/7/contents/enacted (accessed 18 June 2016).

Health and Social Care Information Centre (HSCIC) (2009) Mental Health Bulletin, Third report from Mental Health Minimum Data Set (MHMDS) annual returns: 2004–2009. Available from: http://content.digital.nhs.uk/pubs/mhbmhmds0809 (accessed 5 December 2016).

Hegel, G.W.F. (1967[1821]) *Hegel's Philosophy of Right*, T.M. Knox (trans.). New York: Oxford University Press, section 66.

Herman, D.B., Susser, E.S., Struening, E.L. and Link, B.L. (1997) 'Adverse childhood experiences: Are they risk factors for adult homelessness?', *American Journal of Public Health*, 87(2): 249–55.

Hess, J. (2015) 'Ethics and nursing', *Florida Nurse*, 63(2): 15.

Holtforth, M.G. and Castonguay, L.G. (2005) 'Relationship and techniques in cognitive-behavioral therapy: A motivational approach', *Psychotherapy*, 42(4): 443–55.

Hope, R. (2004) *The Ten Essential Shared Capabilities: A Framework for the Whole of the Mental Health Workforce*. Department of Health (DH), National Institute for Mental Health in England (NIMHE), Sainsbury Centre for Mental Health (SCMH) and National Health Service University (NHSU). London: Department of Health.

Hutcheson, F. (1755) *A System of Moral Philosophy*. London: Millar.

James, I.A. (2001) 'Schema therapy: The next generation, but should it carry a health warning?', *Behavioural and Cognitive Psychotherapy*, 29(4): 401–7.

Jenkins, P., Keter, V. and Stone, J. (2004) *Psychotherapy and the Law: Questions & Answers for Counsellors & Therapists*. London: Whurr Publishers.

Johnsen, T.J. and Friborg, O. (2015) 'The effects of cognitive behavioral therapy as an anti-depressive treatment is falling: A meta-analysis', *Psychological Bulletin*, 11 May. Advance online publication at: http://dx.doi.org/10.1037/bul0000015 (accessed 29 November 2016).

Jones, R.M. (2012) 'Introducing the elephant in the room: Power and collaboration', *Public Administration Review*, 72(3): 417–18.

Joseph-Williams, N., Elwyn, G. and Edwards, A. (2014) 'Knowledge is not power for patients: A systematic review and thematic synthesis of patient-reported barriers and facilitators to shared decision making', *Patient Education and Counseling*, 94(3): 291–309.

Keats, H., Maguire, N., Johnson, R. and Cockersell, P. (2011) Psychologically Informed Services for Homeless People: Good Practice Guide. Available from: http://eprints.soton.ac.uk/340022/1/Good%20practice%20guide%20%2D%20%20Psychologically%20informed%20services%20for%20homeless%20people%20.pdf (accessed 5 December 2016).

Kelly, E.L. (1955) 'Consistency of the adult personality', *American Psychologist*, 10(11): 659.

Kingdon, D. (2007) 'DSPD or "Don't Stigmatise People in Distress": Invited commentary on ... Challenges in the treatment of dangerous and severe personality disorder', *Advances in Psychiatric Treatment*, 13: 333–5.

Kingdon, D. and Finn, M. (2012) *Tackling Mental Health Crises*. London: Routledge.

Kingdon, D.G. and Turkington, D. (2005) *Cognitive Therapy of Schizophrenia*. New York: Guilford Press.

Kingdon, D., Jones, R. and Lönnqvist, J. (2004) 'Protecting the human rights of people with mental disorder: New recommendations emerging from the Council of Europe', *British Journal of Psychiatry*, 185(4): 277–9.

Kingdon, D.G., Farr, P., Murphy, S. and Tyrer, P. (1986) 'Hypomania following cognitive therapy', *British Journal of Psychiatry*, 149: 383–4.

Kingdon, D., Taylor, L., Ma, K. and Kinoshita, Y. (2013) 'Changing name: Changing prospects for psychosis', *Epidemiology and Psychiatric Sciences*, 22(4): 297–301.

Kirkbride, J.B., Errazuriz, A., Croudace, T.J., Morgan, C., Jackson, D., Boydell, J., Murray, R.M. and Jones, P.B. (2012) 'Incidence of schizophrenia and other psychoses in England, 1950–2009: A systematic review and meta-analyses', *PloS ONE*, 7(3): e31660.

Klerman, G.L. and Weissman, M.M. (1994) *Interpersonal Psychotherapy of Depression: A Brief, Focused, Specific Strategy*. Lanham, MD: Jason Aronson.

Kolb, D.A. (2014) *Experiential Learning: Experience as the Source of Learning and Development*. Upper Saddle River, NJ: Pearson.

Komesaroff, P.A. (2001) 'The relationship between law and ethics in medicine', *Internal Medicine Journal*, 31(7): 413–14.

Lago, C. (2005) *Race, Culture and Counselling*. Maidenhead: McGraw-Hill Education.

Lago, C. (2006) *Race, Culture and Counselling: The Ongoing Challenge*. Maidenhead: Open University Press.

Lane, D.A. and Corrie, S. (2006) *The Modern Scientist-Practitioner: A Guide to Practice in Psychology*. Hove: Routledge.

Lane, D.A. and Corrie, S. (2012) *Making Successful Decisions in Counselling and Psychotherapy*. Maidenhead: Open University Press.

Larkin, W. and Morrison, A. (2007) *Trauma and Psychosis: New Directions for Theory and Therapy*. Oxford: Routledge.

Li, Z.J., Guo, Z.H., Wang, N., Xu, Z.Y., Qu, Y., Wang, X.Q., Sun, J., Yan, L.Q., Ng, R.M., Turkington, D. and Kingdon, D. (2015) 'Cognitive-behavioural therapy for patients with schizophrenia: A multicentre randomized controlled trial in Beijing, China', *Psychological Medicine*, 45(9): 1893–905.

Linehan, M. (1993) *Cognitive-Behavioral Treatment of Borderline Personality Disorder*. New York: Guilford Press.

Loades, M. (2016) 'CBT supervision', *Behavioural and Cognitive Psychotherapy*, 44(1): 128.

Locke, J. (1841) *An Essay Concerning Human Understanding*. London: Tegg.

Macdonald, H. and Stalmeisters, D. (2015) 'Greg: A case study of chronic pain', in S. Corrie, M. Townend and A. Cockx (eds), *Assessment and Case Formulation in Cognitive Behavioural Therapy*. London: Sage.

Maguire, N., Fulcher-Cornah, D., Hughes, V., Hulland, D., Nusheen, B. and Kingdon, D. (forthcoming) 'Cognitive behavioural therapy for people who are homeless: A feasibility randomised controlled trial', *Behavioural Research and Therapy*.

Marks, I.M. (1987) *Fears, Phobias, and Rituals: Panic, Anxiety, and their Disorders*. Oxford: Oxford University Press.

Marshall, S. (1996) 'The characteristics of cognitive behaviour therapy', in S. Marshall and J. Turnbull, *Cognitive Behaviour Therapy: An Introduction to Theory and Practice*. London: Baillere Tindall.

Meara, N.M., Schmidt, L.D. and Day, J.D. (1996) 'Principles and virtues: A foundation for ethical decisions, policies, and character', *Counseling Psychologist*, 24(1): 4–77.

Medical Research Council (MRC) (n.d.) 'Developing and evaluating complex interventions'. Available at: www.mrc.ac.uk/documents/pdf/complex-interventions-guidance/ (accessed 4 January 2016).

Mental Capacity Act (2005) Available at: www.legislation.gov.uk/ukpga/2005/9/contents (accessed 18 June 2016).

Milne, D. (2009) *Evidence-Based Clinical Supervision: Principles and Practice*. Oxford: Wiley-Blackwell.

Milne, D. (2011) *Evidence-Based Clinical Supervision: Principles and Practices*. (London: Wiley-Blackwell, 2009), Book Review by S. Sullender, *Reflective Practice: Formation and Supervision in Ministry*, 31.

Moleski, S.M. and Kiselica, M.S. (2005) 'Dual relationships: A continuum ranging from the destructive to the therapeutic', *Journal of Counselling and Development*, 83(1): 3–11.

Moss-Morris, R., Dennison, L., Landau, S., Yardley, L., Silber, E. and Chalder, T. (2013) 'A randomized controlled trial of cognitive behavioral therapy (CBT) for adjusting to multiple sclerosis (the saMS trial): Does CBT work and for whom does it work?', *Journal of Consulting and Clinical Psychology*, 81(2): 251–62.

Muse, K. and McManus, F. (2013) 'A systematic review of methods for assessing competence in cognitive-behavioural therapy', *Clinical Psychology Review*, 33(3): 484–99.

National Health Research Authority (NHRA) (2007) 'Differentiating audit, service evaluation and research'. Available at: www.hra.nhs.uk/documents/2013/10/differentiating-audit-service-evaluation-and-research-version-1-1.pdf (accessed 4 January 2016).

National Institute for Health and Care Excellence (2012) Patient experience in adult NHS services: improving the experience of care for people using adult NHS services. NICE clinical guideline, 138. London: NICE. Available from: https://www.nice.org.uk/guidance/cg138/chapter/1-guidance (accessed 1 July 2016).

National Patient Safety Agency (NPSA) (2004) 'Understanding the patient safety issues for people with learning disabilities', Available at: www.nrls.npsa.nhs.uk/resources/clinical-specialty/learning-disabilities/?entryid45 = 92328&p = 2 (accessed 3 December 2016).

Nelson-Jones, R. (2010) *Theory and Practice of Counselling and Therapy* (5th edn). London: Sage.

Newdick, C. (2005) *Who Should we Treat? Rights, Rationing, and Resources in the NHS.* Oxford: Oxford University Press.

Nicoll, M., Beail, N. and Saxon, D. (2013) 'Cognitive behavioural treatment for anger in adults with intellectual disabilities: A systematic review and meta-analysis', *Journal of Applied Research in Intellectual Disabilities*, 26(1): 47–62.

Oxford English Dictionary (2016) *Oxford English Dictionary*. Oxford: Oxford University Press.

Padesky, C. (2015) 'Best Practices in Depression and Suicide Workshop', University of Derby, 1–2 June.

Padesky, C. (2016) Personal communication between Christine Padesky and Michael Townend. 20 September.

Panksepp, J. (1998) *Affective Neuroscience: The Foundations of Human and Animal Emotions*. Oxford: Oxford University Press.

Patel, V., Araya, R., Chatterjee, S., Chisholm, D., Cohen, A., De Silva, M., Hosman, C., McGuire, H., Rojas, G. and van Ommeren, M. (2007) 'Treatment and prevention of mental disorders in low-income and middle-income countries', *Lancet*, 370(9591): 991–1005.

Patel, V., Chowdhary, N., Rahman, A. and Verdelie, H. (2011) 'Improving access to psychological treatments: Lessons from developing countries', *Behaviour Research and Therapy*, 49(9): 523–8.

Pilgrim, D. (1997) *Psychotherapy and Society*. London: Sage.

Playford, R., Roberts, T. and Playford, E. (2015) 'Deontology and utilitarianism ethics: A brief introduction in the context of disorders of consciousness', *Disability and Rehabilitation*, 37(21): 2006–11.

Proctor, G. (2002) *The Dynamics of Power in Counselling and Psychotherapy: Ethics, Practice and Politics*. Ross-on-Wye: PCCS Books.

Proctor, G. (2008) 'CBT: The obscuring of power in the name of science', *European Journal of Psychotherapy and Counselling*, 10(3): 231–45.

Proctor, G.M. (2014) *Values and Ethics in Counselling and Psychotherapy*. London: Sage.

Rachman, S. and Lopatka, C. (1988) 'Return of fear: Underlearning and overlearning', *Behaviour Research and Therapy*, 26(2): 99–104.

Rahman, A., Malik, A., Sikander, S., Roberts, C. and Creed, F. (2008) 'Cognitive behaviour therapy-based intervention by community health workers for mothers with depression and their infants in rural Pakistan: A cluster-randomised controlled trial', *The Lancet*, 372(9642): 902–9.

Ramesh, R. (2011) 'The truth about suicide', *The Guardian*, 23 August. Available at: www.theguardian.com/y/2011/aug/23/suicide-chronic-illness-study (accessed 30 April 2016).

Rathod, S., Kingdon, D., Pinninti, N., Turkington, D. and Phiri, P. (2015) *Cultural Adaptation of CBT for Serious Mental Illness*. Chichester: Wiley.

Resnicow, K., Soler, R., Braithwaite, R.L., Ahluwalia, J.S. and Butler, J. (2000) 'Cultural sensitivity in substance use prevention', *Journal of Community Psychology*, 28(3): 271–90.

Rojas, G., Fritsch, R., Solis, J., Jadresic, E., Castillo, C., Gonzalez, M., Guajardo, V., Lewis, G. and Araya, R. (2007) 'Treatment of postnatal depression in low-income mothers in primary-care clinics in Santiago, Chile: A randomised controlled trial', *Lancet*, 370: 1629–37.

Roth, A.D. and Fonagy, P. (2010) *What Works for Whom? A Critical Review of Psychotherapy* (2nd edn). New York: Guildford Press.

Roth, A.D. and Pilling, S. (2008) 'Using an evidence-based methodology to identify the competences required to deliver effective cognitive and behavioural therapy for depression and anxiety disorders', *Behavioural and Cognitive Psychotherapy*, 36(2): 129–47.

Rousseau, J.-J. (1920) *The Social Contract and Discourses*. No. 660. London: JM Dent & Sons.

Safren, S.A. and Rogers, T. (2001) 'Cognitive–behavioral therapy with gay, lesbian, and bisexual clients', *Journal of Clinical Psychology*, 57(5): 629–43.

Sandage, S.J. and Hill, P.C. (2001) 'The virtues of positive psychology: The rapprochement and challenges of an affirmative postmodern perspective', *Journal for the Theory of Social Behaviour*, 31: 241–60. doi:10.1111/1468-5914.00157

Savill, R. (2009) 'Former client sues psychologist after he ended their two-year affair', *The Telegraph*, 8 April.

Segal, Z.V., Williams, J.M.G. and Teasdale, J.D. (2012) *Mindfulness-Based Cognitive Therapy for Depression*. New York: Guilford Press.

Selten, J.-P., Slaets, J.P.J. and Kahn, R.S. (1997) 'Schizophrenia in Surinamese and Dutch Antillean immigrants to The Netherlands: Evidence of an increased incidence', *Psychological Medicine*, 27(4): 807–11.

Shillito-Clarke, C. (2003) 'Ethical issues in counselling psychology', in R. Woolfe, W. Dryden and S. Strawbridge (eds), *Handbook of Counselling Psychology* (3rd edn). London: Sage.

Skinner, B. (1938) *The Behavior of Organisms: An Experimental Analysis*. New York: Appleton-Century.

Skinner, B.F. (1963) 'Operant behavior', *American Psychologist*, 18(8): 503–15.

Skinner, B.F. (1971) *Beyond Freedom and Dignity*. Middlesex: Pelican Books.

Social Care Institute for Excellence (undated) *Adult Safeguarding Resource*. Available from: www.scie.org.uk/publications/elearning/adultsafeguarding/ resource/2_study_area.html (accessed 15 May 2016).

Solbrekke, T.D. and Englund, T. (2011) 'Bringing professional responsibility back in', *Studies in Higher Education*, 36(7): 847–61.

Syme, G. (2006) 'Fetter or freedom: Dual relationships in counselling', *International Journal for the Advancement of Counselling*, 28(1): 57–69.

Thorndike, E.L. (1905) *Measurements of Twins*, No. 1. New York: Science Press.

Thwaites, R. and Bennett-Levy, J. (2007) 'Conceptualizing empathy in cognitive behaviour therapy: Making the implicit explicit', *Behavioural and Cognitive Psychotherapy*, 35(5): 591–612.

Tim, B. (2008) 'Towards a new ethic of trust', *Therapy Today*, 19(3): 30–5.

Tseng, W.-S., Chang, S.C. and Nishjzono, M. (2005) *Asian Culture and Psychotherapy: Implications for East and West*. Honolulu, HI: University of Hawaii Press.

Turkington, D., Kingdon, D., Rathod, S., Hammond, K., Pelton, J. and Mehta, R. (2006) 'Outcomes of an effectiveness trial of cognitive-behavioural intervention by mental health nurses in schizophrenia', *British Journal of Psychiatry*, 189(1): 36–40.

United Nations (2007) *Convention on the Rights of Persons with Disabilities*. Available at: www.un.org/disabilities/convention/conventionfull.shtml (accessed 18 September 2016).

United Nations General Assembly (UNGA) (1948) *Universal Declaration of Human Rights*. Paris: UNGA.

van Minnen, A., Harned, M.S., Zoellner, L. and Mills, K. (2012) 'Examining potential contraindications for prolonged exposure therapy for PTSD', *European Journal of Psychotraumatology*, 3.

Van Staveren, I. (2007) 'Beyond utilitarianism and deontology: Ethics in economics', *Review of Political Economy*, 19(1): 21–35.

Värnik, P. (2012) 'Suicide in the world', *International Journal of Environmental Research and Public Health*, 9(3): 760–71.

Watson, J.B. (1913) 'Psychology as the behaviorist views it', *Psychological Review*, 20(2): 158.

Wilkinson, R. and Caulfield, H. (2000) *The Human Rights Act: A Practical Guide for Nurses*. Chichester: Wiley.

Wilkinson, R., Caulfield, H. and Great, B. (2001) *The Human Rights Act: A Practical Guide for Nurses*. London: Whurr.

Williams, M.H. (1997) 'Boundary violations: Do some contended standards of care fail to encompass commonplace procedures of humanistic, behavioral and eclectic psychotherapies?', *Psychotherapy*, 34(3): 238–49.

Willner, P., Rose, J., Jahoda, A., Kroese, B.S., Felce, D., Cohen, D., Macmahon, P., Stimpson, A., Rose, N., Gillespie, D., Shead, J., Lammie, C., Woodgate, C., Townson, J., Nuttall, J. and Hood, K. (2013) 'Group-based cognitive-behavioural anger management for people with mild to moderate intellectual disabilities: Cluster randomised controlled trial', *British Journal of Psychiatry*, 203(4): 288–96.

Wolpe, J. (1968) 'Psychotherapy by reciprocal inhibition', *Conditional Reflex: A Pavlovian Journal of Research & Therapy*, 3(4): 234–40.

World Health Organization (WHO) (2010) *International Classification of Diseases*. Version 10. Geneva: WHO.

World Medical Association (2013) 'World Medical Association Declaration of Helsinki: Ethical principles for medical research involving human subjects', *Journal of the American Medical Association (JAMA)*, 310(20): 2191.

Wykes, T., Steel, C., Everitt, B. and Tarrier, N. (2008) 'Cognitive behavior therapy for schizophrenia: Effect sizes, clinical models, and methodological rigor', *Schizophrenia Bulletin*, 34: 523–37.

Yohannes, A.M., Willgoss, T.G., Baldwin, R.C. and Connolly, M.J. (2010) 'Depression and anxiety in chronic heart failure and chronic obstructive pulmonary disease: Prevalence, relevance, clinical implications and management principles', *International Journal of Geriatric Psychiatry*, 25(12): 1209–21.

Young, J.E., Klosko, J.S. and Weishaar, M.E. (2003) *Schema Therapy: A Practitioner's Guide*. New York: Guilford Press.

Younggren, J.N., Fisher, M.A., Foote, W.E. and Hjelt, S.E. (2011) 'A legal and ethical review of patient responsibilities and psychotherapist duties', *Professional Psychology: Research and Practice*, 42(2): 160–8.

Zur, O. (2008) 'Power in psychotherapy and counselling: Rethinking the power differentials myth and exploring the moral, ethical, professional and clinical issues of power in therapy'. Available at: www.zurinstitute.com/power_in_therapy.html (accessed 30 October 2015).

INDEX

abuse, 30–6; disclosure of, 33, 35–6; types of, 30
Academy of Cognitive Therapy (ACT), 138
acceptance and commitment therapy (AaCT), 8
accountability, 55–6, 59–60, 83
accreditation of therapists, 83, 91, 138
adults at risk, 32–3, 36
advance directives, 73
agenda-setting, 47
Alford, B.A., 51
alternative treatments, 62
American Psychological Association (APA) Code of Ethics, 59–62, 66–7, 98
anonymisation, 76
Aristotle, 19
audit and the audit cycle, 104–5
Australian Association for Cognitive and Behaviour Therapy (AACBT), 138
Australian Psychology Society (APS) Code of Ethics, 18–19, 55, 131–3
authoritarian voice, 59
autonomy, 21–6, 146
  of clients, 56, 58, 66, 79, 132, 143, 145, 151, 157, 160–2
  definition of, 22–3
  relational and *supported*, 22–4
  and suicide, 141–6
  of therapists, 87
aversive techniques, 49

Barnett, J.E., 61
Beauchamp, T.L., 62
Beck, Aaron, 7, 41, 44, 51, 125–6
befriending, 45
behavioural activation, 49
behavioural experiments, 67, 86, 95
behavioural theory, 6–7, 110
beneficence, principle of, 22, 66, 88, 109, 131, 151–5, 158–63
Bentham, Jeremy, 18
'best interests' doctrine, 24–9, 60, 141, 157
Bill of Rights (1689), 12
bipolar disorder, 76, 97
Black and Black British communities, 121–2
Bolam test of medical negligence, 86
Bond, T., 85–6, 142
borderline personality disorder (BPD), 50
boundary crossing, 63–9, 161–3
brief interpersonal therapy, 7
British Association for Behavioural and Cognitive Psychotherapies (BABCP)
  accreditation by, 83, 91, 138
  aims of, 83–4
  Standards of Conduct, Performance and Ethics, 15–16, 18–19, 42, 50–2, 56, 59–63, 66–8, 84–5, 131–2, 141, 152–9, 162–3

capacity, 25–9, 31, 33, 71, 73
Care Act (2014), 14
care plans, 27
Care Quality Commission, 12, 37, 105
carers: involvement of 72–3; support for, 31–2
case studies, 75
categorical imperative, 17
'CBT approaches', 110–16
  as distinct from therapy itself, 113–16
Children Act (1989), 24–5
children's welfare, 72
Childress, J.F., 62
China, 100, 122
chronic illness coping model (Macdonald and Stalmeisters), 132
chronic medical conditions, 129–33
civil liberty, 11
clinical guidelines, 105–6
Cockx, A., 166

codes of practice, 15–16, 18–19, 49–50, 54–5, 59, 68, 82–5, 109, 117
coercion into therapy, 24, 127–9
cognitive behaviour therapy (CBT), 1, 6–9, 21
  core principles of, 87
  criticisms of, 42, 46–52, 125–6
  diversity in, 83
  effectiveness of, 117–18
  fundamental aims of, 109
  overarching framework of, 81
  theoretical model for, 15–16
  see also 'CBT approaches'
cognitive fusion, 8
cognitive restructuring, 86
cognitive therapy, 41
  first, *second* and *third* waves, 7
collaborative approach to therapy, 44–9, 57–8, 63, 81, 102, 109
Committee against Torture, 12
'common-sense' therapies, 85–6, 110, 117
competence, 85–8, 91–2
  conscious and *unconscious*, 117
  definition of, 87
  five domains of, 88
  maintenance and enhancement of, 91
complaints, 78
confidentiality, 17, 36–7, 52, 56, 60, 70–9, 87, 149
  breaching of, 56, 75, 79, 88, 133, 144, 156–61
conscience, liberty of, 10
consequentialism, 18, 154–7, 160, 162; *see also* utilitarianism
contracting with clients, 63, 135, 144–5, 150, 155, 158–63
Convention on the Rights of Persons with Disabilities, 22
'cookbook therapy', 47
Corrie, Sarah, 166
Council of Europe, 2, 9, 11–13
Court of Protection, 29
criminal justice system, 127
criminal records checks, 35
cultural adaptation, 120–4
  challenges in, 123

data protection, 71
death penalty, 85
deontology, 17–18, 22, 131, 140–1, 154, 157–62
depression, 8–9, 34, 41–2, 73, 97, 100–2, 111, 122–3, 130, 159
'deprivation of life' safeguards, 29
diagnosis, 42–4, 50, 117–18
Diagnostic and Statistical Manual (DSM), 43, 100, 106
dialectical behaviour therapy (DBT), 8, 115, 155–6
disclosure: of abuse, 33, 35–6; of information by clients, 56, 60, 71–2, 150; of records to clients and/or carers, 77–8; of traumatic experience, 114–15; *see also* self-disclosure
discrimination, 30
distress, causing, of 96, 109, 114
'downward arrow' technique, 50
'drilling' as an educational practice, 117
Dryden, W., 85
dual relationships, 65–6, 68–9
duty-based ethics, 22, 140
duty of care, 52, 56

Edwards, C.R. 130
Ellis, Albert, 7, 41, 109
emergency situations, 160–1
emotional blackmail, 24
emotional responses to therapeutic intervention, 115–16
emotions in CBT, 51, 126
empathy, 45
employing agencies of therapists, 16, 56–7, 60, 139
Englund, T., 56
ethical decision-making *see* Verb Model
ethical issues, 42, 51–3
ethical principles and standards, 37, 68
  in CBT, 81, 165–6
ethical scenarios, 147, 149–65
ethical theories, 16–20
ethics committees, 103–5
ethics as distinct from the law, 85
ethics of using a CBT approach, 108–18
  as distinct from CBT proper, 115, 118
ethnic minorities, 121–2
European Association for Behavioural and Cognitive Therapies (EABCT), 138
European Convention on Human Rights (1950), 11, 13, 74
European Court of Human Rights, 11
European Union, 13, 104
evidence, assessment of, 97–9
evidence-based practice, 42, 44, 49, 93–101, 111–13, 118
  criticisms of, 99–101
  definition of, 94
  hierarchy of, 96–7
  principles of, 96–7
experiential learning, 117

'expert-by-experience' concept, 23, 126
exploitation of clients, 66
exposure therapy, 48–50, 63, 67, 86

families of therapists, 68
family involvement in therapy, 52, 121–2
family pressures, 24, 139
Feltham, C., 68
fidelity
  ethical principle of, 60–1, 66, 87, 132, 152, 155, 158–62
  to the model of CBT, 87
Fonagy, P., 99
force, use of, 13
formulation, 43, 50, 100, 117
Freud, Sigmund, 6, 75
Friedli, L., 127
Fry, Stephen, 76

Gatchel, R.J., 131
gift-giving, 63–4
Gilbert, P., 57
good practice, 104–5, 118
'graded hierarchies', 117

harm, unintentional, 31; *see also* self-harm
health care, groups excluded from, 112–13, 115, 118, 134–5
Health and Social Care Act (2012), 39
Health and Social Care Information Centre (HSCIC), 121
Hegel, G.W.F., 11
Helsinki Declaration (1913), 13
'here and now' focus in therapy, 47, 49, 116
hierarchy of evidence, 96–7
homelessness, 134–6
'homework', 47–8
hugging clients, 63
human rights, 9, 12–13
Human Rights Act (1998), 11, 15, 141–2
Hutcheson, F., 10
hypomania, 96
hypothesis testing, 94–5, 105

Improving Access to Psychological Therapies (IAPT) programme, 2, 7, 87–91, 99, 102, 111–12
individualised practice, 42–3, 52, 81, 100–1
information sharing, 72–4, 77–8
informed consent, 23, 31, 33, 61–3, 141–2, 154
institutional abuse, 30
International Classification of Diseases (ICD), 43, 100, 106
International Covenant on Civil and Political Rights (1966), 13
International Covenant on Economic, Social and Cultural Rights (1966), 13
international law, 9

James, Ian A., 50
Jenkins, P., 65
job descriptions, 86
jobcentre clients, 128–9
Jones, R.M., 57
justice, principle of, 89, 133, 152, 155, 158–62; *see also* criminal justice system

Kant, Immanuel, 17, 140
Kelly, E.L., 7
Kingdon, David, vi, 1–2, *co-author*

Lane, David, 166
Leahy, R.L., 57
learning cycles, 117
learning disabilities, 136–7
legal rights, 9
Lineham, Marsha, 114
Locke, John, 9
longitudinal research, 101

Macdonald, H., 132
Magna Carta, 12
Maguire, Nick, vi, 2, *co-author*
manualisation of therapies, 100–1
Marx, Karl, 125
Mason, George, 12
Meara, N.M., 19
media contacts, 75
medical malpractice, 38, 86
medical research, 13–14
Medical Research Council (MRC), 112
mental capacity *see* capacity
Mental Capacity Act (2005), 26–9
mental health legislation, 35, 74, 142, 145, 161
mental health practitioners, 14
mentalisation-based therapy, 7
meta-analyses, 102
metacognition, 7
Mill, John Stuart, 18
'mindfulness' techniques, 8
minimal standards for practitioners, 86, 92
money laundering, 56
myalgic encephalopathy/chronic fatigue syndrome (ME/CFS), 130, 132–3

National Institute for Health and Care Excellence (NICE), 39, 98, 105, 111, 142–3

National Patient Safety Agency (NPSA), 136–7
natural rights, 9, 11
negligence, 38–9
New Ways of Working for Psychiatrists, 106
NHS Health Research Authority, 105
non-maleficence, principle of, 66, 88, 152, 155, 158–63
Nuremberg trials, 23

obsessive compulsive disorder (OCD), 48
outcome measurement and assessment, 95–6, 99–103, 117

Padesky, C., 48
'parity of esteem' for mental and physical health services, 39
Pates v. Dungey case, 67
patient preference studies, 101
payment-by-results systems, 99
personal information, 76–7
personal relationships with clients, 65–6
personal therapy for therapists, 51, 91
personality disorder, 8, 34, 49–50, 117–18
Pilling, S., 88
post-traumatic stress disorder (PTSD), 49
power differentials in therapy, 57–8, 62–3, 66, 109, 126
private judgement, right to, 10
Proctor, G., 57, 64, 126
'production-line' approach to therapy, 100
professional liability insurance, 38
professional responsibility, 54–6, 59, 68–9, 147
professional status of therapists, 82–3
protection plans, 36
psychological therapies, 100, 102, 105, 109–10, 134–6
psychosis, 34, 97, 100–2, 122
public interest, 56, 82

qualitative research, 96
quality assurance, 37
questioning skills, 116

randomised controlled trials (RCTs), 42, 96–101
Rape Crisis (agency), 113
record-keeping, 35, 76–7
referrals, 102–3
reflective practice, 117
reflective tools, 166–71
relational frame theory (RFT), 8, 109
religious convictions, 140
religious liberty, 11
reliving techniques, 49
research
  appraisal of primary sources, 98
  carrying out of, 103–4
  as distinct from service evaluation and audit, 104
  involvement of therapists and clients in, 102–3
  use of data for, 71
responsibility, definition of, 54, 57; *see also* professional responsibility
risk assessment, 37
Roth, A., 88, 99
Rousseau, Jean-Jacques, 10

safeguarding procedures, 14, 26, 31–8, 52
safety behaviours, 7–8
safety of practitioners, 37
schema work, 8, 50
schizophrenia *see* psychosis
scientific approach to practice, 81
scientist–practitioner approach to practice, 94, 96
selection bias on the part of therapists, 125
self-disclosure, 45, 63, 121, 124
self-harm, 34–5, 60
service evaluations, 104
sexual abuse, 30
sexual relationships, 59, 66–7, 85–6
shared decision-making, 58
'significant harm', 31
social contract theory, 10–11
social issues, 125
social media, 75
Solbrekke, T.D., 56
'special patients', 68
Stalmeisters, Dzintra, vi–vii, 3, 132, *co-author*
Stearn, R., 127
Suicide Act (1961), 159
suicide and suicide prevention, 38–9, 78, 88, 133, 137–46, 161
  duties of professionals in respect of, 140–1
  values and principles of, 139–40
suicides, estimated numbers of, 137
supervision, clinical, 51, 65–9, 78, 89–90, 126, 147, 149, 152–5, 158, 160, 163

targets, achievability of, 99
terrorism, 56
theory translated into practice, 110
therapeutic relationship, 23, 44–5, 65, 67, 95
therapy as distinct from a therapeutic approach, 113–16

'third wave' therapies, 51, 83, 126
Time for Change, 75
touch, use of, 64
Townend, Michael, vii, 2–3, 166, *co-author*
training in CBT approaches, 83, 111, 115–18
  effectiveness of, 116–17
training materials, 76
trauma-focused cognitive therapy (T-FCT), 113
traumatic experience, 114–15; *see also* post-traumatic stress disorder
triangulation of data, 102
trust, 17–18, 61–2, 132, 157–9
Tseng, W.-S., 123

unalienable rights, 10–11
United States Declaration of Independence (1776), 10, 12
Universal Declaration of Human Rights (1948), 9, 11–13, 15
universalisability, principle of, 17
unwise decisions, acceptance of, 27–8
utilitarianism, 18–19; *see also* consequentialism

validation processes, 114–15
values, 8, 15–17
values-based commissioning and practice, 101–2
Verb Model of Ethical Decision-Making, 4, 133, 147–71
virtue ethics, 19–20, 89
vulnerable people, 14, 16, 24–5, 30–3

'welfare checklist', 25
'what works', 112
whistle-blowing, 37, 151–2
workshops for training purposes, 117
World Health Organization (WHO), 137
World Medical Association (WMA), 13

Young, J.E., 8